BRENDA H MALLEY

SEEKING LIBERTY AND JUSTICE

*A History of the
North Carolina Bar
Association*

1899-1999

J. Edwin Hendricks

Edited by Lynn P. Roundtree

C3

ISBN 0-327-09180-0

Foreword

Most North Carolinians are students of history. When that history is the record of forces and organizations that impact our lives directly, we pay closer attention. This volume is the record of such an organization and its growth, both in importance and power, and therefore merits careful reading.

In great measure, the growth, development and significance of the Bar Association is the reflection of men and women trained in the law, who felt a moral duty to create a public service institution to ensure to each citizen the just and equal protection of the law.

The pages that follow recount the successful efforts of the North Carolina Bar Association to establish stronger academic requirements of legal education, statutory codification, codes of ethical practice, high quality continuing legal education and proper requirements for bar examination and licensure to practice, and to support the continuing and splendid record of the profession in the public service of all citizens.

The movement of a profession from its origins in the founding of our nation to its formidable role in the administration of law and justice today is worth reading. Of special interest is the involvement of the profession and the association in social justice and access to the law by the poor and disadvantaged.

As a member of the Bar Association and of the profession for many years, I have taken special pride in the role lawyers have played to ensure justice, fairness and equity in the administration of the laws of the land. Those men and women who have led us to that cherished achievement are here recognized, and I join in this merited salute.

The book also merits your reading for the substantial history you will learn. It will afford you the opportunity of reflection on the lives of noble men and women, students and practitioners of the law, who individually and through the association afforded you and me a more secure and abundant life and a finer Commonwealth in which to work and live.

William Friday
President Emeritus
The University of North Carolina

Introduction

Throughout the past 100 years the North Carolina Bar Association and its members have influenced the pivotal societal and political events in North Carolina. As the North Carolina Bar Association looks ahead to its next 100 years, it is natural to pause and reflect on our long and proud tradition of service to the public and our profession.

The 1999 Centennial year provides the opportunity to celebrate the rich heritage of the Bar Association, the legal profession, and the significant contributions both have made to making North Carolina a great state. At the North Carolina Bar Association's Leadership Assembly in January 1999, the noted commentator David Gergen, in an eloquent and penetrating analysis of public life, credited North Carolina's remarkable progress in the 20th century to its commitment to education, community and justice. No group of North Carolinians has been more consistently involved in these efforts than have North Carolina lawyers. The lawyers of North Carolina have led the way, making important contributions to the success of our state's education system, the strength of its communities and the administration of justice.

The impact that lawyers have had on the people and institutions of North Carolina is readily apparent. The lawyers who have served as governors of North Carolina listed in the appendix, the public service accomplishments outlined in this book, and the important community service going on every day all over our state provide clear and convincing evidence that lawyers have helped North Carolina in countless ways, and are poised to continue doing so well into the 21st century.

The North Carolina Bar Association is generally recognized as the strongest and best bar in the country. This history book is a testament to the Bar Association's 100 years of dedicated commitment to serve the public and the legal profession by promoting the administration of justice and encouraging the highest standards of integrity, competence, civility and well-being of all members of the profession.

One of the Centennial goals directs us to celebrate the accomplishments of North Carolina lawyers and the vitality of the North Carolina Bar Association. Hopefully, this book helps fulfill that goal. I believe that it does. Although other texts have been written about segments of the legal profession, this book is the first effort to document comprehensively the contributions of the legal profession in the context of the history of North Carolina, from its beginnings as one of the original 13 colonies through its development into one of the most progressive and important states in the Union. This book is designed to be used as a reference book. I hope you find that the marvelous collection of photographs and images reinforces and enhances the text.

The Centennial Celebration has strengthened my belief that we need to celebrate our lives and our profession more readily. In doing so, I believe we enrich our lives and are motivated to be better lawyers and better citizens.

I also believe that our celebration is further enhanced if it takes place with an awareness of our history. Sir Walter Raleigh wrote, "[History] hath triumphed over time, which besides it, nothing but eternity hath triumphed over." This book is a wonderful celebration of the history of the North Carolina Bar Association and the lawyers of North Carolina.

I hope you will use and enjoy this book for many years to come.

John L. Jernigan
President, 1999-2000
North Carolina Bar Association

Acknowledgments

Any undertaking of this scope requires the collective efforts of a large group of individuals and organizations to bring the project to final completion. This is an attempt to acknowledge and thank those whose contributions were critical to our success.

The vision and leadership of the Centennial Celebration co-chairs Nancy Black Norelli and Wade Barber has been extremely important in guiding the project. The members of the History Book Committee—Charles F. Blanchard, Walter L. Hannah, Fred H. Moody Jr., M. Jackson Nichols, Carlton F. Williamson, G. Gray Wilson and Richard W. Wilson under the strong leadership of committee chair Walter H. Bennett Jr.—provided invaluable counsel, as well as dedicated work researching, writing, reviewing and remembering.

Special thanks to William Friday for reviewing the draft and writing our Foreword. Other volunteer lawyers not on the History Book Committee—Charles Becton, Dottie Bernholz, Justice Henry Frye, Ken Kyre, Sharon Parker and Betty Quick—helped in gathering information, writing sidebar chapters and/or reviewing text.

The Centennial year presidents, Larry B. Sitton (1998-99) and John L. Jernigan (1999-2000), provided encouragement, guidance and support at key junctures in the process.

The entire staff of the North Carolina Bar Association under the leadership of Executive Director Allan B. Head provided moral support, with David MacDonald and W. Clifton Barnes III, who helped edit the book, serving as lead staff in the support of the committee, the author, the publisher and the editor. Thomas M. Hull and Julie Dumont Rabinowitz provided leadership in locating and identifying the many photographs which enhance the text and make the book more enjoyable for the casual reader.

Our author, J. Edwin Hendricks, chair of the History Department at Wake Forest University, utilized his broad knowledge of North Carolina history and especially his knowledge of the history of the legal profession within the state to craft an informative text. At a key time during the project, editor Lynn P. Roundtree provided additional historical context to the narrative. His initial work in photograph research was also instrumental in the final appearance of the book.

We especially thank the many lawyers of the North Carolina Bar Association who located photographs in family collections and from archives and local history museums to ensure broad statewide representation. Their names are individually listed in the photograph credits section of the book.

Members of the History Book Committee conducted a series of oral history interviews over several months to collect reminiscences from a number of North Carolina Bar Association members. Thanks to every individual who participated in an interview.

As is often the case in organizations, gaps exist in the records and archives of the Bar Association. We are especially thankful to Past President Richard Elton Thigpen (1948-49), and former Secretary-Treasurer Allston J. Stubbs Jr. (1940-44) for providing key information not available from other sources.

Thanks to Christine Durman, Michael Eisenstein and Leigh Trippe of LEXIS Publishing for their support in making this book a reality. Thanks also go to LEXIS Publishing's Pierre Blondel for the fine work he did in designing the book, and Sarah Truscinski for coordinating the printing.

The thorough indexing by Ann Norcross makes the book easier to use.

A significant number of organizations and individuals helped us obtain accurate historical information and current statistics on the profession. These include:

— North Carolina Supreme Court Library—Louise Stafford, chief librarian.

— Campbell University, Norman A. Wiggins School of Law Library—K.C. Sorvari, librarian.

— Duke University School of Law Library—Gretchen Wolf, librarian.

— North Carolina Central University School of Law Library—Mayo Jeffries, librarian.

— University of North Carolina at Chapel Hill School of Law Library—Professor Laura Gassaway, librarian.

— Wake Forest University School of Law, Professional Center Library—Professor Thomas M. Steele. librarian.

— North Carolina Museum of History—Dr. James McNutt, director; Charles LeCount, curator; Dennis Daniel, assistant curator.

— North Carolina Collection, UNC-Chapel Hill—Donna Tench, Harry McKown, Eileen McGrath, Allice Cotten, and Robert G. Anthony Jr.

Several hundred photographs and images were identified and considered for inclusion in the book. While it was impossible to include every photograph or image brought to our attention, a sincere effort was made to accurately represent the historical record of the North Carolina Bar Association and the legal profession in North Carolina.

Although each individual photograph and image is included in the photograph credit section of the book, there were several organizations and individuals who went the extra mile to track down photographs. They include:

— N. C. Division of Archives & History Photographic Section—Steve Massengill and Earl Ijames.

— UNC-Chapel Hill, North Carolina Collection—Laura Baxley, Jane Witten, Keith Longiotti, Fred Stipe, Jerry Cotten and Neil Fulghum.

— Southern Historical Collection, UNC-Chapel Hill—John White, Dr. Richard E. Schrader.

— Duke University Archives—Dr. William E. King.

— Robinson/Spangler Carolina Room, Public Library of Charlotte and Mecklenburg County—Sheila Bumgardner.

— East Carolina University Library Special Collections — Dr. Donald Lennon.

Table of Contents

Presidents of the North Carolina Bar Association
Chief Justices of the North Carolina Supreme Court
Secretary/Treasurers and Executive Directors of the North Carolina Bar Association
Governors of the State of North Carolina
North Carolina Bar Association Section Chairs
Senior Lawyers Division Chairs
Young Lawyers Division Chairs
Legal Assistants Division Chairs
North Carolina Bar Association Staff 1999
Judge John J. Parker Memorial Award Recipients
General Practice Hall of Fame
North Carolina Bar Association Foundation Justice Fund Honorees
Young Lawyers Division Liberty Bell Award Recipients
Pro Bono Attorney of the Year Award
Outstanding Legal Services Attorney Award
The Chief Justice Award
The Outstanding Pro Bono Services Award For Law Firms
North Carolina Bar Association Annual Meeting Locations 1899-1999
Code of Legal Ethics 1900

*Fayetteville Street in downtown Raleigh after the February 12, 1899, snowstorm —
the second-worst storm of the century. Only two days prior, lawyers from
across the state met to form the North Carolina Bar Association.*

Prologue

The big event of 1899 in North Carolina — weatherwise — was an extreme cold spell in early to mid-February. On the morning of February 10, a low temperature of nine degrees was recorded in Raleigh, the second-lowest temperature on record for that date. A headline on the front page of the Raleigh *News and Observer* announced, "The Polar Wave Will Linger: Several Days Longer Will Jack Frost Tarry; He Breaks the Records."

The newspaper's front page also carried two items of legal news. The first story told of the anticipated recovery of esteemed law professor John S. Manning from an attack of bronchitis at his home in Chapel Hill; the second reported a meeting to be held that evening in Raleigh by a group of the state's lawyers for the intention of forming a statewide bar association.

The object of this organization will be to promote the administration of justice throughout the State, advance the science of jurisprudence, maintain the standard of honor in the profession, establish cordial intercourse among the members and cultivate more intimate relations with National and State Bar Associations.

UNC professor J. Crawford Biggs had sent a letter to attorneys throughout North Carolina requesting that they meet at 7:30 p.m. on February 10 in the Supreme Court building to organize the Bar Association. Even in a time before automobiles and planes, he could not have imagined the difficulties more than 60 attorneys from across the state would have in making that meeting.

The weather on the next day, February 11, was even more severe, as a blinding snow and hail storm wracked Raleigh and much of the Piedmont. Citizens of the capital city awoke on the Sunday morning, February 12, to a city buried in white, as a record 17 inches of snow blanketed the city — the city's second highest snowfall of the century. Weather forecasters predicted a further drop in the temperature the next day, and a snowstorm continued to ravage the eastern Piedmont through the night.

Constructed in 1888, the Supreme Court/State Library Building housed the North Carolina Supreme Court from 1888 until 1914. The building, site of the Bar Association organizational meeting, still occupies the corner of Salisbury and Edenton streets in Raleigh.

Professor John Manning on the porch of his home in Chapel Hill with his family in the 1890s. Manning, who passed away two days after the organizational meeting, was memorialized at the first annual meeting in 1899, establishing a tradition that continues to this day.

On that very evening, down the road from Raleigh in the village of Chapel Hill, John S. Manning collapsed at his home and died. Dr. Manning, a widely respected and much-beloved attorney who had served for nearly 20 years as professor of law at the University of North Carolina, had attended the profession's organizational meeting just two nights earlier. The North Carolina Bar Association thus suffered the death of one of its leaders and charter members almost before it began.

"In tempest and turmoil the association was born," wrote North Carolina Bar Association Executive Secretary William M. Storey many years later. Amongst hail and snow, extreme cold and unexpected loss, the organization began its mission of service to the profession and to the people.

Five months later, at the time of the first annual meeting, the association had grown to 157 charter members with 26 from Raleigh, 13 from Charlotte, seven from Durham, six each from Fayetteville and Winston. The majority practiced law in small towns across the state.

In his inaugural address at that meeting, Platt Dickinson Walker, founding president of the North Carolina Bar Association, spoke of the duties and obligations of the lawyer in North Carolina, those who serve "among a free people devoted to liberty and justice:"

> We appeal to every lawyer who entertains a pride in his profession, and in its past achievements and history, and a hope for its greater destiny, to join us in our endeavor to lift it up, and upon still a higher plane, and to make it a tower of strength in our legislative halls, our councils and our forums, that the gladsome light of jurisprudence may shine in every part of this Commonwealth, and that her people may feel that the supreme law of this land, to which they owe their respect and obedience, is a law of truth, justice and right.

The North Carolina Supreme Court from 1905-1909.
First NCBA President Platt D. Walker had been appointed
to the Supreme Court in 1903.

This is a reproduction of the Hayes Plantation Library owned by James C. Johnston, one of the state's
most prosperous planters and son of attorney Samuel Johnston, governor from 1787-1789.
This library was one of the most significant colonial legal libraries in North Carolina.
It can be viewed today at the North Carolina Collection gallery in Wilson Library
at the University of North Carolina at Chapel Hill.

CHAPTER 1

Law and legal education in North Carolina's early days

Samuel Johnston, governor of North Carolina from 1787-1789, was the first U.S. senator from the state of North Carolina. He was elected president of the first Continental Congress but declined for family reasons. In April 1776, he served as a Chowan County representative to the Provincial Congress in Halifax, which unanimously adopted the Halifax Resolves, making North Carolina the first colony to take official action toward independence from Great Britain.

In colonial North Carolina, the law did not enjoy the respect in the community that it would later command. With powerful governors and a restive populace, laws regarding human conduct or controlling human affairs were few in number and, when present, were but little regarded. Lawyers themselves had a decidedly mixed reputation at best from the earliest days of the colony; indeed, the Fundamental Constitutions of 1669 had discouraged the employment of lawyers altogether:

> It shall be a base and vile thing, to plead for money or reward;
> nor shall any one ... be permitted to plead another man's cause
> till before the judge in open court, he hath taken an oath that
> he doth not plead for money or reward....

Law and politics, those constant bedfellows, were intertwined from the beginning in North Carolina. From the founding of the colony to very near the American Revolution, the licensing of attorneys was left entirely to the governor (though the custom was for the chief justice to give "a perfunctory examination" before recommending them to the executive). Inevitably some men were licensed to practice who had no scruples, or no legal training whatsoever. The low fees available to lawyers in the colony encouraged some to carry over their cases indefinitely, thus running up charges on the client, a situation which only worsened the reputation of the profession.

Despite popular opposition, a number of lawyers appeared before the courts during the colonial period, their names echoing down through the centuries: James Thigpen, Samuel Swann, Richard Henderson, John Baptista Ashe, William Hooper and Abner Nash. A few of these skilled practitioners who enjoyed the governor's favor often gained both wealth and influence; indeed, by the end of the 17th century, some of the most prominent figures in North Carolina were attorneys, men such as Alexander Lillington and Henderson Walker. Still, by the early 18th century, the feelings of most North Carolinians toward lawyers were echoed in a famous letter by a resident of Perquimans County, who wrote that "most who profess themselves doctors and attorneys [here] are scandals to their profession."

From the early 1700s to the eve of the Revolution, many bills were filed in the General Assembly attempting to regulate lawyers' fees in North Carolina. Though a bill was passed in 1731 limiting attorney's fees to "ten shillings for every cause in the General Court," no other measures became law and public sentiment against lawyers continued to grow. By 1760, the assembly was complaining to the governor that "the granting [of] Licenses to persons to practice the Law who are ignorant even of the rudiments of that Science is a reproach to Government, [a] Disgrace to the Profession, and greatly injurious to Suitors." Resentment against lawyers in colonial North Carolina was also directed at what later came to be called "the courthouse crowd" of local public officials.

The same Fundamental Constitutions of 1669 that had discouraged the use of attorneys also vested in the governor the sole power to staff the county courts and appoint justices of the peace. Prior to the Reconstruction era, the county court served as the administrative as well as the judicial branch of government in North Carolina. In addition to levying taxes, this "Court of Pleas and Quarter Sessions" filled the majority of lucrative and influential local offices, such as surveyor, treasurer, register of deeds and overseer of roads. Appointed by the governor on the recommendation of local legislators, the justices of the peace were invariably selected from the county's economic and political elite. Justices served for life or as long as they maintained local residence, and each justice had the power to convene his own magistrate's court when necessary to "maintain, keep and preserve the peace."

Lawyers often held such county offices and therein earned for the profession a none too favorable reputation. That such an attitude was prevalent in the colony is shown by a famous epitaph on a mid-18th century gravestone of Christ Church Cemetery in New Bern:

> "To the Memory of
> CHARLES ELLIOTT
> Late Attorney General for this Province
> Who died Anno 1756
> An Honest Lawyer Indeed!"

Such perceptions of dishonesty, unchecked power and despotism — and real abuses, to be sure, such as extortion of illegal fees by court officers — helped lead to the rise of the Regulator movement, a radical protest for political rights in the face of corruption by some public men and government officials. In

Edmund Fanning, a colonial lawyer and public official, was burned out of his house by the Regulators.

Gov. William Tryon and the Regulators, circa 1771.

September 1770, a group of Regulators stormed the Orange County Courthouse and assaulted two lawyers, John Williams and Edmund Fanning, as set down in the official court records:

> Several persons stiling [sic] themselves Regulators assembled together in the Court Yard ... and many others insulted some of the Gentlemen of the Bar, & in a violent manner went into the Court House, and forcibly carried out some of the attorneys, and in a cruel manner beat them. They then insisted that the Judge should proceed to the Tryal [sic] of their Leaders, who had been indicted at a former Court, and that the Jury should be taken out of their party. Therefore the Judge ... adjourned the Court ... and took the advantage of the night & made his escape.

Edmund Fanning epitomized the worst aspects of the conservative lawyer, planter and merchant elite, these "gentlemen" whom the radicals blamed for all of North Carolina's ills. Fanning's haughty attitude, his ostentatious style of living, and his mistreatment of many people who had to do business with him at the courthouse earned him the enmity of many in the Piedmont back country. The Regulator movement against the conservative elite ended the next year at the Battle of Alamance (1771), and the Regulators' cause — individual liberty and a just political order — was laid aside for several decades. It would take even longer for North Carolina's "gentlemen lawyers" to fully restore their reputation, organize professionally, and take full strides in "preserving the blessings of liberty" for all.

Early Legal Education in North Carolina

If the law were to become a more popular and respectable profession in North Carolina, legal education would have to become more formalized and more readily available. Long before there was any drive to form a statewide professional organization, lawyers in North Carolina began — in fits and starts to be sure — to offer a more rigorous and organized education in the law. Individual study would slowly give way to schools of law, and instruction in jurisprudence and legal history would begin to supplement the strictly practical education offered at first.

From the earliest days of the colony, a young man interested in the law could read the law by himself or under the guidance of another lawyer. In the minds of many, however, the most prestigious legal education to be had was at one of the English Inns of Court. These voluntary associations of law students operated along the lines of medieval trade guilds, making their own rules and, with the approval of the judges, conferring the right to practice in the courts. In the Inns one was not only introduced to the complexities of the common law which governed legal practice in England and in English America, but also to the professional collegiality which was one of the predominant characteristics of the legal profession in England and America. Eleven lawyers in Colonial North Carolina received training at the Inns of Court, including Gabriel Cathcart, the brother-in-law of Samuel Johnston of Hayes Library fame. Yet after the American Revolution only a handful of North Carolinians studied the law abroad or received their education from the Inns of Court.

A few young men did indeed read the law alone, in both the colonial and antebellum periods, with no guidance but the collection of books that they were able to borrow or purchase. Such was the choice of a few talented young North Carolinians in the early 19th century, a time when, in the words of Judge Robert W. Winston, "a Tar Heel banked on horse sense, was gun shy of too much book learning, and generally agreed with Seneca that 'it is much better to be confined to a few authors than to wander at random over many.'"

Colonial attorney Richard Caswell later served as North Carolina's first governor from 1776-1780. Pictured on his desk are his English law books (above), with an example of one of the cover pages (below).

Due to poor road conditions, riding the circuit — for both lawyers and judges — was an arduous journey.

Yet most aspiring attorneys in the late 18th century studied law in the private office of an experienced practitioner. In addition to utilizing the law books in the office, such apprentice lawyers profited from participating in the office work and in observing their mentors in court. In the best apprenticeships they learned how to gather evidence, investigate authorities, prepare legal instruments and try a case in court.

But studying law in a law office was far more haphazard than it was systematic. The student apprentice learned what law he could from watching the practicing attorney, reading his books, and picking up whatever scattered comments he made on the law, but, when the lawyer left town, the student was left to his own devices. Often the lawyers and judges of the day were out of town "riding the circuit," as the General Assembly of 1777 had directed that the Superior Court sit semiannually in each of the "court towns" of the six judicial districts first established by the royal government in 1768. The journey was much more arduous and time-consuming than the travels to the circuit courts of the late 20th century, as depicted in this account of the travels of Justice James Iredell:

> When the courts opened they [the lawyers] followed the judges, from Edenton to Hillsboro, from Hillsboro to Halifax, from Halifax to Salisbury, from Salisbury to Wilmington, and from Wilmington to New Bern. Their way lay through the wilderness, over swollen rivers, through pestilential swamps, through rain and snow, hailstorm and sunshine, their usual conveyance a one-seated gig, and their lodging space as chance and the fortunes of the road might determine.

Jurist William Horn Battle wrote that North Carolina "contributed more than her average share of eminent names to the great roll of American lawyers" during the colonial and early federal periods. Nearly all had studied under a respected attorney or judge. Samuel Johnston had read law under Edenton attorney and political leader Thomas Barker. James Iredell, in turn, studied under Samuel Johnston, who later became his father-in-law. William Hooper learned the law under the Massachusetts Patriot leader James Otis, while Waightstill Avery was tutored by Maryland attorney Lyttleton Dennis. While William R. Davie of Halifax, "the father of the University of North Carolina," read law under Judge Spruce Macay (as did Andrew Jackson), Alfred Moore of Wilmington was taught by his father, Judge Maurice Moore.

James Iredell was appointed by President George Washington to the U. S. Supreme Court in 1790.

Law in Antebellum North Carolina

North Carolina in the early 19th century continued to be an overwhelmingly rural state. Even in the small towns dotting the state — where Carolinians came to trade goods, socialize, talk politics and take care of legal business at the courthouse — the pace of life was decidedly rural, shaped by the rhythms of agriculture. The typical small-town lawyer in the antebellum period bartered farm goods for his services and raised some crops himself, earning a living similar to that of many of his townsmen. What attorney Augustus S. Merrimon wrote in his journal about John W. Woodfin, a Buncombe County farmer-lawyer of the 1850s, could be applied to many antebellum lawyers: "Woodfin has been at the Bar for about ten or twelve years and has succeeded well. He has more taste for his farm than for his Law Office...."

Early in his career, William H. Battle proved the wisdom of starting a small practice and staying with it, even though it was slow to grow. Battle opened a law office in Louisburg in 1825 while continuing to farm. Battle's son, Kemp Plummer Battle, wrote that his father's "learning, integrity and reliability, combined with pleasant manners, procured him clients," and in time eventuated in a large practice.

In the antebellum period, legal education continued to be more practical than theoretical, more informal than organized. A few men, like Edwin Godwin Reade, continued to read law at home with books borrowed elsewhere. But even Reade, who became one of the most brilliant orators and successful practitioners of his day, knew that he had much to learn from other lawyers:

> When I was about to start out to practice law [in 1835] I asked the advice of Judge Mangum. He named the Courts which he advised me to attend. 'But Judge,' said I, 'the oldest lawyers in the State practice in those Courts, and have all the business. And I have neither reputation, nor friends, nor money.' 'No matter,' said he. 'Go where there is business; do not fear competition. The examples of these great men are just what you need. If you want to find tall trees you must go among tall trees.' I took his advice and proved its wisdom.

Since there was no required period of study and no standard curriculum set by the bar, most aspiring young lawyers continued to make individual arrangements to read law with some established practitioner before standing for the bar examination, just as their predecessors had done in the colonial period. To the earlier core text of English common law — Blackstone's "Commentaries" and its kin — was added a steadily growing body of American law.

Though this method of legal education remained deficient in many respects, some of North Carolina's finest lawyers of the antebellum period learned the law individually from a member of the bench or bar. William Gaston, the eminent North Carolina Supreme Court justice whom Daniel Webster called "the greatest of the great men" of the War Congress in which he served, read law under Francois-Xavier Martin in New Bern. George Badger, a forceful and eloquent attorney who later served as U. S. senator and secretary of the Navy, studied under his cousin John Stanley, also of New Bern. And Duncan K. MacRae, a politician and orator ranked as one of the greatest criminal lawyers the state has ever produced, learned the law under the tutelage of Judge Robert Strange of Fayetteville.

Early law offices were often small one or two-room buildings located near the lawyer's home such as this, the Bryan Law Office in New Bern.

John Louis Taylor opened a law school in Raleigh in 1822.

Leonard Henderson, who would later become chief justice of the North Carolina Supreme Court, taught law students in the early 1800s.

William Gaston, a lawyer and state Supreme Court justice, was one of the most prominent men in 19th century North Carolina.

Proprietary Law Schools

The next step in the development of legal education was the evolution of proprietary law schools in the 1820s and 1830s. Owned and controlled by a single lawyer or several lawyers acting together, proprietary law schools provided legal education for a set fee. A lawyer who had one or two students in his office reading law on an *ad hoc* basis and helping with routine legal tasks, might decide, especially as he grew near retirement, to bring order to the system and at the same time increase his income. Several students would be brought in, charged tuition, and instructed on certain legal topics. The teaching of law remained a sideline in this period, as nearly every lawyer-instructor continued to earn his living chiefly from the practice of law.

Nearly all the proprietary law students in North Carolina lived in the attorney's home or with neighboring families. A few instructors constructed small structures away from the primary dwelling to give their families and the students a modicum of privacy. Board and basic supplies were charged to, if not provided by, the students themselves. In towns and villages, many students secured room and board in boarding houses. Fees for instruction and board varied greatly, ranging from $100 to $225 per year. Students were responsible for their own supplies, though they could use books belonging to the sponsoring attorney. Some proprietary law students studied for only a few months at $10 a month, but most completed their course of study in one to two years.

The first place for legal education in North Carolina which could legitimately be called a school was opened by John Louis Taylor. Taylor had taught students for a number of years but formally opened a school in Raleigh in 1822. An advertisement in the *Raleigh Register* that year announced "The Subscriber having lately, at the request of some of his friends and pupils, undertaken the professional tuition of an additional number of Students, to whose improvement his constant residence at home enables him to pay more attention than heretofore, is encouraged to believe that his mode of instruction may be rendered more extensively useful by being made public."

When the Supreme Court of North Carolina was established in Raleigh in 1818, John Louis Taylor became its first chief justice. He taught at his school throughout the 1820s while serving on the Supreme Court. David Lowry Swain, later governor and president of the University of North Carolina, was one of Taylor's most celebrated students during that period. In his will, Taylor bequeathed his Raleigh home, "Elmwood," to his son-in-law, William Gaston, himself the teacher of such noted lawyers as Hamilton Chamberlain Jones of Mecklenburg County, seventh president of the North Carolina Bar Association.

Leonard Henderson, another pioneering law instructor, studied law near his home in Williamsboro in the law office of Judge John Williams. After serving as clerk of the district court in Hillsboro, he began teaching law students, first in his office and then at a separate school in Williamsboro in 1819. Three years earlier he had resigned from the Superior Court bench and returned to the full-time practice and teaching of law. In 1818, he was chosen as one of the three justices of the newly established Supreme Court. After the death of John Louis Taylor, Henderson became chief justice and served in that capacity until his death. Henderson's students were well-trained in the law, their knowledge based on a variety of cases which he carefully selected. Among his students were Richmond M. Pearson, who would later establish a famous law school on the Yadkin River, and William Horn Battle, who founded the law school at the University of North Carolina.

Little is known of the proprietary teacher Richard Trapier Brumby, a South Carolinian who appears to have read law with George Badger and Leonard Henderson. While Brumby's first advertisements for law students appear in the *Raleigh Register* of December 1829, it appears that he moved to Lincolnton in 1828 to establish a law practice there. Brumby and his brother established a small school there after Brumby's health declined and he was no longer able to attend court. In addition to Latin, Greek and mathematics, Brumby taught law, promising that he could devote more time to his students than most lawyers, for in his words, "it is a notorious fact that practicing lawyers have neither time nor inclination to direct the studies of their students, and that they do not examine them as often as once a month." Richard Brumby closed his school in 1831 and moved to Tuscaloosa, Alabama, where he became a professor of mineralogy and an ardent nullificationist.

Archibald DeBow Murphey, attorney, legislator, jurist and strong proponent of public education and internal improvements, had outstanding individual pupils such as Thomas Ruffin, Jonathan Worth and John Motley Morehead. Newspaper advertisements in 1831 announced that he had recently settled in Hillsboro and would receive a few law students there. Unfortunately for the profession, the plans of the man called "the father of the common schools of North Carolina" were cut short by his death early the next year.

John Lancaster Bailey began teaching law students in his office in Elizabeth City about 1835, after studying under James Iredell. In May 1845, he announced that he would establish a law school in Hillsboro to be open "during the time he is not necessarily attending his Courts." He later joined forces to conduct a law school with Frederick Nash, a justice on the state Supreme Court. Three years earlier Nash and Hugh Waddell had proposed opening a school in "the seclusion of [the] quiet Village of Hillsboro," provided that at least eight students enrolled.

In 1859, following Nash's death, Bailey moved to a farm in Black Mountain where his son, William H. Bailey, joined him briefly. The new school, on the north fork of the Swannanoa River, opened on March 1, 1859. Instruction was interrupted by the Civil War, but Bailey resumed teaching after the end of hostilities. Some of his notable students were state attorney general Theodore Davidson and Judge James Merrimon of Buncombe County.

From the 1840s through the 1870s, Richmond M. Pearson and William H. Battle were the pre-eminent teachers of law in North Carolina. Students of Judge Leonard Henderson, Pearson and Battle were also fellow graduates of the University of North Carolina.

The Richmond Hill Law School

Richmond Mumford Pearson opened a law school at Mocksville around 1836. About 10 years later, he moved his family to a sizable plantation in what is now Yadkin County on the south side of the Yadkin River. There, on his Richmond Hill plantation, he opened a law school familiarly known as "Logtown" or, more often, "Richmond Hill." At Richmond Hill, Pearson utilized a rigorous Socratic method of discussion, questioning students on the law and its principles. He prepared beginning students for their county court license as well as advanced students for their license to practice in the superior courts.

A number of Richmond Pearson's students became judges; indeed, three served with him on the state Supreme Court, and three others followed him on the Court after his death. The Richmond Hill school also produced three governors of North Carolina and a trio of United States congressmen, as well as countless numbers of local public officials. Some sources credit Pearson's law school with producing more than 1,000 lawyers during the 19th century.

Archibald DeBow Murphey's plan to instruct law students was cut short by his death in 1832.

Frederick Nash (above) and John Lancaster Bailey (below) joined forces to open an early law school in Hillsborough around the year 1845.

The Richmond Hill Law School (1848-1878), located in Yadkin County, became well known and highly regarded for its exceptional instructors and successful students.

William Horn Battle trained for the law in Chief Justice Leonard Henderson's office and was admitted to the bar in 1824. He served as reporter to the state Supreme Court and worked to revise the statutory laws of the state in the 1830s. In 1840, Battle was appointed a superior court judge, and the next year he and James Iredell Jr. jointly taught law students in Raleigh. By 1843, William Horn Battle had moved to Chapel Hill for the purpose of educating his sons at the university. That same year he opened a law office on the grounds of his home to teach students when the court was not in session.

The George N. Folk Law School

Little known to history is the law school of George Nathaniel Folk, a Virginia native who, in 1852, had moved to Watauga County, an area of the state which he was elected to represent in 1856 and again in 1861. After serving as a colonel of the 65th N.C. Regiment during the war, George N. Folk settled in Lenoir in 1866, where he opened a law school for the "ragged Confederate veterans" of the region. By the 1870s, Folk's Caldwell County law school was said to have been "a well-known institution, drawing boys from many sections of the state," the students living in small houses about the grounds of Folk's home, "Riverside." Folk called his law school "Blackstone," after the famed English jurist. His students included Thomas A. Love, a prominent attorney in Mitchell and Avery counties and a founding trustee of Appalachian State University; and Edward J. Justice, a Rutherford County native and leading Progressive legislator from Guilford County, who was also a founding officer of the North Carolina Bar Association.

Richmond M. Pearson, founder of the Richmond Hill Law School, was said to have instructed more than 1,000 students in his career.

THE STATE OF NORTH CAROLINA.

To the several Courts of this State:

Samuel Hinsdale MacRae

having applied to the undersigned Chief Justice and Associate Justices of the Supreme Court, to be examined with the view to be admitted to practice as an

ATTORNEY AND COUNSELLOR AT LAW, in said Courts:

We do certify, that he hath produced before us such sufficient testimonials of his upright character, and upon examination before us has been found to possess such competent Knowledge of the LAW as entitle him to be so admitted.

Given under our hands at Raleigh, the 24 day of September 1892

A. S. Merrimon Chief Justice.

A. C. Avery Associate Justice.

Jas. E. Shepherd Associate Justice.

Walter Clark Associate Justice.

Jas. C. MacRae Associate Justice.

TAX PAID $20.

Thos. S. Kenan
S.C.C.

Late 19th century law license of Samuel Hinsdale MacRae, signed by members of the North Carolina Supreme Court. Future Bar Association President Thomas S. Kenan (1904-1905) served as clerk of the Supreme Court.

Early Law in Western North Carolina: A Note

Lawyers were more scarce, and legal institutions (such as Colonel Folk's Law School) more slow to develop, in the isolated western part of North Carolina, a section hampered by geographical barriers, limited means of transportation, and political domination by the landholding elite in the east. As late as the early 1830s, the western part of the state was seen as little more than a jumping-off point for points further west. As the society and economy of the state stagnated, a Raleigh journalist commented that "between the Eastern and Western parts of this State is as great [a] dissimilarity in the face of the country, productions, and means of subsistence as usually exists between different and widely separated nations." The entire state was suffering industrially, educationally and politically.

The lack of suitable farm land, along with inadequate transportation facilities, tight credit and an undemocratic political climate, caused many residents to leave the state altogether, rather than further settle the back country and western sections. In 1830, North Carolinians themselves seemed asleep, heedless of the fact that hundreds of thousands of people were leaving the state for good, so much so that others began to call North Carolina "the Rip Van Winkle State."

But beginning in 1835, with the advent of a competitive two-party system in the state and a revised constitution — which for the first time gave western citizens an effective political voice — the population in western North Carolina began to grow. State investment in transportation increased, mineral resources were developed, and commercial agriculture grew. New counties were formed, and a western Superior Court circuit encompassing Buncombe, Madison, Cherokee, Jackson, Haywood, Henderson and Yancey counties would be established by the early 1850s.

In the 1830s, western North Carolinians had reasons both to praise and to criticize the state's new Supreme Court, founded in 1818. Lawyers in the western counties, already predisposed to criticize an unresponsive, distant state government dominated by eastern planters, protested the long journeys they had to make in order to argue cases appealed to the Supreme Court. (By 1846 the General Assembly would require the Court to hold an August term in Morganton.) In the reformist democratic spirit of the Jacksonian years, many westerners thought the Court an elitist institution too far removed from the people, its justices chosen rather than elected and given "extravagant" salaries of $2,500 per year (the governor's salary was only $2,000). But it was the same Supreme Court — under the leadership of Justice Thomas Ruffin — whose decisions transformed the common law of North Carolina into an instrument of economic change. Ruffin's writings on eminent domain paved the way for the expansion of railroads and other public improvements, enabling the Rip Van Winkle state to embrace the nascent industrial revolution.

Still, the legal system in parts of western North Carolina of that day was relatively undeveloped. Respect for the law was not uniformly present, and in some counties a legal system which could only be called "rough justice" seems to have prevailed. A. S. Merrimon, a young Asheville attorney at the time, describes the scene at the Yancey County Courthouse during the January term, 1854:

> Several cases of little importance have been disposed of today, and the court is a perfect mockery of justice. I feel confident in saying that I have never seen a court behave so badly and *keep* such confusion. There is during this Session of the court a continual fuss, a continual talking, so that the Court, the Council nor the jury cannot hear the testimony. It is disgraceful... There has

been quite a crowd in attendance today and they have tried to see how badly they could behave themselves. Scores were drunk and tonight are snoozing away over the drunkenness of today. The more I see of the County Courts, the more I wish to see them abolished.... A portion of the Court has been drunk all day. How shameful! A portion of the time, while suits were trying the whole court were [sic] off of the bench.

Meanwhile, a few hundred miles east, two law professors at the state university were a few years into their experiment of training "classically educated young gentlemen" in the law, with the hope that they would lead in the creation of that "virtuous and orderly" society envisioned by the founding fathers.

The First University Law School: Chapel Hill (1845)

Americans in the middle of the 19th century trusted in the promise of social reforms, and North Carolinians shared in that hope of a more orderly and virtuous society. The expanding interest in higher education in the state in the 1840s and 1850s both reflected and reinforced the reform impulse. The University of North Carolina, chartered by the state Legislature in 1789, had been vilified by some as a "school for the rich." Yet during the 19th century, university administrators would broaden its classical curriculum and "popularize" the institution by opening enrollment and emphasizing the importance of training the state's brightest young men for careers in public service.

In 1845, University of North Carolina President David L. Swain established a law department headed by William Horn Battle. Battle continued to teach out of his Chapel Hill office and received no salary from the university. He was "entitled to demand from each member of the Independent Class fifty dollars per session for the first two sessions of the course, and twenty-five dollars per session afterwards."

In order to make up for the absence of the "laboratories" of law office and courtroom which legal education was leaving behind in moving from private

Founder of the University of North Carolina's law school, William H. Battle later served as a legislator and president of the university.

University of North Carolina law students (1892).

Robert Paine Dick, co-founder of the Greensboro Law School, also known as the Dick & Dillard Law School.

office to private school, Battle decided to require his students to "from time to time draw pleadings and other legal instruments" and test them out "in a moot court held occasionally." The judge also established a two-year course of study in order to receive the LL.B. degree.

Samuel Field Phillips was added to the law faculty in 1854. A student of Battle, Phillips took the judge's place when he was at court and remained at the university for five years before going on to a distinguished career in the law. The law school, along with the rest of the university, closed for five years after the Civil War. In 1894, the same year that Wake Forest College opened its law school, the University of North Carolina trustees put the law school on the "same footing" as other departments of the university. James Cameron MacRae was named as "Professor of Common and Statute Law and Equity" in 1899, and Dean of the Law Department the following year. (MacRae, a Fayetteville native, had become a charter member of the North Carolina Bar Association in February 1899 and attended its first annual meeting at Morehead City that summer.)

Greensboro Law School ("Dick and Dillard")

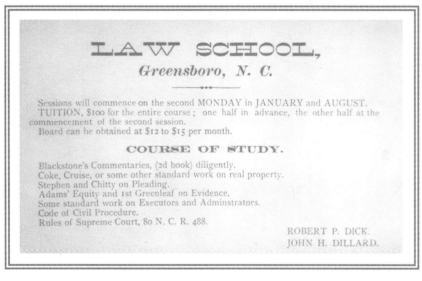

An advertisement for the Greensboro Law School.

Richmond Pearson died in 1878, and William H. Battle died the following year. Pearson's school appears not to have continued after his death, but the University of North Carolina law school continued to develop into a modern legal education program. A few proprietary law schools continued to flourish. The Greensboro Law School was founded in 1878 shortly after the death of Richmond Pearson. Its founders, Robert Paine Dick and John Henry Dillard, had both served with Justice Pearson on the Supreme Court. Popularly known as the "Dick and Dillard Law School," it provided sound legal training for many of the state's lawyers in the latter part of the 19th century, including Francis D. Winston, 14th president of the association. It apparently did not survive the deaths of its founders.

Shaw University Law School

In December 1888, Shaw University in Raleigh opened the only law school for "colored" students in the South. John S. Leary of Fayetteville was appointed dean of the Shaw University Law Department. Leary, a graduate of Howard University Law School and only the second black admitted to the North Carolina bar, had represented Cumberland County in the state House of Representatives from 1868 to 1870. While at Shaw, he also served as president of the North Carolina Colored Industrial Association, an organization devoted to improving the welfare of blacks in the state.

Edward Augustus Johnson, the first graduate of the Law Department of Shaw University, became a member of the law faculty after graduation and remained at the school until 1906, serving as dean for part of his tenure. The Trustee Board minutes for 1893 describe Johnson's curriculum as "Instruction in the drawing of papers technically called 'Pleadings,' a very difficult and important part of the science. He also instructs in shorthand and typewriting. ... Because the young lawyer who can write shorthand or operate the typewriter can find many openings...."

Johnson was probably the best-known black lawyer in North Carolina at the turn of the century, respected for his founding of the Raleigh's Pickford Sanitarium "for consumptive Negroes." While still in law school he had published *A School History of the Negro Race in America*, a textbook used by black fourth-graders in North Carolina. After leaving Shaw he moved to New York, where, in 1916, he became the first black man elected to the New York state Legislature. The 1894 commencement program for the Shaw University Law Department listed seven law graduates and two faculty members (Leary and Johnson), with R. H. Battle of Raleigh, a charter member of the North Carolina Bar Association, delivering the annual address.

Shaw University in Raleigh (circa 1908) was home to a law school from 1888-1914.

Shaw President Henry Martin Tupper boasted that the law school "seems to command the respect of the Judges of the Supreme Court of North Carolina before whom our law students appear for examination before they commence to practice in court." But few students enrolled, and only 54 students graduated from the law school between 1890 and its closing in 1914. Although no official reason was given for closing the Shaw Law School, it was likely due to the high cost of professional education programs and low enrollment. During the school's last term (1913-1914), there were only four enrolled students. Still, the school produced some prominent graduates — including a United States congressman and a municipal judge in the District of Columbia — and trained most of the black lawyers in North and South Carolina until the mid-1930s. Even as late as 1940, it was reported that one quarter of the practicing black lawyers in North Carolina were Shaw graduates.

Wake Forest Law School

In 1894, Wake Forest College opened a law school under the direction of Needham Y. Gulley, who had read law under E. W. Pou, one of the founding members of the North Carolina Bar Association. Gulley's success rate was

Pictured left to right are Edward W. Timberlake Jr., Dean Needham Y. Gulley, and Robert B. White, who were called the "Great Triumvirate" of the Wake Forest Law School.

The first admissions brochure for Wake Forest Law School.

remarkable. When he resigned as dean in 1935, more than 1,600 of his students had been licensed to practice law, and approximately half of the practicing attorneys in North Carolina had attended Wake Forest. Gulley resisted changes in legal education, including increased educational requirements, large library resources, and the case method of legal education.

When Wake Forest hired a new law school dean, Dale Foster Stansbury, in 1935, the administration made the commitment to hire more faculty, increase the size of the library, and implement the case study method in all its classes. Such changes finally won the law school accreditation from the American Bar Association. During World War II, Wake Forest participated in a wartime joint program with the Duke University School of Law. The college's law students and faculty traveled to Durham for joint classes, but the program met with only mixed results. Wake enjoyed a large increase in the number of law students during the postwar years just as it was planning for the move of the campus to Winston-Salem.

Carroll W. Weathers became dean at Wake Forest in 1950 and devoted the next 20 years to building and strengthening the law school in its new home. When the time came for the move in 1956, he had already ensured a separate building for the law school on the new campus; increased the number and quality of its law school faculty, as well as the number of volumes in the library; and expanded the impact of the school on the legal profession in North Carolina, the region and the nation. Dean Weathers always stressed the importance of commitment to one's legal studies and the practice of law, along with the need for absolute integrity in one's personal and professional dealings.

Trinity College School of Law

Although a school of law had operated at Trinity College from 1868 to 1882 under President Braxton Craven — and again for three years (1891-1894) under Justice Alphonso C. Avery when the college relocated to Durham — the modern law department dates to 1904. That year, James B. Duke and Benjamin N. Duke provided the endowment to reopen the Trinity College School of Law. Samuel Fox Mordecai, a prominent member of the Raleigh bar and a part-time lecturer on law at Wake Forest, was appointed senior professor of law. After a study tour of some of the leading American law schools, Mordecai returned to

North Carolina to reorganize the law school. Two years of pre-law study became the new requirement for admission, a three-year program leading to the LL.B. degree was established, and the case method of study was adopted as the basis of instruction. In 1905, the university named Professor Mordecai dean of the law school, and the next year Trinity became the second Southern law school accepted by the Association of American Law Schools. Trinity continued to flourish as the college gained more financial support from the Duke family and foundations, and, in 1924, became the Duke University School of Law upon the acceptance of the Duke Endowment from James B. Duke. Sixteen years would pass before another new law school was established in the state.

Claude Love's Law School

Most of the proprietary law schools disappeared with the changes in requirements for legal education and admission to the bar in the 1930s. One notable exception — along with the "Wilmington Law School" (1913-1941) of Harry Edmund Rodgers — was Claude Love's law school, which operated in Asheville from 1926 until 1951. With no other schools operating west of Chapel Hill and the curriculum becoming more rigorous, Love's private law school filled a need. Claude Love's annual summer review course, designed to prepare candidates to take the bar examination, proved even more popular. Love, an Asheville lawyer, served terms as a state legislator, assistant attorney general and president of the Buncombe County Bar Association prior to his death in 1959. Many prominent attorneys were Love students and, at the time of his death in 1959, it was reported that Love had prepared at least 1,000 young lawyers for the bar examination.

An Evolving Story

Clearly, in the years immediately following the founding of the North Carolina Bar Association, legal education under the auspices of educational institutions was flourishing. Other law schools, all associated with colleges and universities, would be founded in the 20th century. (The continuing story of the schools of law associated with the University of North Carolina, Wake Forest and Duke and their roles in the practice of law in North Carolina will be discussed in later chapters, as will the stories of the other schools of law created in the 20th century: The North Carolina Central University School of Law, chartered in 1940, and the Campbell University School of Law, founded in 1975.)

In reviewing the early years of legal education in North Carolina, it is clear that each of the previous institutions for the teaching of law — the private home, the private office, the proprietary law school and the early college law school — added something new and valuable to the prior method. Over time, a consensus developed in North Carolina on the proper elements of a legal education, but a variety of institutions offering legal instruction persisted for decades to come. As society and culture continued to change, so would the practice of law. In the 20th century, the North Carolina Bar Association would play a significant role in preparing the profession for what Justice Felix Frankfurter called "the overwhelming task of governing modern society by law."

Samuel Fox Mordecai, founder of the modern law school at Trinity College in Durham (now Duke University).

Tobacco wagons travel down one of Winston's main streets around the turn of the century.
The separate towns of Winston and Salem merged into Winston-Salem 1n 1913.

∞

CHAPTER 2

Law and Society
in North Carolina
1865-1899

T he Civil War had ravaged North Carolina. Property damage was enormous, wealth had been wiped away almost overnight, and the economy was in ruins — to say nothing of the loss of life, which had touched nearly every family in the state in some manner. Those who had remained at home during the war — nine out of 10 Tar Heels — had already endured four years of deprivation, exorbitant prices and depreciating currency. Now there were hardships anew: scores of wounded and demoralized soldiers; the collapse of the social order and local government; an acute labor shortage; and an uncertain future, both politically and economically.

Still, the state would slowly rise from the ashes of war; indeed, the social crisis in North Carolina brought on by the war would, in time, create new possibilities. More than 100,000 Tar Heels had traveled hundreds of miles from their localities and seen a wider world. Women had managed farms and businesses while the men in the family had gone to fight. Black North Carolinians were now free from slavery.

The law profession continued to change in reaction to the political and social disruptions that rippled through North Carolina during most of the last half of the 19th century. In the half-century after the Civil War, a new industrial society emerged in the United States, renewing the nation's historic promise as a land of opportunity for all. But prosperity would be unevenly distributed, and opportunities not always as promised. A gnawing question would emerge in the minds of nearly every North Carolinian—who would control this increasingly productive and powerful society, and who would ensure these "blessings of liberty" for all?

This collection letter from Wilmington attorney Frederick D. Poisson, dated January 23, 1877, was sent to give the recipient a chance to avoid the "unpleasantness and expense" of a lawsuit. The amount in question: $29.35.

The Politics of Reconstruction

The Reconstruction period was a time of political confrontation and social upheaval in North Carolina. With federal troops still garrisoned in the state, Republicans gained control of state and local governments for several years from

Zebulon Baird Vance was a U.S. senator and two-time governor of North Carolina.

The final page of the state constitution of 1868. Among other things, this constitution eliminated county courts and replaced them with county commissioners.

the Conservatives (Democrats). A new, more egalitarian state constitution was passed in 1868, broadening suffrage, democratizing elective offices, and reforming the county courts. Blacks gained the right to vote and a number of black Republicans were elected to municipal, county and state offices. George H. White, a black attorney from New Bern, served in the U.S. House of Representatives from 1897 to 1901. He was the last black man — in the North or South — to serve in the Congress for a quarter of a century. White, who went on to practice law in Washington, D.C., and later settled in New Jersey, is reported to have said that he left his native state because he "could not live in North Carolina and be a man."

Most of the wealthy, land-holding Conservative elite were threatened by the loss of political control to these unproven officeholders. Many feared reprisals and a possible collapse of the social order from a government run by white subsistence farmers and poor blacks, but particularly by blacks. The presence of 20 black members in the General Assembly of 1868-69 — as well as many northern "Carpetbagger" Republicans — spurred many of the Conservatives to act against what they saw as a corrupt government. An instrument was already at hand in the Ku Klux Klan, which had been founded just a few years earlier.

In the Reconstruction period, nearly every prominent lawyer in the state was a Conservative, but most probably agreed with Judge Richmond Pearson's nonviolent stance toward the Republican takeover: "When the storm is over, the Conservative party representing as it does, the property and intelligence of the State, will take the guidance of affairs, and all will be well."

However, the judge's advice was not taken, and heavily armed bands of Klansmen terrorized blacks as well as white sympathizers. The vigilantes at times resorted to murdering the most prominent black Republicans, and their campaign of terror proved effective: Gov. W.W. Holden, a Republican, was impeached in 1871; the Conservatives regained control of the General Assembly, and by 1876 the Conservatives — now called "Democrats" — had reclaimed the governorship from the Republicans.

Law in the 1870s: Crisis and Opportunity

Most attorneys continued their law practices during Reconstruction, but the focus of many attorneys changed. With money scarce and the market economy diminished, many North Carolinians returned to a simpler, more self-sufficient existence, whether on the farm or in town. The need for legal services decreased proportionally in the immediate aftermath of the war, leaving many attorneys to retrench and rebuild their practices. Perhaps the scene in many a North Carolina village of the 1870s was not unlike that described by Albion W. Tourgee, a Guilford County judge during Reconstruction, in his book, *With Gauge & Swallow, Attorneys:*

Before the reorganization of the court system, local justices of the peace acted in numerous legal capacities.

> During court-week the little town was populous and prosperous, the inn, of course, being the centre of population, if not the chief recipient of this recurrent prosperity; but the lawyers, officers of the court, and even the merchants, as well as the landlord, looked forward to the coming of the judge as an epoch when prosperity should wipe out the memory of the dull and profitless interval since his last departure.

STATE OF NORTH CAROLINA.
EDGECOMBE COUNTY.

ON this the 25 day of *Aug.* 1866, personally appeared before me, *W. W. Parker* a Justice of the Peace in and for said County, *Aaron Proctor* and *Rosa Taylor* residents of said County, both of whom were lately slaves, but now emancipated, and acknowledge that they have cohabited as man and wife for 5 years, 2 *Children* *W. W. Parker* J.P.

In western North Carolina, "court week" may have played an even more important role, as historians Ina and John Van Noppen contend:

> The courthouse was to the county seat what the cathedral was to a medieval city: it expressed the hopes and aspirations of the people. It was the heart's core of the western counties, the shaper of human lives and destinies.... It was the focal point of the social life, the occasion when those from one cove could meet and gossip with their neighbors from other coves and ridges.... They came to meet their friends and relatives, to buy and sell, and to barter their home-grown products for store-bought goods, needed supplies of salt, coffee, medicines, and tools.

In small towns, court week was a legal, political and social occasion. Court proceedings and the lawyers' oral arguments often served as entertainment.

Court Week.

N. C. Hughes.
W. H. Oliver.
L. F. Ives.

Job Printing Offices

W. T. Hill.
Richardson's Printing Office.

Junk Dealers.

D. Becker & Co.

Lawyers.

A. D. Ward.
D. L. Ward.
C. R. Thomas.
R. B. Nixon.
L. J. Moore.
O. H. Guion.
M. D. W Stevenson.
H. C. Whitehurst.
R. A. Nunn.
E. W. Carpenter.
W. D. McIver.
P. H. Pelletier.
W. W. Clark.
S. M. Prinson.
W. J. McSorley.
J. E. & R. O'Hara. (col.)
R. W. Williamson, (col.)

Laundries.

O. K. Steam Laundry.
Hop Wah.
Long Wah Sing.

Leather Dealers.

L. H. Cutler & Co.
W. S. Phillips.
Gaskill Hardware Co.
P. M. Draney.
J. C. Whitty & Co.

Lumber M'f'rs and Dealers.

The Blade Lumber Co.
The Trent Lumber Mills.
Elm City Lumber Co.
Pine Lumber Co.
S. E. Sullivan.
C. W. Monger.

Machinery Dealers.

The Hyman Supply Co.

Machine Shops.

Willis & McIntosh.

Marble Works.

Joe K. Willis.

Masons and Builders.

J. L. Hartsfield.
B. F. Delamar.

Mattress Manufacturers.

W. P. Jones.

Millinery and Fancy Goods

Mrs Duncan & Whitcomb.
Simmons-Hollowel Co.
J A Barfoot.

Mineral Water Bottlers.

C. D. Bradham.

Medicine Manufacturers.

F. S. Duffy.
C. D. Bradham.
T A Henry.

Music Teachers.

Miss Carrie Hendren.
Miss Fannie Holland.
Miss Mary Hatch Harrison.
Miss Emma Powell.
Miss Cathryn Griffin.
Miss Alma Speight.

Musical Instruments.

George A. Ennett.
E. Walnau.

Naval Store Dealers.

John Ellis.

Officers Cotton Exchange.

OFFICERS—President, J. E. Latham;
Vice-President, E. H. Meadows; Treasurer,
T. A. Green; Secretary, James Redmond.

Newspapers and Editors.

THE JOURNAL—Charles L. Stevens, Ed.

Oil Dealers.

Hollister & Cox.
George Clark.

Painters.

Edgar T. Hollowell.
Wm. E. Charlotte.
R. B. Blalock.
C. F. Hargett.
W. J. Osteen.

Paper-Hangers.

Guilford Lewis.
R. B. Blalock.
E. T. Hollowell.
C. F. Hargett.

Paint and Oil Dealers.

J. C. Whitty & Co.
E. W. Smallwood.
L. H. Cutler & Co.
Gaskill Hardware Co.
P. M. Draney.
B. B. Davenport.
J. F. Taylor.

Plumbers.

J. C. Green.
A. B. Wallace.
J. P. Wood.
L. M. Cannon.

Produce Dealers.

Hollister & Cox.
C. S. Hollister.
Broadstreet Fruit Co.
N. C. Hughes.
W. F. Rountree.
J. D. Swindell.
J. A. Parish & Co.

Retail Grocers.

J. F. Taylor.
Hudson & Co.
B. B. Davenport.
J. F. Clark.
Armstrong and Matthews.
H. W Jewell.
F. Ulrich.
R. L Thornton.
Lucas & Lewis.
K. R. Jones.
S. W. Willis.
John Dunn.

This 1904 directory listing of New Bern lawyers included the names of James Edward and Raphael O'Hara. Raphael graduated from Shaw University's law school in 1895 and joined his father, former Congressman James Edward, working extensively in real estate.

The 1870s saw a watershed change in the actual practice of law in the courts for every North Carolina lawyer. The Constitution of 1868 had adopted the Code System of procedure to replace the old modified common law practice. Under the old procedure, pleadings were not required to be signed by counsel or even read in open court, except to state the nature of the action and its defense. John D. Bellamy, a prominent Wilmington attorney, described the reaction of the "old lawyers" to the Code System which went into effect in 1875:

> The Code System of Pleading [was] an innovation not at all relished by the lawyers of the old school. It was most interesting and flattering to the young lawyers trained under the Code System, to have the old and experienced lawyers of the olden time to seek their aid and advice as to the manner of preparing and filing pleadings and conducting causes under the new system — the hateful, new innovation, as they termed it, forced unwillingly on them and for which they had no respect....

Economic conditions began to improve in the 1870s, particularly for those working outside of agriculture. Slowly but steadily, towns and small cities were becoming magnets for the ambitious and the restless, as well as havens for those forced off the land by rural poverty. Only one in 25 North Carolinians made town their home in 1870; by 1900, it was one in 10. In the growing economies of the state's towns professionals found new opportunities, including lawyers.

This was also a time of increased opportunities for African-Americans in North Carolina. In 1871, James Edward O'Hara, a Republican activist and Howard University law graduate, became the first black man licensed to practice law in the state. He was the first of a small but steady number of African-Americans, mostly associated with the Republican Party, to establish a practice in North Carolina cities and towns. By 1876, five black lawyers had obtained licenses from the Supreme Court, and, by 1890, there were 14 black lawyers in North Carolina.

James Edward O'Hara — the first African-American licensed to practice law in North Carolina — was elected to the U.S. Congress in 1882.

The "First Ladies" of the Law

Likewise, the decade witnessed the opening of a window of opportunity for women lawyers in the state. Although women's suffrage movements were growing across the nation, the state Democratic Party remained an exclusively white male organization, as did the Republicans. Despite this climate, and against the strong opposition of many attorneys, in 1878 Tabitha Anne Holton of Guilford County became the first woman licensed to practice law in the state. North Carolina became the sixth state — and the first Southern state — to grant a woman a law license.

Many years later Tabitha Holton's examiner, Supreme Court Associate Justice Edwin Godwin Reade, recalled the scene:

> It fell to my lot to conduct the examination; and I did it so gently and sympathetically that my associate justices said enviously, that I did not ask her a single question that would have bothered a child. Well, whether it would have bothered a child or not, it did not bother her; for she answered promptly and correctly and got her license.

The same steadfastness and strong preparation shown by Miss Holton would be demonstrated by other pioneering women lawyers in North Carolina in succeeding years.

Few North Carolinians know that a woman appeared in a North Carolina court on behalf of a client in North Carolina's earliest days. As recorded in the *Colonial Records of North Carolina*, Ann Marwood Durant of Perquimans County successfully represented one Andrew Ball at court in 1673 in his effort to recover wages owed him. Ann Durant, who died in 1695, appeared before North Carolina colonial courts on at least 20 other occasions on behalf of her husband, herself or others. Her husband, George Durant, was an early planter who later served the colony as speaker of the assembly and attorney general. During her husband's frequent absences, Ann Durant ran the family plantation and store at "Durant's Neck" and, as we have seen, appeared in court on his behalf. Such was their prominence that prisoners were sometimes held at the Durant plantation, and it was on their land the first public structures erected in North Carolina — stocks and pillories — were built.

In 1878, Tabitha Anne Holton became the first woman to be licensed to practice law in North Carolina. She reportedly passed the bar examination without missing a single question.

Main Street and the Courthouse Square: N.C. Lawyers, 1880-1900

Railroads not only helped rebuild the state after the war, they reshaped the physical, economic and social landscape. In North Carolina, a town's access to a rail line usually meant the difference between prosperity or stagnation. With

Tarboro residents await boarding on the Atlantic Coast Line Railroad in the 1890s. Railroad lines ensured the prosperity of many North Carolina towns.

North Tryon Street in Charlotte about 1900.

A listing of minimum fees for legal services published by the Caswell County Bar sometime around the 1850s.

A. C. Zollicoffer's law office in Henderson, one of the oldest, continuously occupied law offices in North Carolina.

a railroad connection, Tarboro expanded as a marketing center for cotton and tobacco, and Hamlet became a flourishing junction for rail passengers. With a rail line a town might add tobacco factories, as did Durham and Winston, or become a center of the textile industry, as did Charlotte and Greensboro. In the western part of the state, the railroads were an even greater catalyst, furthering development of the bountiful natural resources of the region and making tourism possible. Once-isolated villages became towns, and by the end of the 19th century Asheville was a booming small city.

A vigorous middle class prospered in North Carolina's towns and created and supported a diverse array of stores and services — including legal services. Even the smaller North Carolina towns shared in the passion for growth and became connection points between the local rural world and a wider urban one. The many ambitious young men who wanted to live in a community with a courthouse square, a newspaper, a doctor, drugstores and banks could find himself a comfortable town without difficulty and flourish there. A young lawyer named A. C. Zollicoffer typified the movement of North Carolinians from rural life to town life.

Allison Caulincourt Zollicoffer moved from Weldon in Halifax County to Henderson at the age of 28 to open a law practice, hanging out his shingle on Henderson's Garnett Street. Much of his practice focused on the usual staples of the law — deed work, judgments, bankruptcy. Zollicoffer's sense of judgment, and his reputation as an attorney who could skillfully litigate a suit but who preferred to prevent rather than promote litigation, won him loyal clients over the years. It was a measure of the lawyer's standing and the community's enterprise that he also represented the town's largest corporations: its cotton mill, bagging company and biggest bank.

The average lawyer in turn-of-the-century North Carolina was not unlike A. C. Zollicoffer. They were middle-class residents of modest towns. Not out to make a fortune, they practiced their profession and raised a family, living a full life in a small place. Their life may have looked uneventful to the outsider, but it had its pleasures: a close-knit community of neighbors and fellow worshipers; the gossip and daily drama of the courthouse; the bustle of visitors on market days.

Down on the Farm: Unrest and Protests, 1880-1898

It was a different story for North Carolina farmers. Until the turn of the century, notwithstanding moments and scattered instances of prosperity, most North Carolina farmers were locked in a struggle to subsist. By the 1880s, lured by the possibilities of cash crops made possible by the railroads, North Carolina's farmers found themselves married to the marketplace at the very moment when prices for farm products were about to collapse worldwide. In 1890, one in three white farmers and three in four black farmers in the state found themselves tenants or sharecroppers.

Some farmers dealt with the dilemma of an agricultural depression by migrating to the city; others tried new methods of "scientific agriculture;" but many others chose to band together and fight against the stranglehold of sinking farm prices and high costs for supplies, equipment and credit. In North Carolina, and in the nation at large, the Farmers' Alliance became a powerful democratic movement prepared to take on the vast private interests — bankers and merchants, railroads and warehousemen — who held them in thrall through policies of scarce credit and tight money.

In North Carolina, most farmers perceived lawyers as part of the problem, rather than part of the solution, so much so that the president of the North Carolina Farmers' Alliance, Elias Carr, ruled in 1890 that "no licensed and practicing lawyer [was] eligible for membership in the Alliance under any circumstances." Similarly, the Knights of Labor, a union formed in North Carolina in the 1880s, had also barred "lawyers, bankers, gamblers and liquor dealers" from joining its ranks.

Many farmers left the Democratic Party in the 1890s to join the People's Party (Populists), a movement for greater economic democracy and social reforms. In 1894, the state Republican Party allied with the Populists in a "Fusion" ticket which gained control of the Legislature and elected Republican Daniel L. Russell governor in 1896. The stage was set for a showdown between the old order and this upstart alliance of farmers and laborers.

Farmers cure their tobacco at a Nash County farm. Tobacco and cotton were the only crops to surpass prewar production levels, but conditions for farmers in the state were harsh and wages were low.

Leonidas L. Polk organized the North Carolina Farmer's Alliance, which successfully lobbied for a state agricultural college (North Carolina State University).

The North Carolina Farmer's Alliance, which published The Progressive Farmer magazine, also published this songbook.

The Search for Order: Attorneys' Organizations in the Late 19th Century

The coming of the railroad, the growth of towns, and the growing complexities of the industrial age brought substantial change to the practice of law and the courts. In many ways the movement toward bar associations in the late 19th century was simply the search for a new form to accommodate the changed circumstances of modern life. A North Carolina attorney described the shift:

> In the earlier days of the profession in this country the members of the bar of a given Circuit rode in goodly company with the judges and solicitors from court to court; they were an association in themselves and came to know each other well and learn from each other as they traveled and ate and slept together. But with ... the swift modes of conveyance [of this day], the absorbing office practice, [and] the argument today in this court, rest for the night in the sleeper, and the appearance in the morning before another judge and jury in a distant town or city, the old companying together has vanished. The necessity has come for these new associations, the meetings in vacation, the renewals of friendship, the addresses on matters of interest.

Downtown Kinston at the turn of the century.

In these tumultuous times, with corruption and malfeasance present in Reconstruction governments in the South and in municipal and state governments in the North, attorneys also sought ways to address needed social changes and improve the standards of their profession. The most common and most useful of these efforts were associations of lawyers organized to apply pressure for improvement in the legal profession at all levels: from individual practitioners to state legislatures, and from local courts to the highest courts on the state and national level.

Attorneys were the last of the major professions to form a permanent organization in North Carolina. The North Carolina Medical Society had been in existence since 1849, and the North Carolina Press Association was organized in 1873 by lawyer-editor William Biggs. It would be another 26 years before Biggs' 26-year-old son, James Crawford Biggs, would call a meeting to consider the formation of "The North Carolina Bar Association."

Local bar associations were formed in many municipalities across the United States in the early and middle years of the 19th century. Wilmington, for one, had some type of association of attorneys by the 1850s. While it would be several decades before these New Hanover County attorneys formally established the Wilmington Bar Association, they were holding conventions, sponsoring resolutions, and selecting a "Dean of the Wilmington Bar" as early as 1853.

William Pollock's 1888 law license featured the signature of Joseph J. Davis, president of the short-lived predecessor to the present North Carolina Bar Association.

Kentucky was the first state to form a bar association (1871). North Carolina's neighboring states followed with their own statewide organizations in the 1880s — Tennessee in 1882, Georgia in 1883, South Carolina in 1884 and Virginia in 1888. The American Bar Association — with which the North Carolina Bar Association would become affiliated — was founded by 100 lawyers from 21 states in 1878 at a convention in Saratoga Springs, New York.

An earlier "North Carolina State Bar Association," founded in Raleigh in February 1885, proved to be short-lived. Fifty-six leading attorneys — about half of them from Wake County — attended the inaugural meeting and elected Joseph J. Davis as president. Reform of the state's judicial system (including the abolition of judicial elections and increase in the number of judgeships) seems to have been the main reason for the group's formation.

In his October 1885 address to these elite "gentlemen of high character," the Hon. J.J. Davis, a former Congressman and soon-to-be member of the state Supreme Court, spoke of lawyers as "the defenders of public and private rights" and "advocates of civil liberty" just as the firestorm of agrarian protest against the state's business interests was about to ignite. In Davis' eyes the state's lawyers had always been the protectors of the people:

> The legal profession, by its training, its regard for forms and precedents could hardly be otherwise than conservative, and [in] our own beloved State we find that in the past ... the law abiding, honest and conservative character of her people has been fitly represented by her lawyers.

Though membership in the association would increase to 125 and a second meeting was held, within a few years the organization "fell into innocuous desuetude," as a reporter for the Raleigh *News and Observer* described it.

Order in the Midst of Tumult: The North Carolina Bar Association

By 1899, 20 states had organized functioning associations of attorneys. In that year, New Jersey and the territory of Hawaii would join North Carolina in creating state bar associations. Since the antebellum period, North Carolina's leading lawyers had been members of the state's elite, a gentry of wealth and social position; in 1899 such was still the case, and the founders of the North

Carolina Bar Association were largely men of that aristocracy of privilege. They were gentlemen active in public affairs, whose families socialized together and often intermarried. Many were truly men of superior education, character and achievement. Several of the early presidents of the association — Platt Dickinson Walker, Charles Manly Stedman and Harry Skinner, to name just a few — were some of the finest public-spirited men of their generation.

The gentlemen who gathered to form the North Carolina Bar Association in 1899 did so in the shadow of social turmoil in the state. The triumph of the Fusion movement of white farmers and black Republicans prepared the ground for a campaign of terror in 1898 in the name of "white supremacy." Democratic newspapers in the state stirred many white citizens into a frenzy with lurid tales of impending "Negro domination" of the political and social order, as "Red Shirt" vigilantes threatened black citizens in broad daylight in some sections of the state. A number of the leading Democrats orchestrated the white supremacy campaign in the name of order and "good government," even as the rights of citizens and the values of democratic government were being violated.

Anti-black rhetoric also spurred the resurgence of the Ku Klux Klan; incited a race riot in Wilmington in 1898 which killed at least five black citizens; and contributed to the lynchings of an untold number of African-Americans around the turn of the century. By 1898, the Democrats had returned to power on a white supremacy platform and began a systematic campaign of disenfranchising blacks. In 1899, state legislators passed a "Suffrage Amendment" requiring a literacy test and creating various obstacles designed to strip blacks and poor whites of the right to vote. North Carolina voters ratified it in 1900. Now solidly in control of what was essentially a one-party state, Democratic leaders spoke of "the dawn of a new day" of progressive legislation, especially "universal education." In reality the party's legacy was single-party domination of the state and a system of legal, social and economic segregation that would strongly influence North Carolina politics and society until the 1950s.

The North Carolina Bar Association was born in the midst of this maelstrom. Perhaps the sense of disorder abroad on the land only stiffened some of the founders' resolve to firmly establish the association as a bulwark of law and justice, particularly in light of early failures. In his address at the first annual meeting of the North Carolina Bar Association in 1899, President Platt D. Walker spoke of those "fundamental principles of liberty" enshrined in the state's first constitution:

> If the laws are bad ... the respect and confidence of the people ... are either lost or impaired, and what should be a well-regulated system of government and law ... becomes an intolerable system of oppression and tyranny. Such a condition should not exist and should not be possible in a free country, and *among a free people devoted to liberty and justice*, and where the supreme law of the land should be the sure hope and our temples of justice the safe refuge, for any and all who may seek the vindication of a right or the redress of a wrong.

Despite the leadership of men like Justice Walker and the high ideals of the founders of the association, it would take several decades before all in the legal profession would enjoy the full blessings of liberty, and before all North Carolinians received equal justice under the law.

∽

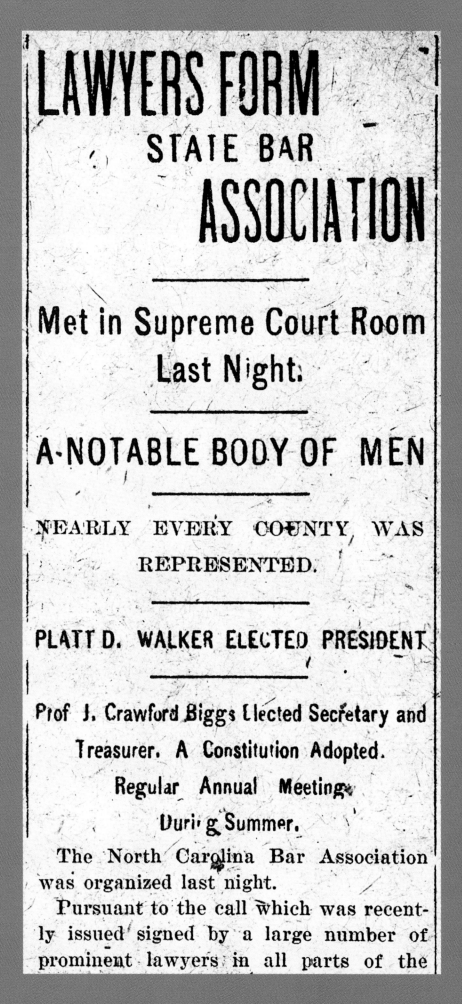

LAWYERS FORM
STATE BAR
ASSOCIATION

Met in Supreme Court Room Last Night.

A-NOTABLE BODY OF MEN

NEARLY EVERY COUNTY WAS REPRESENTED.

PLATT D. WALKER ELECTED PRESIDENT

Prof J. Crawford Biggs Elected Secretary and Treasurer. A Constitution Adopted.
Regular Annual Meeting
During Summer.

The North Carolina Bar Association was organized last night.

Pursuant to the call which was recently issued signed by a large number of prominent lawyers in all parts of the

News & Observer, Raleigh, February 11, 1899.

"Call and Response"
The First Year of the North Carolina Bar Association
(1899)

Wh…hen J. Crawford Biggs, professor of law at the University of North Carolina, issued a call for an organization of the lawyers of North Carolina in January 1899, there was no statewide bar association in North Carolina nor any regional association of attorneys. Both an early "Bar Association of Western North Carolina" and the old "North Carolina State Bar Association" had ceased to exist some years earlier.

The young Biggs may well have been inspired by the example of his father, William Biggs, who as editor of the *Tarboro Southerner* had issued the call for the formation of the North Carolina Press Association in 1873. Other North Carolina attorneys were also well aware of the precedent set by the state's journalists. Henry Armand London, lawyer and editor of the *Chatham Record*, had served as the first president of the North Carolina Press Association, and would be elected to the six-man executive committee of the North Carolina Bar Association at its first annual meeting. Likewise, E.F. Lamb, attorney and publisher of the Elizabeth City *Falcon*, had been present at the founding of the Press Association, and would be on hand for the North Carolina Bar Association's inaugural meeting as well.

Charles W. Tillett, the North Carolina Bar Association president from 1910-1911 who strongly encouraged the publication of a North Carolina Bar journal, is shown here with his family at their Charlotte home. His son, C.W. Tillett Jr., served as NCBA president from 1934-1935.

A Call to Organize

The Raleigh *News and Observer* of February 9, 1899, announced that a meeting of the state's lawyers would be held the following day. Editor Samuel A. Ashe spoke approvingly of the gathering:

> There are many reasons why the organization of members of a learned profession is to be desired. It elevates the tone, gives a community of interest, and stimulates the whole membership.

J. CRAWFORD BIGGS

The efforts to establish and sustain a state bar association in the 1880s failed due to a lack of continuity and communication among the members. The key component which was missing was the position of secretary-treasurer. During the next effort at the turn of the century it would be the secretary-treasurer who provided "the glue to hold it all together," as a fledgling association was organized.

As professor of law at the University in Chapel Hill, J. Crawford Biggs was "the indispensable man" for the new North Carolina Bar Association created in 1899. It was his letter, written on January 21, 1899, that sent out the call to lawyers for the establishment of a new statewide bar association. Even in his own day, he was called the "Father of the Association." As Judge Robert W. Winston remarked, "It is perhaps saying not too much when we affirm that the North Carolina Bar Association owes more to J. Crawford Biggs than to any other lawyer in the state."

Born in 1872 in Oxford, N.C., Biggs was part of a family known for being among the community's leading citizens. He attended the Horner Military School in Oxford and the University in Chapel Hill, graduating summa cum laude. He was licensed to practice law in 1894 after reading the law under Dr. John Manning. He returned to Oxford, which had one of the best local bars of the day, and practiced law for four years serving twice as mayor and as chair of the executive committee of the Democratic Party in Granville County.

During the first year of the association, more than a thousand pieces of correspondence were mailed from his university office on behalf of the new group. Due to Biggs' efforts, more than 65 lawyers met on Friday evening, February 10, 1899, in the Supreme Court courtroom in Raleigh. This successful meeting was recounted in the February 11 issue of the Raleigh *News & Observer* as a meeting of the most prominent members of the bar from across the state. Biggs was identified in newspaper accounts as the father of the movement.

At this organizational meeting officers were elected, a constitution and bylaws proposed, committees appointed and charter members enrolled. A summer annual meeting at the Atlantic Hotel in Morehead City was organized and successfully concluded on July 7, 1899, largely due to Biggs' efforts.

He served as secretary-treasurer (predecessor of the current executive director position) until 1906. Interestingly his resignation as secretary-treasurer coincided with his marriage to Miss Marjie Jordan that same year. In those first years, Biggs and others established traditions and procedures that have continued even unto today.

In later years, he also served as a legislator for Durham County, Supreme Court Reporter and as a Superior Court judge. He briefly served on the law school faculty at Trinity College in 1911-12. In 1914, he was honored by his peers and was elected president of the North Carolina Bar Association. The American Bar Association elected him vice president in 1933, and he served as Solicitor General of the United States under President Franklin D. Roosevelt from 1933 to 1935. Over several decades he maintained a private law practice in Washington, D.C. and Durham until his retirement in 1950. He died on January 30, 1960.

The lawyers in all ages have been in the forefront of struggles for the preservation of liberty regulated by law. In North Carolina they have been the foremost leaders of the people from the days of Iredell. The profession never embraced so many able and learned men as now. Their organization for mutual good will not be confined to the membership, but will have a salutary influence upon the men of all callings.

The attorneys were invited to a meeting in the Supreme Court room in Raleigh on February 10, 1899, at 7:30 p.m. Biggs called the meeting to order and asked J. B. Batchelor, a Raleigh lawyer, to act as temporary chairman. In short order, those present chose Biggs to act as temporary secretary of the fledgling organization.

Charles W. Tillett, a leading member of the Charlotte bar, stated that the object of the meeting was to organize the bar of North Carolina into an association. The mission of the new organization was spelled out in the draft constitution:

> This Association is formed to cultivate the science of jurisprudence; to promote reform in the law; to facilitate the administration of justice; to elevate the standard of integrity, honor and courtesy in the legal profession; to encourage a thorough and liberal legal education; and to cherish a spirit of brotherhood among the members thereof.

Biggs had prepared a constitution and bylaws based on those of the Virginia Bar Association, and suggested that they be referred to an appropriate committee for consideration. William R. Allen, a Goldsboro attorney, argued that the group should first see which lawyers intended to join. W. B. Shaw of Henderson responded that this was "like putting the cart before the horse," since he believed that no one would want to join without knowing what sort of provisions he was agreeing to. In response, Tillett commented that the organization was starting off "powerful suspicious" of one another, but that surely any member could resign if dissatisfied with the group's bylaws and constitution.

During the organizational proceedings of the new association, W. J. Peele, treasurer of the 1885 bar association, reported that he had the sum of $80 from the defunct group. On the motion of T. M. Argo, former secretary of the "Old Bar," members of the old association who were present retired to discuss the relationship between it and the new association. The members of the 1885 group decided to dissolve that association and turn over books, records, minutes and the $80 to the new group. The *News and Observer* commented that "this generous offer on the part of the members of the defunct association was received with thanks."

A committee on permanent organization was appointed. J. Crawford Biggs read the proposed constitution and officers were suggested by the permanent organization committee. Biggs' constitution and bylaws were debated, amended slightly and adopted. Any white member of the bar of North Carolina was eligible to join the Bar Association. An admission fee of $5 and annual dues of $2 were charged. Judges of the Supreme, Superior and criminal courts — as well as judges of federal courts in North Carolina — were made honorary members of the Bar Association.

The constitution provided that the president, 12 vice presidents (from each of the judicial districts), and the secretary-treasurer should be elected annually. Standing committees on membership, legislation and law reform, the judiciary, legal education and admission to the bar, memorials, grievances and legal ethics were to be appointed by the president within 10 days after the annual meetings. Those present at the annual meetings were to constitute a quorum for the purposes of voting. The constitution also provided that the president should deliver an address at the annual meeting on a subject of his choice.

The organizers directed the secretary to secure a charter of incorporation from the Legislature. (Biggs would do so that spring, and on March 6 the Legislature granted it.) Ultimately a total of 157 charter members were recognized. Biggs was made secretary-treasurer; as such, he was to receive the sum of $100 per year. Platt Dickinson Walker of Charlotte was chosen as president. In accepting the office, he stated that the "highest honor that can come to any man in North Carolina is the expression of confidence of the representatives of the bar of the State."

Platt D. Walker, native of Wilmington, practiced in Charlotte until his election to the North Carolina Supreme Court in 1903.

PLATT D. WALKER

Upon his election as first president of the North Carolina Bar Association on February 10, 1899, Platt D. Walker said, "This honor comes to me when I am so young in years and so unexpectedly that I hardly have words adequate to express my appreciation and to thank you for the honor you have conferred on me by electing me president of this association. ... There is no honor in this state, whether it came from the legislature or the people that I would value more highly."

Walker's modesty reflects a degree of humility often not found in those of patrician background. Yet his statement also appears to acknowledge that recognition by one's peers has been and continues to be one of the highest possible compliments.

Platt Dickinson Walker was born on October 25, 1849, in Wilmington, the largest city in antebellum North Carolina. His lineage demanded that he pursue a profession appropriate to a Southern gentleman. He entered the University of North Carolina in 1865 as one of only 15 freshman applicants. When the university was forced to close the following year in the wake of the war he transferred to the University of Virginia. At Virginia he completed his elective literary course and then studied law under Dr. Minor, the dean of the University Law School. His license to practice in North Carolina was issued in June 1870, before he was 21 years of age.

As a junior partner, he first practiced in Rockingham, and was elected to the State Legislature in 1875. However, he relocated to Charlotte when his mentor Col. Walter L. Steel was elected to Congress in 1876. The Civil War had impoverished the smaller country towns, so that many leading lawyers gravitated to the cities for professional advancement. During the next quarter century, he represented varied business interests in and outside of the courtroom as North Carolina struggled to regain economic prosperity.

As a Democrat, he offered himself in the 1884 primary for the office of attorney general, yet was defeated by a small percentage of votes. He did not seek elective office again until after the turn of the century.

During his term of office as president of the North Carolina Bar Association, establishing a strong framework for the organization was the first priority. Committees on Permanent Organization, Constitution and Bylaws, Legislation and Law Reform, and an Executive Committee would report to the officers of the association, which included the president, 12 vice presidents (one from each judicial district), and a secretary-treasurer. With this structure in place, the organization was prepared to grow.

With widespread urging, he stood for election to the N.C. Supreme Court in November 1902. With his election, he went to Raleigh for service on the Court. He had been engaged in the private practice of law for 32 years and would now sit on the bench for the next 20 years.

Justice Walker filed his first opinion in the case of *Board of Education v. the Town of Greenville* reported February 24, 1903, 132 N.C., 4 and his last opinion was filed in the case of *Erskine v. Motors Co.*, 185 N.C., 479 May 26, 1923, four days after his death. He wrote nearly 2,000 opinions during the 20 years he was a member of the Court and was generally viewed to be a conservative jurist who strictly interpreted the laws of his state.

As a faithful member of the Episcopal Church, he served as a vestryman for many years. The degree of Doctor of Laws was conferred upon him by both the University of North Carolina and Davidson College. He was also a vice president of the American Bar Association from 1916-1918.

He was married to Miss Nettie Settle Covington of Richmond County in 1878, who died at her home in Charlotte in 1907. In 1910 he married Miss Alma Locke Mordecai of New Orleans. After his death on May 22, 1923, in Raleigh, he was buried in Wilmington. Although he never had any children from his two marriages, a nephew, Thomas W. Davis, served as president of the North Carolina Bar Association in 1920-21, and as secretary-treasurer of the association for many years.

Upon the unveiling of his portrait at the North Carolina Supreme Court on April 20, 1926, Chief Justice Walter P. Stacy said, "In 54 volumes of our published *Reports*, his opinions afford convincing proof of the unusual ability, the marked accuracy of learning and the constant devotion to duty, which were his."

The receipts of the office since the meeting of organization, to July 5, 1899, as will appear from the accounts filed herewith, have been $838.10, as follows:

Cash from W. J. Peele, Treasurer of the Old North
    Carolina State Bar Association, - - - $ 78.10
Admission fees collected from 152 members, - - 760.00

        Total receipts, as above, - - - $838.10

The expenditures are classified as follows:

University Press Company, - - - - - $ 44.00
University Press Company, - - - - - 1.50
Check Book, Stamped - - - - - 1.00
Alfred Williams & Co., - - - - - 2.65
Capital Printing Co., - - - - - 2.50
C. B. Poland, copy of Charter, - - - - 2.00
Postage, - - - - - - - - 10.50
News & Observer, - - - - - - 5.00
Postage, - - - - - - - - 8.10
Salary of Secretary and Treasurer from February 10
    to June 30, 1899, - - - - - 38.88

Total Expenditures, - - - - - $116.13
Net balance on hand July 6, 1899, - - - $721.97

*This is the Bar Association's budget report
as of July 6, 1899.*

*Thomas M. Argo, a prominent Wake
County attorney, was a founder of
the "Old Bar Association," and its
long-serving secretary.*

An Address to Remember

Large advertisements in the *News and Observer* in the first week of July 1899 announced that the Atlantic Hotel in Morehead City would give special rates to all members of the Bar Association who attended the first annual meeting. The session opened on July 5, at 10:30 p.m. F. H. Busbee of Raleigh, chairman of the executive committee, called the meeting to order and President Walker was introduced. Walker announced that the executive committee had recommended that the night's program be postponed until the following day, "owing to the late hour of the night, and to the fact that the train is late."

Platt Walker addressed the body the next day, taking as his subject the mission and functions, duties and responsibilities of a bar association. He began by urging the members to look to the future, not to past failures:

> I am quite sure that we have come to this
> meeting with the single and determined purpose
> that nothing shall be left undone hereafter in
> our efforts to establish this association upon a
> firm and enduring foundation, and to make it
> what it shouldbe, an honor to the profession
> and the State.

Walker reminded his colleagues of their high calling as lawyers, urging them to live up to the ideals upon which the association was being founded:

> We [must] inspire the profession with the confidence that we propose
> to make it what it was designed to be — a society organized in truth
> and in fact to cultivate the science of jurisprudence; to promote the
> reform of law; to facilitate the administration of justice; to elevate the
> standard of integrity, honor and courtesy in the profession; and to
> cherish a spirit of brotherhood. We must believe that these principles
> and purposes commend themselves to every lawyer who loves his
> profession and is proud of its prestige and past history.

He would countenance no selfish motives for the organization, nor entertain any hint of self-promotion or self-aggrandizement by its members, because the association was to be — first and foremost — a public service institution:

> The pursuit and practice of this profession imposes upon us
> responsible duties and obligations to ourselves and to the public....
> Our daily practice and experience is ever presenting to us the
> deficiencies and imperfections of the law, where any exist; and by
> reason of these special qualifications, it is a sacred duty we owe
> to the State and its people to...ensure to each and every citizen
> the just and equal protection of the law.

For Platt Walker, the Bar Association was the ideal organization, not only for the securing of good laws and the effective administration of justice, but also for the ennobling of the legal profession itself:

We seek through it [the Bar Association] to accomplish what is best for the profession, because, and only because, it is best for the State and its citizens. Good laws administered by an upright and able judiciary, and constantly sustained and strengthened by a Bar daily increasing in learning and wisdom and a better knowledge of the science of the law, and refined by obedience to the highest precepts of honor and integrity, are some of the ends which we shall strive to attain; and what greater blessings can be conferred upon a people than these?

All that was needed to attain such lofty goals was the participation of all members of the Bar, or as the president put it, "every worthy and honorable lawyer" in North Carolina:

We appeal to every lawyer who entertains a pride in his profession, and in its past achievements and history, and a hope for its greater destiny, to join us in our endeavor to lift it up, and upon still a higher plane, and to make it a tower of strength in our legislative halls, our councils and our forums, that the gladsome light of jurisprudence may shine in every part of this Commonwealth, and that her people may feel that the supreme law of this land, to which they owe their respect and obedience, is a law of truth, justice and right.

Platt D. Walker's eloquent speech set a high standard of excellence for future presidential addresses. The *News and Observer* reported that it was "able, eloquent and ... enthusiastically received." The *North Carolina Law Journal* noted the historic nature of Walker's keynote: "As the first President, Mr. Walker goes on record as holding up to the profession high ideals, great principles of honesty, justice and liberality, ideals and principles that should commend themselves to every lawyer who loves his profession and is proud of its prestige."

Getting Down to Business — and Pleasure

The establishment of a law periodical was another major item of business at the first annual meeting. Charles W. Tillett, a member of the Committee on Permanent Organization, was firmly convinced that a law journal was necessary and expressed the opinion that the editor should be a lawyer, "even though," he added, "good lawyers are too busy to edit a magazine." Paul Jones of Tarboro, a young lawyer and editor of the war monthly *Our Living and Our Dead*, indicated his intention to publish a legal periodical. The matter was finally referred to a committee of three, which was given full power to act, though not to commit the association financially. Within a year, the *North Carolina Law Journal* would be started.

Raleigh News & Observer advertisement touting the Atlantic Hotel, Morehead City, and special rates for the first annual meeting.

This etching shows the Atlantic Hotel, built by the Atlantic and North Carolina Railroad in 1880, the leading resort on the Carolina Coast. Bar Association business meetings were held in the Teachers' Assembly Building, to the right of the hotel.

Above: Ladies and gentlemen stroll along the waterfront of the Atlantic Hotel, circa 1899.

Left: The Atlantic Hotel in Morehead City was the site of four Bar Association annual meetings between 1899 and 1912. It was destroyed by fire in 1933. At the height of its popularity, the hotel could accommodate 750 guests in rooms and cottages.

In many ways, the Morehead City meeting set precedents which would be followed in annual meetings until the present day. Since 1899, an address by the president, along with addresses by invited speakers, have been highlights of the meetings. Concerns about the legal system and the practice of law in North Carolina were addressed then and subsequently.

Other traditions established at the first annual meeting included the provision of some form of entertainment for the members and a fine banquet for the attendees. In 1899, Edward Chambers Smith of Raleigh, son of state Supreme Court Justice W.N.H. Smith, extended an invitation for the members to "take a sail with [him]," which was unanimously accepted. That same year, the association had a long discussion about its proposed banquet. F. H. Busbee told the group of his difficulties with hotel officials in arranging for wine to be included at the price of $1.50 a plate, admitting that "we only got them to concede to us native wines."

The 1899 meeting was deemed very successful. Paul Jones wrote that the first annual meeting "was marked for its enthusiasm and determination on the part of those present to make the Association a success." Charles F. Warren, a leading member of the Washington bar, was elected the new president for the year 1899-1900. Biggs reported that the total membership, including honorary members, had reached 269; but since more than 800 lawyers were practicing in North Carolina at the time, he felt that many others should join the association. In an article in the *North Carolina Law Journal* after the convention, Charles W. Tillett wrote eloquently of the professional obligation of lawyers to join their association, words that many presidents of the Bar Association would echo in later years:

> It is the duty of every lawyer in North Carolina, whose name appears not on the roll of the Association to become a member at once. It is a duty he owes to himself, as well as to the Profession. It is a duty imposed upon him by the very nature of things, which he should not shirk, and which he cannot afford to put aside for some convenient season. The Bar Association of North Carolina needs the presence, the sympathy, and approval and support of every licensed Attorney in the State. If the Association is to stand, it should stand as a Profession united.

"A Much-Needed Organization"

Unlike the "Old Bar Association," the new North Carolina Bar Association had secured the membership of a higher percentage of the state's attorneys and of nearly all the leading lawyers from across the state. Fifteen of the charter members went on to serve the association as president. Four of the first group of members later served on the state Supreme Court: Henry Groves Connor, Walter Clark, Heriot Clarkson and Platt D. Walker. It is also notable that all seven governors who served North Carolina between 1901 and 1929 were original members of the Bar Association: Charles B. Aycock, Robert B. Glenn, William W. Kitchin, Locke Craig, Thomas W. Bickett, Cameron Morrison and Angus W. McLean.

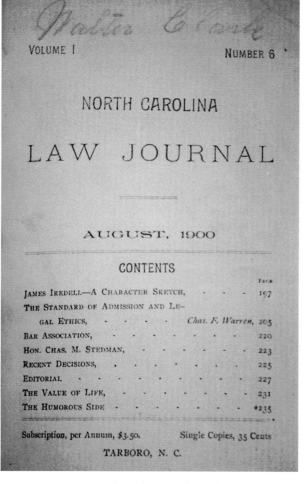

VOLUME I   NUMBER 6

NORTH CAROLINA

LAW JOURNAL

AUGUST, 1900

CONTENTS

PAGE

JAMES IREDELL—A CHARACTER SKETCH,   - - -   197

THE STANDARD OF ADMISSION AND LE-
    GAL ETHICS,   - - - -   *Chas. F. Warren,* 205

BAR ASSOCIATION,   - - - - - -   220

HON. CHAS. M. STEDMAN,   - - - - -   223

RECENT DECISIONS,   . - - - -   225

EDITORIAL   - - - - - -   227

THE VALUE OF LIFE,   - - - - -   231

THE HUMOROUS SIDE   - - - -   235

Subscription, per Annum, $3.50.   Single Copies, 35 Cents

TARBORO, N. C.

The earliest North Carolina law journal was published by Paul Jones of Tarboro from 1900 until 1902.

Wayne County's Charles Brantley Aycock was a lawyer, school administrator and newspaper editor. As governor (1901-1905), he worked to improve the state's public schools.

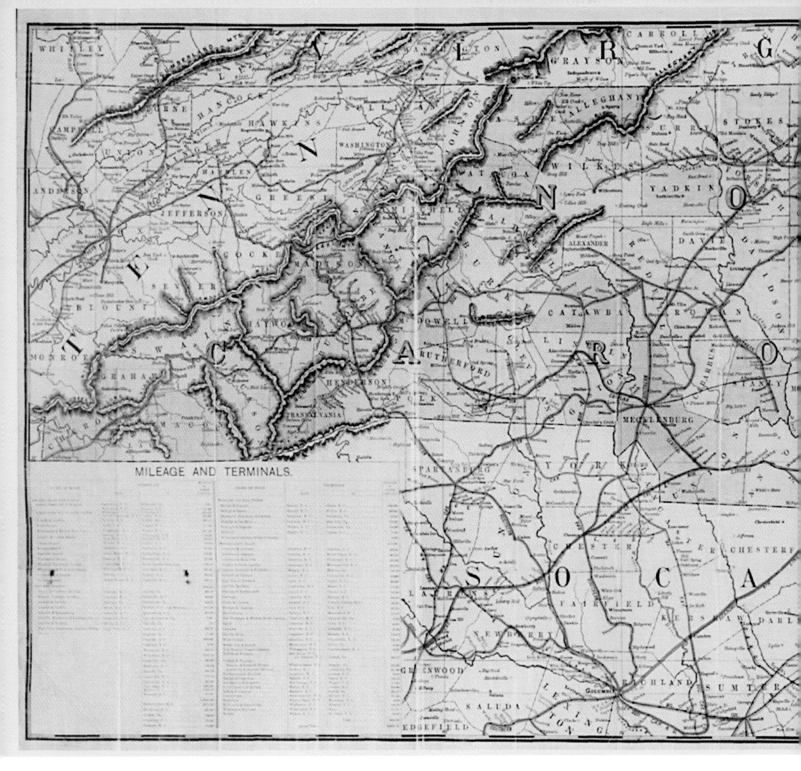

MILEAGE AND TERMINALS.

This 1900 railroad map shows major train routes in North Carolina. Trains were the primary means of transportation to both the Raleigh organizational meeting and the early annual meetings.

Daniel K. Russell, a former judge and Republican governor of the state during the founding of the North Carolina Bar Association, did not become a member of the association until 1901, after the end of his term as governor. His reluctance to join was no doubt due to political considerations. The 1899 annual meeting must have had something of the feel of a Democratic state convention, with the party's leading candidate for governor, Charles B. Aycock, a visible presence at the meeting and very few Republicans on hand.

RAILROAD MAP
...OF...
North Carolina
· 1900 ·

With the close of the 1899 annual meeting, it was evident that the North Carolina Bar Association was well organized and showing promise. Most of the members, it seems, were happy to finally have an organization and hopeful about its prospects. Platt D. Walker spoke for many when he observed:

> We have needed such an organization for many years.... I believe had the Bar been organized thirty years ago and its organization kept up, the Bar of North Carolina would not have been misrepresented individually and collectively, as it has been. It would have been better understood and better appreciated. I pray the blessings of God to rest upon these efforts.

*Toxaway Inn,
Lake Toxaway,
site of the 1905
annual meeting.*

*Battery Park Hotel,
Asheville, site of the
1900 and 1902
annual meetings.*

*Seashore Hotel,
Wrightsville Beach,
site of the 1901
and 1906 annual
meetings.*

Annual meeting sites of the early 1900s are depicted in postcards of the era.

∞

CHAPTER 4

"A Firm and Enduring Foundation" 1899-1906

After its first annual meeting, the North Carolina Bar Association passed through a few years in which it determined its priorities and established its importance to the legal profession. The early years were difficult, and the association might have suffered the same fate as the "Old Bar Association" without the leadership of the first presidents, and particularly the skill and determination of J. Crawford Biggs. Instrumental in founding the association, Biggs was named secretary-treasurer of the organization and served in that capacity until the conclusion of the eighth annual meeting in June 1906.

Biggs carried on the correspondence of the association, kept records of the finances, coordinated the annual meetings and arranged for the printing of the annual meeting reports. He kept the members in compliance with the constitution and bylaws at the annual meetings, frequently made motions to advance the business of the association, and occasionally admonished debating delegates as to the proper form of conducting business. When he resigned to become judge of the Ninth Judicial District of North Carolina in 1906, the members of the association expressed their thanks for his "efficient and loyal work." The resolution concluded: "We consider him to have been the chief moving power in making the North Carolina Bar Association a social, professional and business success." Biggs would be elected president of the association in 1914.

The first years of the Bar Association, especially those under Biggs' careful supervision, set the tone for its operation in the years and decades to come. By the time Biggs resigned as secretary-treasurer, the North Carolina Bar Association was an established organization with firm traditions and practices.

One of the earliest traditions of the North Carolina Bar Association was that of holding the annual meeting at or near a popular tourist attraction, so that the attorneys and their spouses might take pleasure in recreation. "Our meetings are partly business, partly social," President E. F. Aydlett would remark in 1919. The association generally alternated its meetings between the mountains and the coast (with an occasional stop in the Piedmont) as the sites for the first eight annual meetings attest. It was Morehead City in 1899 and 1903, Asheville in 1900 and 1902, Wrightsville Beach in 1901 and 1906, Charlotte in 1904, and Lake Toxaway in 1905.

Biggs described the annual meetings as "not only pleasant reunions of the brotherhood, but [an] opportunity for the discussion of important topics bearing upon the welfare of the profession and, of consequence, of the people."

A Legal Journal for North Carolina

One of those topics, the prospect of a statewide legal periodical discussed at the 1899 meeting, soon became a reality. In 1900, the president of the association reported that Paul Jones was publishing *The North Carolina Law Journal* in Tarboro. Jones announced that he had published four issues, sent sample copies to lawyers in the state, and was seeking additional subscribers. The journal contained biographical sketches of outstanding lawyers, articles on North Carolina law, digests of court opinions, editorials, humorous notes, book reviews and other items of interest to attorneys. A Bar Association committee appointed in 1899 had studied the situation and approved Jones's proposition to publish a journal, but offered no financial support.

The North Carolina Law Journal was published as the organ of the North Carolina Bar Association for approximately two years. At the 1903 meeting, Jones reported that he had discontinued the publication of the journal because he did not see how he could "in the future issue from 500 to 800 journals gratis in the State year after year." Another committee was appointed to confer with Jones, but support from the association was not forthcoming.

The next publication, the *North Carolina Journal of Law*, was issued from Chapel Hill, under the patronage of the North Carolina Bar Association with university law school Dean James C. MacRae as editor. Despite requests from MacRae to sponsor the journal, the Bar Association agreed to contribute $300 for the first year only. In the first issue, MacRae announced:

> As a result of the action of the Bar Association the editor has, with some misgiving, undertaken the task of presenting this publication for the year 1904.... As, while under the patronage of the North Carolina Bar Association, it is, nevertheless, a private enterprise and not an eleemosynary institution, it cannot succeed unless it has ... the liberal financial support of those who shall be interested in the undertaking.

The publication was discontinued in 1905 after just two years. No other legal journal would publish in the state until the law school of the University of North Carolina established the *North Carolina Law Review* in June 1922.

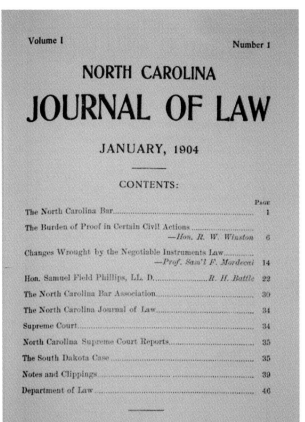

Volume I   Number 1

NORTH CAROLINA

JOURNAL OF LAW

JANUARY, 1904

CONTENTS:

SUBSCRIPTION, $3.00 PER ANNUM
SINGLE NUMBER, 35 CENTS

Jones' Tarboro-based law journal was succeeded by The North Carolina Journal of Law, *edited by University of North Carolina Law School dean James C. MacRae.*

Legal Education and Admission Standards

Proposed requirements for legal education and admission to the bar came before the association at many meetings in its early years. Legal historian Albert Coates has argued that "no one can read the proceedings of the North Carolina Bar Association since its organization ... without feeling its keen and enthusiastic interest in standards of admission to the bar." In 1900, the committee recommended that two years' study be required for legal education. The opposition favored a more stringent bar examination, arguing that increasing the course of study would instead prevent poorer students from entering the profession.

The University of North Carolina's law course at the turn of the century consisted of one year preparatory to the bar examination, with the awarding of the LL.B. degree if the student completed two years of study. Biggs believed that more study would produce better lawyers. The Bar Association agreed and voted to recommend to the Supreme Court that the requirement for legal study be raised to two years. In 1902, the newly elected president, Charles M. Busbee, reported that the Court had consented to the association's recommendation and added a requirement that "a work on legal ethics" be read.

A discussion of the texts used in legal study occupied the attention of those attending the 1903 annual meeting. Much time was spent debating the merits of Blackstone versus Ewell's *Essentials*, a condensed version of Blackstone. The debate was heated but inconclusive. (A student of Samuel Fox Mordecai, Sidney Alderman, later recalled Mordecai's devotion to the venerable Blackstone: "Thank God that he gave us no Ewell's Essentials, no dehydrated pablum passed through the dessicating process of extraction, but Blackstone *tout pur*, and then 'Mordecai on Blackstone' as well.")

A key issue at the 1903 meeting was a proposal that the Legislature make the Bar Association responsible for the examination and licensing of attorneys. A resolution in favor was passed but the matter was held over until the next annual meeting. In the interim a study was made of the method of examination in other states. Only Idaho, Montana, Oregon, South Dakota, Vermont, Alabama, South Carolina, Virginia and North Carolina made their supreme courts responsible for the bar examination. The association's Committee on Legal Education and Admission to the Bar reported in 1904 that "outside of our sister southern states, the other states which follow the North Carolina plan are not states that North Carolinians feel a pride in following." It would be many more years before the profession gained the right to administer the bar examination and license new attorneys.

The bar not only wanted to regulate the admission of new members; it also wanted power to regulate the behavior of and expel undesirable lawyers. The association's Committee on Legal Ethics reported a set of general rules of ethical behavior, which formally adopted a Code of Ethics of the North Carolina Bar Association on June 28, 1900. The code, printed thereafter in every annual report, specified 51 general rules or "duties" to guide the behavior of members of the bar. Amongst the code's recommendations were provisions which formed the foundations of subsequent ethical codes: that lawyers refrain from public criticism of judges; that they not seek special favors in court; that they be frank in dealing with one another; that they be punctual; that they control their tempers; and that they be faithful to their clients, to the law, and to God.

In 1901, the association began efforts to establish procedures for disbarment of attorneys and passed a resolution to that effect. The next year a special committee was appointed to draft such a bill. In 1903, Biggs made the statement that North Carolina had little legislation on the important subject of disbarment; therefore, he moved that the matter again be referred to committee, which was done. A draft bill was prepared in 1905 and finally passed by the Legislature in 1906.

COMMENTARIES

ON THE

L A W S

OF

E N G L A N D.

BOOK THE FIRST.

BY

WILLIAM BLACKSTONE, Esq.
VINERIAN PROFESSOR OF LAW,
AND
SOLICITOR GENERAL TO HER MAJESTY.

OXFORD,
PRINTED AT THE CLARENDON PRESS.
M. DCC. LXV.

Blackstone's Commentaries on the Laws of England remained the dominant law text well into the 20th century.

REPORT OF COMMITTEE ON LEGAL ETHICS. 87

RERORT OF COMMITTEE ON LEGAL ETHICS.
To the North Carolina Bar Association :
The Committee on Legal Ethics respectfully report that they find their labors much lightened by the Codes upon this subject which have been adopted by the Bar Associations of sister States.
They present a Code of Legal Ethics for the consideration of this Association, which is substantially the same as that which has been adopted by the Bar Associations of Alabama, Georgia, Virginia and perhaps other States.
Respectfully submitted,
JAS. C. MACRAE, Ch'm'n.
ARMISTED BURWELL,
Committee.

REPORT OF COMMITTEE ON LEGAL ETHICS.
CODE OF ETHICS.
Adopted by the Bar Association, June 28th, 1900.
The purity and efficiency of judicial administration, which under our system is largely government itself, depends as much upon the character, conduct, and demeanor of attorneys in their great trust as upon the fidelity and learning of courts or the honesty and intelligence of juries.
"There is, perhaps, no profession, after that of the sacred ministry, in which high-toned morality is more imperatively necessary than that of the law. There is certainly, without any exception, no profession in which so many temptations beset the path to swerve from the lines of strict integrity; in which so many delicate and difficult questions of duty are constantly arising. There are pitfalls and mantraps at every step, and the mere youth, at the very outset of his career, needs often the prudence of self-denial, as well as the moral courage, which belong commonly to riper years. High moral principle is his only safe guide; the only torch to light his way amidst darkness and obstruction."—*Sharswood.*
No rule will determine an attorney's duty in the varying phases of every case. What is right and proper must, in the

The establishment of a Code of Ethics was a priority of the new association. It was adopted on June 28, 1900.

WALTER CLARK

Although born into a family of prominence and wealth, Walter Clark placed service to state, country and God before himself. In 1860, at the early age of 14 years, he entered the service of his state and became the youngest lieutenant-colonel in either army at age 17 years during the Civil War.

Upon admission to the bar in 1867, he initially practiced law in northeastern North Carolina in Scotland Neck and Halifax and then removed to Raleigh in 1873 to establish a general practice of law. His career on the bench began in 1885 upon appointment to the Superior Court by Gov. Alfred M. Scales. Four years later, he was appointed associate justice of the Supreme Court.

At the time of his death in 1924, his total service of 39 years one month and four days as a judicial officer was the longest on record. His service of 34 years is the longest service ever on the North Carolina Supreme Court. At the close of his long tenure, he had participated in more than one-half of all opinions written by the Court in its entire history.

As a charter member of the North Carolina Bar Association, he actively participated in the affairs of the association at numerous bar meetings and conventions for 25 years. He also spoke at bar meetings in many other states including New York and Pennsylvania since his oratorical skills were acclaimed and his range of topics broad.

Efficiency and punctuality were among his many trademarks which resulted in unclogged dockets and an efficient administration of justice. Upon his direction, clocks were installed in courtrooms and the court ran by the clock.

As stated by James A. Lockhart when Clark's portrait was presented to the Supreme Court on Oct. 28, 1924, "He was the first prominent Southerner to advocate woman's suffrage, and the case of *Crowell v. Crowell*, 180 N.C., 516, completely removes the last vestige of the inequality of women in North Carolina and fulfills Judge Clark's early prediction, in a dissenting opinion, that the time would come when women would not in any particular be classed with infants, idiots, convicts and persons."

Walter Clark, chief justice of the state Supreme Court (1903-1924), was a progressive reformer long active in bar activities.

Legal and Judicial Reforms

Lawyers frequently expressed dissatisfaction with crowded dockets and emphasized the need for additional judges. The existing system of rotation of judges — Superior Court judges were required by law to regularly preside in other judicial districts in the state — was discussed, but efforts of some members of the Bar Association to abolish the rotation system did not succeed.

After heated discussions on the threat to "democratic simplicity" posed by formality in judicial dress, the association proposed at the 1902 meeting that the state Supreme Court justices be asked to wear robes in court. A year later came the Court's reply, from Chief Justice Walter Clark: "With the greatest deference to the wishes of your Association, we are constrained to say that we do not feel at liberty to institute such an innovation upon the habits and traditions of the Court." (Whatever the reasons for the Court's reluctance — sensitivity to charges of elitism, a reaction against form and ritual, or a simple desire "to *be*, rather than to seem" — 37 years would pass before the Court would don robes for the first time, on August 27, 1940.)

The Bar Association was more successful in its efforts to bring about a new codification of the laws than it had been in persuading the judges to wear robes. There had been no codification since 1885. As a result of the efforts of the association, a revision was soon begun. In 1902, the *Asheville Citizen* went so far as to say that "the lawyers are considering the problem of codification because the laws were so intricate that they could not be understood." In 1903, Secretary Biggs reminded the members that at the two previous meetings the association had favored a code commission. He announced that the N.C. General Assembly had created a commission of three members, its chairman being the president of the Bar Association. In 1905, a revisal of the laws was approved by the Legislature.

The working of the jury system in North Carolina troubled many members of the association. In a widely published 1903 essay, "Jury Service," Clement Manly of Winston had praised the juror as "the most dignified person that God Almighty ever created." Many of his fellow North Carolina attorneys did not agree. They pointed out that many prospective jurors merely wanted to be excused from jury duty. The question of exemptions, particularly for ministers and physicians, was discussed at length. In the end, the association recommended that, except for ministers, there should be no exemptions without specific cause.

Clement Manly of Winston was the ninth president of the North Carolina Bar Association, serving from 1905-1906. He was an early partner in the law firm now known as Womble Carlyle Sandridge & Rice.

"Setting the Tone"
The First Presidential Addresses

A major reason for the success of the Bar Association in its early years was the quality and stature of the first presidents. The founding president of the association, Platt D. Walker, was recognized not only as one of the state's great lawyers, but as a man of character who cultivated "those graces of dignity, honor and courtesy that should ever bind brother to brother."

President Walker's inaugural address in 1899 had been a clarion call to the profession to hold to the high ideals of honesty, justice, liberality and service. His speech not only set a standard for oratorical excellence, but set the tone for the entire organization. The second president, Charles F. Warren, was similarly well known and well regarded throughout the state, a man whom J. Crawford Biggs called "a good lawyer, a fine advocate, a courteous gentleman [whose] personal character is without reproach." It was through Warren's initiative that the Supreme Court restored to two years the length of study before a candidate could apply for a law license.

While Warren's presidential address on "The Standard of Admission and Legal Ethics" lacked the flights of oratory in Platt Walker's inaugural, it did set the organization on a steady course of high professional principles and public service. In addition to improved standards for legal education, President Warren called for the association to scrutinize more closely the professional conduct of members of the bar, it being a high aim of the association to "promote clean practice and suppress the shyster." In his closing remarks, Warren reminded his brethren of their mission:

> The annual meetings of the Association are not alone for social recreation and the discussion of abstract questions, but the higher purpose is to achieve results which shall strengthen the Bar and make it more efficient and useful to society. It can become a power for great good in the State, if it shall exert every effort and influence to elevate the Bar and to simplify and purify the administration of justice.

The association's third president, Charles Manly Stedman, was one of the most respected men in North Carolina, popular with Democrats and Republicans alike. A man of force and considerable personal magnetism, he was known throughout the state for his courtliness and generosity. In the words of his law partner, Guilford County attorney A. Wayland Cooke, "a characteristic of his entire life was his opposition to monopolies and oppression of every kind.... He was ever the friend of the weak and oppressed, no matter whether white or black."

Charles F. Warren of Washington was the first lawyer to serve a full term as president, 1899-1900.

Stedman's 1901 presidential address, "The Lawyer," was instantly hailed as a classic. He began by recalling the state's tradition of great judges and learned lawyers, noting that De Tocqueville had called the judicial bench and bar "the aristocracy of America," a class by nature disposed to be "the friends of order and the foes of anarchy, yet at the same time the steadfast friends of freedom, too."

Declaring "moral courage" to be one of the defining characteristics of the practicing attorney — "a high and most rare trait," Stedman noted — he described the fruits of the practice of that virtue:

> The capstone of the arch of a lawyer's fame is that moral courage which sustains him upon every theatre of conflict where he stands for the honor, the fortune or the life of his client.... The blessings we enjoy as the result of our form of government have been brought about by lawyers.... The courage of lawyers to enforce the natural rights of man, to perpetuate his love of liberty, and to preserve it hallowed free and true for all those who are worthy of its blessings are the lawyers' grand monuments.

After listing some of the distinguished 19th century lawyers of the North Carolina bench and bar who had advanced civilization and achieved "intellectual and moral greatness, " Stedman expressed concern as to whether the *fin de siecle* "frenzy and insane desire for wealth" would prove to be a blessing for the state and nation. He asked whether America was actually living in a purported "golden age" of excellence:

> What constitutes the greatness of this republic? Not alone its unparalleled wealth.... Great and wonderful as are its natural and material resources, its chiefest [sic] glory will not be discovered in them. It will be found in the constitution of our common country and its legal institutions which maintain and enforce justice for all, with no discrimination and give an equal chance to each in the battle of life. This is the supreme essence of its greatness, the most radiant jewel in its crown of glory. To preserve [the] constitution inviolate, to maintain our legal institutions, to improve and adjust them to the new wants and requirements of advancing civilization and an ever

increasing population is their highest and greatest duty. Let not the behest of any party nor the prejudice of any creed interfere with its faithful and courageous performance....

In his annual address of 1902, President Charles M. Busbee returned to the issues of legal ethics and admission to the bar addressed by President Warren two years earlier. A leading member of the Raleigh bar, Busbee spoke of his concern that the bar did not enjoy the reputation in the community that it had a century ago, and called for legislative authority to disbar unworthy lawyers, whether members of the association or not. If the bar could demonstrate good faith, he argued, then popular approval would surely follow:

> Just as soon as we demonstrate that we have no other aim than the good of the people — just as soon as we make it evident that professional selfishness abideth not among us, and that no faithless or disreputable lawyer can be found within our ranks, then will this Association become what it ought to be, a power in the State, a power to be exercised at all times for the welfare of the people and the safety of this State.

No presidential address was delivered in 1903, due to the illness of the president, Charles Price. The other presidential speeches in this period were: "The North Carolina Bar," by William Dossey Pruden (1904), who called for a symposium on the subject of legal education; Thomas S. Kenan's untitled address of 1905 on the lawyer's moral principles and the great underlying principles of jurisprudence; and "The North Carolina Lawyer," by Clement Manly (1906), a plea for reform of the legal curriculum. (Kenan filled the unexpired term of Charlotte's Hamilton C. Jones, the first president to die in office.)

William Dossey Pruden, sixth president of the Bar Association (1903-1904), descended from several generations of Edenton lawyers.

Convivial Conventions

At each annual meeting, a prominent local citizen welcomed the visitors to the host city. The opening remarks at the 1900 convention in Asheville provides evidence — if any were needed — that not all was serious business at these legal gatherings. Thomas A. Jones of Buncombe County extended greetings and courtesies on behalf of the western section of the state:

Social events, such as a streetcar tour of Asheville in the early 20th century, have been popular bar meeting attractions.

> Our customs and usages will not be disagreeable to you, but in order to follow them you need not consult Gould on Waters, but you may casually examine Black on Intoxicating Liquors. All your demurrers to our customs will be overruled, and no devices of yours can change them. . . . We will covenant and guarantee to you a good time, if you will only follow our advice — which, different from our usual custom, we will give you free of charge.

SECOND ANNUAL BANQUET.

Battery Park Hotel, Asheville, N.C., June 29, 1900.

MENU.

Cocktails.   Caviar Canape.   Consomme Printaniere.   Sherry.
Olives.   Salted Nuts.   Striped Bass, Hollandaise.
Cucumbers.   Saratoga Chips.
Saddle of Spring Lamb, Mint Sauce.   Claret, Calvet & Co.
Green Peas.   New Potatoes.
Roman Punch.
Broiled Spring Chicken on Toast.   Lettuce and Tomato Salad.
Neapolitan Ice Cream.   Fancy Cakes.   Fruits.
Cheese.   Coffee.   Cigars.

Toastmaster, CLEMENT MANLY, Winston.
TOASTS.
1. THE BAR ASSOCIATION — Its Benefits to the State and the Legal
   Profession ....B.F. LONG, of Statesville.
2. ASHEVILLE — The Queen of the West .... LOUIS M. BOURNE, of Asheville.
3. THE LAWYER — His Part in the Development of Constitutional
   Government .... W.D. PRUDEN, of Edenton.
4. THE JUSTICE OF THE PEACE — His Sphere of Influence ..... F.H. BUSBEE, of Raleigh.
5. THE BENCH AND THE BAR — Their True Relations ..... J.E. ALEXANDER, of Winston.
3. THE STATE OF NORTH CAROLINA — Its Motto: "Esse Quam
   Videri" .... E.J. JUSTICE, of Marion.

Good company and good food have been enduring hallmarks of bar conventions through the decades.

The gatherings provided much entertainment for the visiting lawyers and their families. A variety of excursions were provided at the various meeting sites. The afternoon of June 28, 1900, they rode street cars around Asheville and had refreshments at the Swannanoa Country Club. The next day the members enjoyed a special tour of the Biltmore Estate. In 1901, the attorneys were invited to inspect Fort Caswell, a military facility generally closed to civilians.

In 1902, the Asheville bar invited members and their families to a trolley ride to Overlook Hill. The following year, at Morehead City, the attorneys enjoyed mackerel fishing and, later, a trip down the Trent River at New Bern, as recounted by James C. MacRae:

> The forces of Nature added all their blandishments to the three days' stay at Morehead. By day the sun shone upon the sparkling waters and the ocean breezes tempered its glowing warmth, while at night the pale moonlight made beautiful the summer sea.... The ladies were in full evidence, music added to the charms of the gathering, delightful sails and fine fishing filled up the intervals, and the session came to a happy conclusion....

"Flourishing Like a Green Bay Tree"

Members of the North Carolina Bar Association included many of the state's civic and political leaders; the *Charlotte Daily Observer* went so far as to call the profession the "ablest in the State." The organization, according to a *News and Observer* prophecy, was "destined not only to live, but to flourish like a green bay tree."

By 1905, the association had expanded to 421 members (including honorary members). Attorneys who attended the meetings found fellowship and social opportunities, heard learned addresses, and discussed serious matters of professionalism, public policy, and legislative and judicial reform. Attorneys recognized the need for their association and realized its importance. By 1906, the Bar Association was not only growing in membership but had its customs and practices well in place. Deliberations on legislative and judicial reforms had resulted in the betterment of the laws. And while some social and economic injustices in the state continued to be accepted without question, others were beginning to be addressed.

Bar Association convention attendees visiting Asheville throughout the century have enjoyed excursions to the Biltmore Estate.

In 1906, J. Crawford Biggs resigned as secretary-treasurer. During his term in office the membership of the association had grown, a code of ethics had been adopted, the law code had been revised, the requirements for licensing were strengthened, and a procedure for disbarring unscrupulous attorneys had been approved by the state Legislature. The North Carolina Bar Association had backed each of these major reforms, and had become a viable organization, thanks largely to Biggs.

The association owed its beginning to the painstaking and enthusiastic work of the young Biggs. Upon Biggs' appointment to the bench, Judge Robert W. Winston said, "We affirm that the Bar Association owes more to Judge Biggs than to any other lawyer in the State. It was he and his law partner who prepared the charter for the Association. He was its first and only Secretary, and his diligence, discrimination and levelheadedness did much to make of it what it is today."

In the words of Paul Jones, the North Carolina Bar Association was truly on its way to becoming an organization "of the lawyers, by the lawyers, and for the lawyers."

∞

North Carolina lawyer and United States Army Col. Albert Cox leads World War I troops in a "welcome home" parade down Fayetteville Street in Raleigh on March 23, 1919.

CHAPTER 5

"Taking Flight"
1906-1921

The North Carolina Bar Association, its traditions and practices well established and its importance to the legal profession demonstrated, faced familiar struggles — sustained membership growth and continued legislative and judicial reforms, among others — and new challenges in the first two decades of the 20th century, as it sought to maintain momentum and respond to new currents of thought and new social conditions in the state.

While the 1910 census showed North Carolina to be still an overwhelmingly rural state of small tobacco and cotton farmers, changes were afoot. Although only seven cities in North Carolina had populations larger then 10,000 in 1910 — Charlotte, Wilmington, Winston-Salem, Raleigh, Asheville, Durham and Greensboro — towns and cities were growing rapidly, and Charlotte had just passed Wilmington to become the largest city in the state. For the first time in the state's history, more than 10 percent of the population lived in an urban area.

Wilmington in the early 1900s.

By the beginning of the century's third decade, the first World War had ended; industrialization and urbanization had proceeded apace; public schools were preparing a new generation of North Carolinians for the future; a statewide system of all-weather roads for the automobile was being planned; and women had gained the right to vote. The old "Rip Van Winkle" state was wide awake, modernizing and changing rapidly — but not without some bumps along the way.

Still, for many years, the fabled North Carolina "country lawyer" would be the mainstay of the legal profession in the state. Frank M. Drake, a Kentucky lawyer who was the father of the legal institute movement in his state and a great admirer of the country lawyer, offered this definition:

> 'Country lawyer' does not mean a hill-billy lawyer. It means a lawyer who is a leading citizen and respected influence in those smaller communities of a state who mold public opinion and who furnish the best thought on problems of a civic and governmental nature. It describes the best and most influential group of citizens in any state.

Lillian Rowe Frye (front row, middle) of Bryson City, the first female member of the North Carolina Bar Association, in attendance at the 1913 annual meeting at the Battery Park Hotel in Asheville.

The same year that women got the vote, Lillian Exum Clement became the first woman elected to the state House of Representatives. A Democrat, she was also known as "Brother Exum," and she was one of only two women elected to state office before World War II.

Young girls at a suffrage meeting, circa 1920, in an automobile festooned with banners and placards reading "Votes for Us when We are women."

The Progressive Era in North Carolina

Although the state contributed to and participated in the progressive movement that impacted the national scene, the state itself continued to be dominated by a monolithic Democratic Party, which worked to maintain the status quo. North Carolina welcomed the election of Woodrow Wilson, a Southerner, to the presidency in 1912, as a number of Tar Heels gained positions of influence in Washington. Josephus Daniels, publisher of the Raleigh *News and Observer*, served eight years as Secretary of the Navy. North Carolina Democrats headed the U.S. Senate's Finance and Rules committees; they also headed the Rules and Judiciary committees of the U.S. House of Representatives. Walter Hines Page of Cary served as U.S. Ambassador to England and played a prominent role in Wilson's cabinet.

The "North Carolina Equal Suffrage Association" had been organized as early as 1894, but the movement for voting rights for women lagged until 1913, when local suffrage league chapters began to form in quick succession across the state. In spite of this momentum, and despite the support of prominent men such as Chief Justice Walter Clark — who spoke often and forcefully in favor of suffrage — powerful political interests blocked action by the Legislature year after year. Women in North Carolina finally gained the right to vote in 1920, not by action of the General Assembly, but by federal law, as provided in the 19th Amendment of the Constitution.

Across the nation, women were gradually entering the professional fields, but progress was slow — especially in medicine and law. North Carolina generally lagged behind the western and urban eastern states in terms of progressive legislation. The most nativist state in the Union (the 1900 census had shown that more than 99 percent of North Carolinians were native-born), North Carolinians had less exposure than other Americans to people from other regions and different backgrounds.

Not until the fall of 1911 would Lillian Rowe Frye, wife of attorney and association member A.M. Frye of Bryson City, become the second woman licensed to practice law in North Carolina. Two years later, Lillian Frye would become the first woman member of the North Carolina Bar Association. Lillian Exum Clement, an Asheville Democrat, passed the bar examination in 1916 and became the first woman in North Carolina to begin her own law practice. In 1920, "Brother Exum," as she was called, became the first woman elected to the N.C. House of Representatives.

In the wake of the Wilmington race riot and the spate of lynchings in North Carolina, only a relative handful of blacks applied for a law license, and fewer passed the bar exam. Some of the state's most talented black lawyers, including Shaw University's Edward A. Johnson, left the state during this period. The Bar Association's constitution, adopted at the height of racial turmoil in the state, had limited membership to "any white person...who [is] a member of the Bar of this State in good standing."

During the Progressive era, the profession became more "professional," with higher ethical and educational standards. Fewer and fewer attorneys were licensed who had not had at least some formal legal training. Most North Carolina lawyers continued to have a general practice in a small town. Those who practiced law in the cities saw an expansion of the scope and type of their practice as the state slowly became more urban and modern, with increasing ties to the wider world of commerce and industry.

Certainly change was afoot in the law, and progress was being made in North Carolina. But still, on occasion, lawyers found themselves in the midst of citizens who took the law into their own hands — as happened in Wilmington in 1898. In Watauga County in 1908, attorney Thomas Anderson Love paid a high price for being a lawyer, as recounted in a 1965 reminiscence by his daughter, Florence Love Halas:

> Papa was an expert in murder cases. He was called to another murder case in Boone, N. C. (A Luther Banner was charged with murdering a Mr. Cline.) It seems Banner had a post office in Banner Elk and had some simple quarrel with Cline over a letter or groceries and killed him. Anyway, Banner received a first degree murder sentence. Well that night they got revenge on Papa.... We were all sleeping except Annie, who was a great reader of books, and she was reading 'On the Trail of the Lonesome Pine' upstairs and saw the light from the outside of the house through a glass door. What a fire.... Seventeen rooms and no way to extinguish it. We barely escaped with our lives. Papa's grand law library was entirely lost, and all we possessed. We saved nothing.

Thomas Anderson Love's reported response to the destruction was typically laconic: "Being a lawyer was not without risks in the mountains in 1908." While the frontier had vanished in the Tar Heel State before the American Revolution, the frontier spirit lived on well into the 20th century.

Expanding law firms, such as Manly, Hendren & Womble of Winston-Salem, employed the legal technology of the times. Shown here are Bunyan Snipes Womble in the firm law library, and secretaries (believed to be) Jo Marshall with her Remington typewriter and Kate Wurreski on the telephone, around 1915.

THOMAS WALKER DAVIS

Thomas W. Davis of Wilmington was the second secretary-treasurer of the North Carolina Bar Association.

Thomas W. Davis was born in Wilmington May 27, 1876, into a family of prominent legal professionals. Davis' mother was a sister of North Carolina Supreme Court Justice Platt D. Walker, the first president of the North Carolina Bar Association. As a youth, Davis began working for the Atlantic Coast Line Railroad and remained until 1898 when he enlisted in the U.S. Army for service in the Spanish-American War. Upon his return, he began his legal training under his father and then at the University of North Carolina. He was admitted to the bar in 1900 and began practicing with his father. After his father's retirement due to ill health, Davis continued practicing in Wilmington focusing on corporate and industrial clients, especially the Atlantic Coast Line Railroad.

Davis became secretary and treasurer of the North Carolina Bar Association in 1906 and served in that capacity until he resigned in 1920 upon his election as association president. During his tenure he continued his practice in Wilmington, but led the association in many areas. He was an active member of the American Bar Association and was instrumental in the North

Carolina organization's approval of the ABA Canons of Ethics in 1908. He was also active in the Association's leadership when it admitted its first woman member in 1913. When World War I began, Davis again went into the Army in the Judge Advocate General Department and served until his discharge in May 1919.

While secretary and treasurer of the Bar Association, Davis saw the association make many, mostly fruitless, efforts to improve legal education and to raise the requirements for admission to the North Carolina bar. In 1920, he was elected president of the body he had served so faithfully for 14 years. In his July 1921 presidential address, Davis introduced the idea of a state bar organization consisting of all practicing attorneys in the state possessing authority over the requirements for taking the bar examination, the examination itself, and disciplining attorneys. His call for action, like many annual meeting suggestions, did not result in immediate action, but set in motion events which would eventually change the legal profession in North Carolina.

At the end of his presidency, Davis remained active in the association and continued to lead efforts to create a state bar. This movement gained strength after 1926 and when the legislature finally approved the idea in 1933, Davis was hailed as one of those responsible for its success and implementation. He remained active in the association, serving on various committees as long as he was active professionally. He died in 1951.

The Second Secretary-Treasurer

George F. Rountree of Wilmington was president of the Bar Association from 1906-1907.

In many ways, Thomas W. Davis was destined to become a leader of the North Carolina Bar Association. A prominent lawyer of the Wilmington bar in his own right, he was the nephew of Platt D. Walker, the first association president; the son of Junius Davis, general solicitor of the Atlantic Coast Line Railroad Company; and the grandson of George Davis, attorney general for the Confederate States of America.

Davis served as secretary-treasurer from 1906 until the annual meeting of 1920, when he was elected president. According to long-established tradition, only a few insiders knew that Davis was being proposed for the presidency. When he was elected, the leaders of the association "drafted" prominent attorney A. B. Andrews of Raleigh to serve as secretary-treasurer. Davis had served the association diligently and well, in the tradition of J. Crawford Biggs. But it seems that Davis often faced formidable opposition in the annual elections. His opponents usually came from the central part of the state, perhaps indicating some regional concerns about the location of the association's office and records in Wilmington, and the dominance of the New Hanover bar in the association's early years. (Thomas W. Davis' law partner during the latter years of his tenure was George Rountree, an organizer of the North Carolina Bar Association and president in 1906-1907.)

Legal Ethics

In August 1908, the American Bar Association adopted "Canons of Legal Ethics" which were then sent to the bar associations of the various states for their consideration. The New York Bar Association approved them, as did all the associations that had considered them prior to the next meeting of the North Carolina Bar Association, in June 1909 at Asheville. Secretary Thomas W. Davis sent copies of these canons to all members of the Bar Association well before the Asheville meeting. Clement Manly, of Winston, chairman of the Committee on Legal Ethics, proposed that the canons be formally adopted by the North Carolina Bar Association.

Recognizing that the association had adopted a Code of Legal Ethics in 1900, Manly recommended the Canons of Legal Ethics as an elaboration on the code, and an improvement of it.

In the 1909 *Report* of the annual meeting, both the Code of Legal Ethics and the Canons of Legal Ethics were printed. Thereafter, only the canons were included until 1918, when they were omitted. In 1919, they appeared again, with the notation that they were "Adopted Session of 1919." No record of their being considered or voted upon exists in the 1919 *Report*. A possible explanation is that Davis returned to Army service with the beginning of World War I. He is listed as secretary of the association in both 1918 and 1919, but someone else undoubtedly supervised the printing of the *Reports*.

Members of the Wake County Bar gather for a picnic and meeting at the home of attorney Thomas S. Fuller in April 1907.
Front row (sitting): *Will Pace, Claude Benson, Buck Jones, Jim McKee, Robert Boyd, Ed Battle, Hayden Clement, Walter Clark Jr., Ed Chambers Smith.*
Second row: *Thomas S. Kenan, R.T. Gray, Thomas Badger, W.T. Grant, B.C. Beddingfield, Ashby Lambert, Perrin Busbee, Will Russ, J.C.L. Harris, Staples Fuller, Will Snow, Sam Rogers, —— Brown.*
Third row: *James Shepherd, Carl Duncan, Willis Briggs, Jones Fuller, Judge George H. Brown, Bart Gatling, Samuel Ashe, unidentified, Richard H. Battle, —— McNeil, William H. Peele, Elmer Long, W.N. Jones, the next three men are unidentified, Thomas Argo, S. Brown Shepard, James I. Johnson.*

Legal Education

The issue of educational and other requirements for admission to the North Carolina bar also received regular attention from the association. From the beginning, the Bar Association had a standing Committee on Legal Education and Admission to the Bar, and early on the *North Carolina Journal of Law* had urged a progressive stance toward legal education:

> Such is the progress of the law that one who confines himself to the old black letter of the science can never fit himself for the active duties of professional life. One who goes to Coke or Blackstone for the law of corporations will be as unprepared for the practice in this branch of law as the astronomer who stops at Galileo, or the scientist who is content with what he learns from Newton.

In its first decade, the North Carolina Bar Association had led a successful effort to require two years of study before admission to the bar, and had debated the nature of the educational requirements that should be established. In 1909, the association submitted to the Supreme Court a request:

> 1. That the Court carefully inquire into the preparatory legal training of each candidate; and,

> 2. That the Court make the legal questions asked of candidates on examination of a nature that will demand a display of knowledge and legal reasoning, such as can be required by an average law student only after a period of two years study; and,

> 3. That, in the holding of examinations, the Court devise some method of preventing deception being practiced by candidates upon the Court and upon the profession.

Given such a request by the Bar Association, clearly all was not well with the training and certification of attorneys in North Carolina.

University of North Carolina law students pose in front of the law school in 1909. Dean James C. MacRae is pictured in the third row, center. Professor Thomas Ruffin is seated to the right of MacRae.

1909

The issue surfaced again at the 1910 annual meeting. Needham Y. Gulley, dean of the School of Law at Wake Forest College, chaired the Committee on Legal Education and Admission to the Bar that year. When called upon to give his report, he said, "I asked the Committee to meet in Raleigh in June, but couldn't get anybody there but Judge [Francis] Winston and myself." He then presented a report that addressed several of the issues that had been raised in 1909. The proposals included a requirement that a certificate of at least two years of study be required from a law school or an attorney who directed the candidate's course of study. A list of books to be studied during the first and second year was included:

> *First Year*—Blackstone's Commentaries, Bispham's Equity, Hughes on Evidence, May's Criminal Law, Croswell on Administrators, Hopkins on Real Property, Clark on Contracts, Clark on Corporations, Bigelow on Torts, Cooley's Constitutional Law, Clark's Code of Civil Procedure, Constitution of United States, Constitution of North Carolina and Revisal of 1905, Vol. 1.

> *Second Year*—Hale on Bailments and carriers, Bigelow on Bills, Tiffany on Sales, Bigelow on Wills, Richards on Insurance, Huffcut on Agency, Boone on Banking, Conynton on Corporate Management, Clark on Criminal Procedure, Shipman's Common Law Pleading, Bryant on Code Pleading, Hughes on Federal Procedure and Sharswood's Legal Ethics.

The committee also proposed that "candidates for admission to the bar be advised not to begin the study of law until they have at least such educational attainments as are required for admission to the academic departments of the leading colleges of this State."

Noting that Gulley's proposals included increasing the course of study required for admission to the bar, J. Crawford Biggs proposed that a new committee be constituted, with Gulley as chairman, to report the following day. But obstacles — perceived or real — obviously existed to this project. When Gulley

Downtown Goldsboro in May 1914.
Note the different forms of transportation —
the horse and buggy, streetcar, and automobile.

The Lewis West Gang trial was held in the Wilson County Courthouse in March 1911. West was convicted and executed for the first degree murder of Deputy Sheriff George W. Mumford.

Aubrey Lee Brooks, one of eight Greensboro lawyers who have served as Bar Association president, was president from 1916-1917

Members of the North Carolina Supreme Court 1911-1920. From left to right: W. A. Hoke, Platt D. Walker (first NCBA president), Chief Justice Walter Clark, George H. Brown and William R. Allen.

rose to present his report the next day he said, "The Committee was of the opinion that nothing could be done, so we just recommend that the Court do what it pleases." The committee's formal report, submitted later, read more discreetly: "We recommend to the Association that it suggest to the Supreme Court the advisability of extending the course of study prescribed for applicants for license to practice law." Progress in this area, as well as in many others, was slow.

Growing Pains

The spirit of agreement that existed in the areas of examination, ethics and discipline did not, unhappily, prevail in other areas as the association began its second decade. The organization seemed to be overburdened with committees, and largely ineffective ones at that. Most of these committees were appointed extemporaneously at the annual meeting, usually because of some issue of momentary interest. Most never met, and only a handful ever reported any activity during these years. Time after time these committees were called upon to report at the annual meetings, and in the great majority of cases the answer was "the committee has no report."

Aubrey Lee Brooks of Greensboro temporarily stirred the association out of the doldrums of inaction by his remarks at the 1911 annual meeting. Frustrated by the ineffectiveness of the Bar Association's committees and the organization's inability to press for meaningful legislative reforms, Brooks rose to challenge the members to live up to that "sacred duty of procuring the adoption of good laws" of which Platt D. Walker had spoken:

> In view of the fact that I am a charter member of this Association, and have a deep interest in the Association, I think I may be permitted to say that in my opinion the North Carolina Bar Association will soon cease to have any justification for its existence, unless it begins to do something.

Brooks' barb apparently had the desired effect, at least for a time. Within a few years the association's efforts had resulted in more judicial districts, improved selection of jurors and speedier trials. Brooks' own career did not suffer as a result of his criticism. Already one of the most successful lawyers in the state, his colleagues elected him president of the North Carolina Bar Association in 1916.

"Judges and Juries"
Presidential Addresses of
the Second Decade

Over the years, presidential addresses had tended to fall in three categories: important public issues or professional challenges facing the bar, needed legislative and judicial reforms, or reminiscences of one's legal career. In 1914, President Thomas S. Rollins of Asheville delivered an address titled "Our Bar Association, its Past, its Present and its Future." The address focused primarily on future reforms which the association might endorse including: reforming the jury system to permit a jury to render a verdict in civil cases with only a three-quarter or five-sixths majority; placing the selection of jurors in the hands of a jury commission; passing a workmen's compensation law; and providing salaries for solicitors. Rollins' talk dealt only briefly with the origin and history of the association, but his topic may have diverted the next president, J. Crawford Biggs, from talking about his work as first secretary of the association.

Biggs, who had resigned as secretary in 1906 to become judge of the Superior Court for the Ninth Judicial District of North Carolina, served only five years in that position and returned to Durham to practice law and teach at the Trinity College School of Law. In 1912, he moved to Raleigh where he became a partner with Robert W. Winston. Biggs had remained an active member of the association during this entire time.

Judge Biggs chose as the topic of his 1915 presidential address, "The Power of the Judiciary over Legislation." In a lengthy and scholarly presentation, he discussed "the most unique and at the same time the most important feature of American constitutional law...the power exercised by the courts to declare legislation null and void when in conflict with the written Constitution." Biggs noted that "this is an

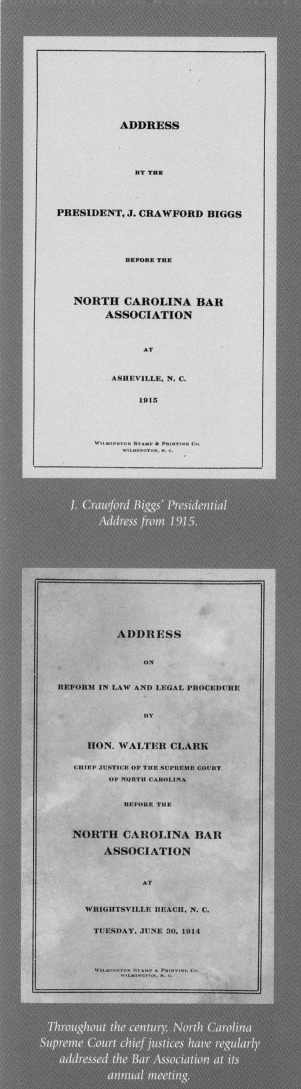

J. Crawford Biggs' Presidential Address from 1915.

Throughout the century, North Carolina Supreme Court chief justices have regularly addressed the Bar Association at its annual meeting.

American doctrine and had its rise in the formation of the several State governments in 1776," and proceeded to establish North Carolina's primacy in the development of this practice.

As many other Bar Association speakers had done before, Biggs took the opportunity to highlight North Carolina's contributions to the legal profession. He outlined the work of James Iredell in the famous North Carolina Supreme Court case of *Bayard v. Singleton*. In that landmark case the North Carolina court established the principle of judicial review, well before the decision by the U.S. Supreme Court under Chief Justice John Marshall in the case of *Marbury v. Madison*.

Biggs then examined the actions of other state courts and legislatures as well as that of the Constitutional Convention in support of this judicial power. He noted the American origin of the doctrine of judicial review and its evolution. He described the impact of the doctrine on the creation of a strong national government, and concluded with numerous judicial and scholarly tributes to "the wisdom of the fathers in lodging the ultimate protection of the Constitution in judicial authority."

Harry Skinner, president in 1915-1916, was one of the most exceptional figures in the history of the North Carolina Bar Association. From a politically prominent Perquimans County family, Skinner came to prominence in the 1880s through his writings on agricultural economics, including the subtreasury scheme later adopted by the Farmers' Alliance. As a lawyer, he was not eligible to join the alliance, but he nonetheless became a strong supporter of the farmers' movement in the General Assembly, where he served as a representative for

Pitt County, advocating for farm relief and state support for the downtrodden. Although a staunch Democrat, he joined the People's Party and was elected to the U.S. Congress as a Populist in 1894. His legislative proposals — the subtreasury plan, bimetallism, and a cotton price stabilization plan — were far ahead of their time, and were later adopted as parts of the Federal Reserve Banking Act and the farm programs of President Franklin Roosevelt's New Deal.

In a high-minded address to the association, Skinner argued that the law should be the protector of the powerless, and lawyers the bold protectors of the rights of all citizens:

> Lawyers should be impressed with the importance of their profession.... The greatest and most important matters of the world are committed to his care. He is the protector against the encroachments of power; the preserver of freedom; the defender of weakness; the unraveller of cunning; the investigator of artifice; the humbler of pride; the scourger of oppression. As long as our profession retains character and learning, the rights of our people will be well arranged. As long as it retains the character for virtuous boldness, these rights will be well defended.

Also in 1915, a woman of exceptional character and learning, Margaret Kollock Berry, was graduated from the University of North Carolina School of Law, the first woman to be granted a degree from one of the state's law schools. (Women applied for admittance to the Wake Forest College School of Law in 1915, but the school's board of trustees voted to deny admission to women.)

World War I and Its Aftermath

The state, including many of its attorneys, strongly supported World War I, whether in military service in the armed forces or in the war effort on the home front. President Angus W. McLean described the scope of the lawyers' involvement in his opening remarks at the 1918 meeting at Wrightsville Beach:

> There is a reason why the attendance here is small. There are a number of the members of this Association on the battlefield and in camp, and a large number are engaged in war work at various places, particularly this week with the drive for War Savings Stamps. I think I can say in all candor that no calling or profession has contributed more to war service than the members of the legal profession, so that we ought not to feel disturbed because there is a small attendance [here].

The North Carolina Council for Defense, a civilian coordinating committee designed to mobilize social and industrial resources for the war effort, was established in May 1917, by Gov. Thomas W. Bickett, a charter member of the Bar Association. The council quickly established a statewide system of county councils of defense headed by local professionals, businessmen and county officials. Lawyers chaired 28 of these county defense councils in North Carolina. In Pasquotank County, J.C.B. Ehringhaus, later a governor of North Carolina, chaired the council; and in Wake County, J. Melville Broughton, governor and U.S. senator in later years, presided over the Raleigh area council. On the state level, the North Carolina council was one of the first in the nation to appoint a legal committee to advise draftees on settling their business affairs before induction into the armed forces. The state's lawyers, of course, formed the backbone of these legal advisory boards but also worked on Red Cross campaigns and Liberty Bond drives.

Lumberton's Angus W. McLean, president from 1917-1918, later served as governor of North Carolina from 1925-1929. McLean and J. Melville Broughton are the only two attorneys who first served as president of the Bar Association before later serving as governor.

Sam J. Ervin Jr. of Morganton served with distinction in France during World War I.

A military parade in Statesville during World War I.

More than 300 North Carolina lawyers served in the armed services in World War I, including several who would later hold high public offices. Henry M. London, a future secretary-treasurer of the association, served in the 1st North Carolina Reserve Militia. Secretary Thomas W. Davis served in the Judge Advocate General's Department, while fellow future presidents of the Bar Association — Willis Smith, Kenneth C. Royall and Charles W. Tillett Jr. — also served in the Army. R. Gregg Cherry, a future governor of North Carolina, organized a machine gun troop of the First North Carolina Cavalry. William Bradley Umstead, another future occupant of the governor's office, also served as a machine gunner, in the 317th Machine Gun Battalion. Two Bar Association members who would become U.S. senators were also soldiers — Robert R. Reynolds of Asheville and Samuel J. Ervin Jr. of Morganton.

State Adjutant General R. E. Denny later summarized the service rendered by his fellow attorneys during the Great War:

> From the very moment and even before a status of war was declared to exist practically every lawyer in the State was either heading or performing most important parts in the work of assembling industries and converting others to the purposes of war. With the establishment of the selective draft the legal profession found its offices crowded with many needing help with question-naires. Liberty and Victory loan drives required of the lawyers much time and energy in the speaking and selling campaigns conducted, and with the sprinkling of the drives for war charities and welfare work coming sometimes in doubles the attorneys-at-law were almost unanimously attorneys-at-war.

During the war years, many women worked in jobs previously held by men in offices, shops, factories and farms, proving their ability and gaining valuable experience. And nearly 200 North Carolina nurses served in the armed forces from 1917 to 1919. Those men and women who had gone "over there" — including lawyers — had experienced other ways of living, and seen a broader world beyond their home state. Some returned with a greater openness to progressive ideas, and a greater tolerance for points of view different from their own.

Perhaps in reaction to the horrors of the World War and out of respect for the war dead, the site of the first postwar meeting (1919) was neither in the mountains nor along the coast. For only the second time in its history the membership gathered in the Piedmont, at Greensboro, the executive committee having concluded that "no better place could be found for holding a real business annual meeting." For one year at least, the social side of the annual meeting was being downplayed.

President E. F. Aydlett's address that year, "Problems of the North Carolina Bar Association," was similarly businesslike and practical. Aydlett advocated a series of court and procedural reforms as President Rollins had done five years earlier — including minimum educational standards for the legal profession and a call for a state constitutional convention study commission — but also called for change on the part of the association: that a county-level canvass for new members be instituted; that the terms of the standing committees should be extended to five years; and that the association erect its own building in Raleigh.

Reform and progress were the watchwords of the age, and the end of the war had brought a new sense of possibility to the lives of many North Carolinians. The state was a significantly different place from what it had been just 20 years earlier. In 1900, North Carolina counted only 10,932 telephones in the state but, by 1920, that number had ballooned to 123,000. In 1910, there were only 2,400 motor vehicles in the state but by 1921 that number had skyrocketed to 150,000. North Carolina was no longer an isolated, rural state. Her laws — and her lawyers — would have to respond to these new conditions.

Looking down Hay Street towards the old Marketplace in Fayetteville, around 1920.

A Legal Giant Speaks

One of the most distinguished speakers ever to address the North Carolina Bar Association was Professor Roscoe Pound, dean of the Harvard University School of Law. Recognized as one of the world's foremost legal thinkers, Pound implemented many reforms in the teaching of law, and was a proponent of the case study method of Christopher Langdell. (Trinity's law school had pioneered the use of the case study method in 1904, when Samuel Fox Mordecai reorganized the law school. The University of North Carolina School of Law began using the case method in 1919, with Wake Forest following in 1935.)

Pound advanced the idea that the legal profession must recognize the needs of humanity and take social conditions into account. This concept of "sociological jurisprudence" — how the legal system can further justice and a desired social order — would ultimately be credited with inspiring the New Deal programs of the 1930s. In his 1920 address to the attorneys of a still predominately agricultural state, Pound chose to speak on the topic of "The

Dean Samuel F. Mordecai, a Raleigh lawyer and previous part-time law instructor at Wake Forest College, stands with his Duke University law faculty. Mordecai instituted the case method as the basis of instruction at Duke.

Prominent Wake County resident Armistead Jones, a senior member of the Raleigh Bar who had volunteered for the Confederate Army at age 16, is shown here with his secretary, Alice Little, about 1920.

Pioneers and the Common Law." Rural and small-town attorneys may not have agreed with the ideas Pound expressed in his talk and elsewhere, but lawyers in the rapidly growing industrial and commercial cities may have had a better understanding.

Dean Pound began by noting the origin of the common law in England and asserting the idea that American law was generally based on the same concepts. He stated: "Our judicial organization, then, and the great body of our American common law are the work of the last quarter of the 18th century and the first half of the 19th century." He then noted that the emergence of large American cities and "the social and legal problems to which they give rise are of the last half of the 19th century. Our largest city now contains in three hundred and 26 square miles a larger and infinitely more varied population than the whole thirteen states contained when the federal constitution was adopted." He continued:

> Demand for socialization of law, in the United States, has come almost wholly, if not entirely, from the city. We have no class of agricultural laborers, demanding protection. The call to protect men from themselves, to regulate housing, to enforce sanitation, to inspect the supply of milk, to prevent imposition upon ignorant and credulous immigrants, to regulate conditions and hours of labor and provide a minimum wage, and the conditions that require us to heed this call, have come from the cities. But our legal system has had to meet this demand upon the basis of rules and principles developed for rural communities and small towns—for men who needed no protection other than against aggression and overreaching between equals dealing matters which each understood....
>
> Although much has been done and comparatively rapid progress is now making, it is perhaps still a chief problem to work out a system of legal administration of justice which will secure the social interest in the moral and social life of every individual under the circumstances of the modern city, upon the basis of rules and principles devised primarily to protect the interest in general security in a rural community of seventy-five years ago.

Pound concluded that the social and legal problems created by the cities and their large populations had changed the nature of the legal system. He called for the transference of common law ideals into a new legal structure that would make "courts and bar efficient agencies for justice."

There is no record of the immediate response of the members of the association to the address of the professor, who was speaking of a problem many there had not experienced. His speech did become the basis of his next book, *The Spirit of the Common Law* (1921), a classic of American jurisprudence. It also seems that the visionary ideas spoken that day by Dean Pound in Asheville took root in the minds of some of the association's leaders, for we see a growing concern for "modernization" challenges in the presidential addresses of the next decade.

A Valedictory Address

A year after Roscoe Pound's speech before the bar, President Thomas W. Davis delivered his farewell address as a leader of the North Carolina Bar Association. In "The Bar, Its Duties and Burdens," Davis called for a robust state bar organization with expanded authority and significant responsibilities to the profession. He began with a characterization about lawyers that is still largely true today:

> The lawyer has been scolded, exhorted, criticized, held up to ridicule, scorned and damned so long that he would think something was radically wrong with the whole world, that he was being neglected, if this should cease. This cheap wit has emanated alike from ministers, merchants, doctors, politicians, professors; in fact, from all classes of people.

Davis proposed "a remedy for all of this. I believe that every lawyer, upon becoming a member of the Bar, should become a member of the (Bar Association)." He lamented that many lawyers in the state were not members of the North Carolina Bar Association and that many who were members saw the annual meeting "simply as a means and a place for the foregathering of good fellowship."

Davis envisioned a state bar organization — to which all practicing attorneys would belong — as a means to regulate legal education; to control the licensing and disbarment of attorneys; and to elevate the reputation of the profession in the public mind. Davis continued to bring this proposal before the association in the years that followed. His efforts and those of others who joined him in urging such action would continue for more than a decade.

The Granville County Bar Association of 1920.
Seated in the front row: *Judge A.W. Graham, B.S. Royster Jr., Dee Hunt, Judge Henry A. Grady, Cam Hunt, James Taylor and A.A. Hicks.*
Back row: *Dennis Brummitt, T. Lanier, J.P. McLendon, Gen. B.S. Royster, B.K. Lassiter, A.W. Graham Jr., T.G. Stem and F.W. Hancock Jr.*

This 1927 Norman Rockwell painting, titled The Law Student (Young Lawyer),
evokes nostalgic feelings about the challenges of learning the law.

CHAPTER 6

"Currents and Crosscurrents"
1922-1931

T he America of the postwar period was far different from the progressive country that had entered the war in 1917. An exaggerated sense of patriotism expressed itself in the development of a "Pure Americanism" movement whose darkest elements lashed out against "nontraditional" groups such as foreigners, Jews, Catholics, labor organizers and Communists. In North Carolina, paradoxically, progressive advances continued to be made at an even faster pace, and the state remained an island of relative tolerance in an increasingly reactionary South.

North Carolina's success was due in no small part to 12 years of excellent leadership from three governors in the 1920s: Cameron Morrison, Angus W. McLean and O. Max Gardner — all attorneys, all members of the North Carolina Bar Association. Morrison (1921-1925), known as the "Good Roads Governor" for his successful highway program, also did much to improve public education. McLean (1925-1929) greatly modernized the administration of state government. Gardner (1929-1933) added workmen's compensation and the secret ballot to the list of reforms, and continued the Morrison program of road-building and school reform.

For all the progress that North Carolina was making, problems remained. Even though the Ku Klux Klan was not as active in North Carolina as in other Southern states, the Klan was readily accepted in many quarters of the state. And even if the number of lynching victims in North Carolina was only a fraction of the annual number in Georgia or Mississippi, the Tar Heel state still ranked 20th in lynchings among all the states in the 1920s.

Cameron Morrison, known as the "Good Roads Governor," worked to improve road conditions such as these depicted in this photograph of Franklin Street, Chapel Hill, during the 1920s.

O. Max Gardner, lawyer and governor of North Carolina from 1929-1933, reorganized state government during his administration.

Association member Albert Coates founded the Institute of Government in 1931. It became affiliated with the University of North Carolina at Chapel Hill in 1942.

While never an issue before the Bar Association, the decade's conflicting crosscurrents of modernism and traditional values saw their most public clash in the furor over the teaching of "Evolution" in the public schools. A 1925 bill to prohibit the teaching of evolutionary science, the so-called "Poole Bill," failed by a single vote in the Education Committee of the North Carolina House of Representatives. Most teachers in the state avoided the subject altogether, in the classroom anyway, but the vote was an important symbolic victory for the modernists — and North Carolina's progressive image.

Whatever prosperity and social progress that the state was beginning to see came to an abrupt halt with the panic of 1929 and the Great Depression. While the average North Carolina lawyer would not experience the hardships of hunger and unemployment faced by many Tar Heels, the profession was seriously affected, and membership in the association would soon begin to decline.

"A Difficult and Delicate Transition"

Legal historian Albert Coates described the 1920s in North Carolina as "a period of industrial upswing" following the social changes brought on by World War I and preceding the economic depression of the 1930s. His description of the challenges facing the state's law schools also applied to the state's lawyers and the Bar Association of that day:

> Economic, social and political horizons are rapidly extending, as little local businesses are forced to grow or combine or perish, as long established practices, customs and beliefs are stretching in the ever lengthening currents and cross currents playing through our life, as counties and states and sections are brought by rapid transit and instant communication into competition or cooperation. ...
> It is the Law School's business now to train lawyers equal to the task of guiding human relationships through these difficult and delicate transition days, lawyers who in the transactions of every day's routine are mindful of the fact that not merely agriculture and industry, a superstructure of trade and transportation, commerce and finance, but a civilization is in the making....

Professor Coates was right, the currents of modernity were sweeping over North Carolina. But the old ways hung on in certain corners of the state, and the old values persisted in the person of some in the profession. One lawyer who embodied the virtues of courtesy and compassion was Judge John H. Bingham. A Watauga County native, Bingham managed a farm and taught school before going to Wake Forest and passing the bar at age 45. Known for his friendliness and generosity, his home became an open house for any passerby who needed food or shelter, so much so that he came to be known as "The Hospitable Judge" in the western counties.

The story is told of one trip the judge was making to Boone on horseback from his Sugar Grove farm. It seems that along the way he passed a country store from whence a certain "hardshell" Baptist preacher called out to the judge in a loud voice, "Woe unto ye Doctors and Lawyers!" Judge Bingham looked back with a smile and replied, "...Scribes, Pharisees and Hypocrites."

Change at the Top

The Bar Association prospered during the postwar era but also faced significant changes, not just in leadership but in becoming a modern profession. The association began the decade with 762 active members on June 30, 1920, and had 1,203 active members by the end of the annual meeting in 1930. Members focused their activities through existing committees of the association, with an occasional special committee to address a pressing issue. During the 1920s and on through the 1930s, the staff consisted almost exclusively of a one-person secretary-treasurer elected at each annual meeting. This had been the situation from the first years of the association and seemed to work well in that day and time.

The early secretary-treasurers were practicing attorneys, often with larger firms that could supply them clerical assistance. From the beginning, addresses and reports of business conducted at the annual meetings were published *verbatim* — indicating that persons skilled with transcription had assisted in their preparation.

The first two staff executives served terms of eight and 14 years respectively. Both J. Crawford Biggs and Thomas W. Davis were very active before, during and after their terms of service, and both later served as presidents of the association.

Alexander Boyd Andrews Jr., third secretary-treasurer of the association, was elected in 1920 when Thomas W. Davis resigned to become president. A civic-minded Raleigh attorney and amateur historian, Andrews was a charter member of the Bar Association. He was particularly interested in the development of the legal profession at all levels. In 1928-29, he was president of the Wake County Bar Association and, at the same time, president of the North Carolina Bar Association. He also served on the American Bar Association's committee on legal education and chaired its Special Committee on Judicial Salaries from 1922 to 1943. Andrews was also an accomplished statistician who regularly issued statistical reports on legal and judicial topics. He was not a candidate for the secretary-treasurer job for a second year and Henry M. London, also of Raleigh, was elected to the position.

A.B. Andrews, shown with his wife in a "flying machine" at Atlantic City, New Jersey, in 1914. Andrews later served as secretary-treasurer in 1920 -1921.

While in Charlotte for the 1921 annual meeting held at the Selwyn Hotel, members and spouses posed for the traditional Bar Association group photograph.

Henry M. London:
"A Genius for the Details of Great Affairs"

Henry Mauger London was a native of Pittsboro who graduated with honors from the University of North Carolina in 1899. For two years he worked as a clerk in the census office in Washington, D.C., while he also studied law at Columbian University (now George Washington University). Returning to Chapel Hill, he completed his legal studies and was admitted to the North Carolina Bar in 1903. For 10 years he practiced law in Pittsboro and assisted his father in editing the *Chatham Record*.

London returned to Raleigh in 1913 and served as chief deputy collector of internal revenue until 1919 when he became legislative reference librarian. In this position he directed the drafting of bills for the state Legislature. He assisted in drafting an estimated 5,000 bills before his death in 1939. When asked about the quality of the legislation passed by the General Assembly, London had a ready answer. "Some of the bills were wise," he said, "and some were otherwise."

Elected secretary and treasurer of the North Carolina Bar Association in 1921, London served until his death. Upon the creation of the North Carolina State Bar as a state agency in 1933, London was named its secretary, a position he held concurrently until 1938. As further testimony to his keen secretarial abilities and executive acumen, Henry London also served as treasurer of the Episcopal Diocese of North Carolina for 20 years and as secretary of the University of North Carolina Board of Trustees for 18 years.

Secretary London was appreciated by the members for his work in easing the work of association committees by arranging most of the scheduling and correspondence. As President John A. MacRae said in 1922, he was "prompt, efficient and systematic." His genius for the details of public affairs made him the Bar Association's "indispensable man" in the 1920s and 1930s, so much so that a journalist at the time remarked that "Henry London is as much a part of the association as its constitution."

Henry M. London was the Bar Association's secretary-treasurer from 1921-1939.

"Modernizing the Law and the Profession"
Presidential Addresses, 1922-1931

In 1922 the Bar Association returned to Wrightsville Beach, where the president, John A. MacRae of Charlotte, gave a practical address on "The Importance of the Organization of the Bar." Perhaps anticipating the Junior Bar Association movement of the next decade, MacRae called on his colleagues to emulate the medical profession in "organizing the Bar from top to bottom" through strong local organizations linked to the state association:

> The Medical Society of Charlotte, for instance, meets every two weeks.... What the doctors of Charlotte are doing, why can't the lawyers do? Let the local Bar Association meet monthly or quarterly or even annually and discuss professional standards, changes in the statute law, recent decisions of the Courts, and remedies for defects in the law, and the administration of the law, and the result will be a higher professional standard....

President E.S. Parker delivered "The Evolution of Democracy Under the Law" at the 1924 meeting in Pinehurst. Parker's was the first of several presidential addresses in the decade to build on Dean Roscoe Pound's

Charlotte's Law Building in the late 1920s. The offices of most of the Queen City's lawyers were housed in this building.

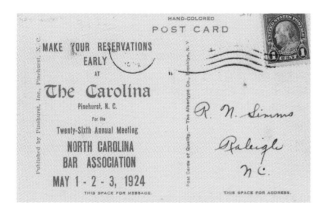

A penny postcard encourages early reservations for the 1924 annual meeting at The Carolina in Pinehurst.

The corner of Front and Market streets, Wilmington, in the 1920s.

Kathrine Robinson Everett, pioneer woman attorney whose career spanned seven decades, symbolizes the evolution of the role of women within the legal profession.

idea of modernizing the law. In a learned speech addressing U.S. Supreme Court decisions on such issues as child labor and the federal income tax, the Alamance county native gave a balanced address on the genius of the Constitution devised by the founding fathers, and the need for it to evolve:

> The Constitution could not be what Mr. Justice Story said it was to be — an instrument not merely for the exigencies of a few years, but one to endure through a long lapse of ages — unless by some method it could meet changing conditions; unless it could grow to keep pace with national growth, and could progress to keep abreast of — while exercising the necessary restraint upon — National progress.

Another event at the 1924 convention — though unremarked at the time — proved the rewards which can, at times, redound to one from attendance at the annual meeting. It was at the Pinehurst meeting that Kathrine Robinson, the young Fayetteville attorney who had been the first female graduate of the UNC law school, met Robinson O. Everett, a leading trial lawyer in Durham. They would be married two years later, and both would continue to have distinguished careers at the bar.

The task of the 1927 presidential address fell to John D. Bellamy, a founding member of the association and a self-described "old and experienced practitioner." The venerable member of the Wilmington bar delivered a call to the members to be men of virtue and live up to the organization's high ideals "for truly the profession of law is the noblest, the most influential and the most patriotic of all the professions." Yet even Bellamy recognized the need for the law — and the lawyers — to live out the old virtues in a new way. Reform should begin with admission standards for the bar:

This short term of study of the law [two years] is hardly sufficient, in this era of great advancement in science, with all the developments in the various subjects of trusts, unlawful combinations, electricity, the telegraph, the telephone, the phonograph, the aeroplane, the hydroplane, the radio, the submarine, and the complicated questions of prohibition as a national measure, and the numerous new phases of international laws, to enable a man to enter upon the practice of law....

Not every speech at the annual meetings was so solemn, nor the proceedings so serious as to rule out a generous amount of laughter and socializing. In his welcoming remarks to the 1927 meeting at Pinehurst, attorney H. F. Seawell of Moore County began with a humorous anecdote about fires in the longleaf pine forests of the Sandhills:

It was when arguing an appeal in a damage case on account of one of these forest fires about Pinehurst that the distinguished lawyer, Mr. Douglass, of counsel for the defendant, stated to the Supreme Court that the particular fire in question was the biggest, the hottest, and most ruinous ever known in history. 'Why sirs,' he said, 'it burned up a mule in a ten-acre field, and burned up Nick's Creek.' Chief Justice Faircloth, with puzzled look, asked: 'Does the counsel desire the Court to understand him to say that the fire really burned up a creek?' 'Yes, your Honors,' Mr. Douglass replied, 'and it burned down it, too.'

Golf remains one of the favorite recreational activities at annual meetings. The first of 23 Bar conventions during the 1900s at the Grove Park Inn in Asheville was held June 28-30, 1928.

In a light moment in his own address, President Bellamy recounted a story about a young North Carolina lawyer who had appeared before the Supreme Court seeking his license:

I am told by a reputable practitioner and member of this Association that at a not very remote examination by our Supreme Court one of the questions asked was, 'What was the Magna Carta,' and the answer of one applicant for admission to the bar was that it was the Colonial home of Thomas Jefferson.

Even the ever-efficient Henry London seems to have joined in the fun of the 1927 meeting at Pinehurst, for at one point in the proceedings he announced:

For such as wish to pitch horseshoes—a new and modern game— arrangements have been made and prizes offered for the best score at the Country Club this afternoon. At the same time, those who wish to engage in rifle or trap shooting or archery may do so at the Gun Club. We have had a carload of lemon wood sent in from Cuba for your use.

For all the levity of the 1927 meeting, an air of sadness hung over President Kenneth C. Royall's address to the 1930 annual meeting. The shadow over the convention was not just due to anxiety about the deepening economic depression but to "a death in the family." Royall, a Goldsboro native, had been chosen by the executive committee to fill out the unexpired term of the late president T. L. Caudle of Wadesboro, who had died in September. (It was only the second time in the association's history that a president had died in office, the first having been Hamilton C. Jones in 1904, who was replaced by Thomas S. Kenan.) Thirty-five at the time of his election, Royall became the youngest person ever to head the Bar Association.

In "The Bar Association and the Country Lawyer" Royall addressed a practical problem which he said faced every lawyer in North Carolina. Using a national standard for urbanization as his yardstick, Royall declared that "every North Carolina lawyer is a country lawyer." Yet, even in a state of country lawyers practicing in small country towns, unsettling changes had already arrived:

> We were once communities with a fine leadership of independent
> business and professional men — men with small businesses, it is
> true, but men of independence of judgment and action who by their
> own initiative worked out their destinies.... But in our small towns
> today we are confronted with an entirely different situation. We buy
> our groceries and our clothing from a clerk who acts upon instruc-
> tions from some store system, with headquarters located away from
> our town.... There was a time when the town banker was a big man in
> his community. He is rapidly being replaced by a teller of a chain or
> branch banking system.... The spirit of independence and initiative,
> which in the past have made our country towns such fine places to
> live in, is being replaced by a spirit of submission to routine tasks and
> admission that the real brains of the nation must be in our cities.

For North Carolina's "country lawyers" Royall identified worrisome trends, chiefly a narrowing of the field of practice due to encroachments by insurance companies, title companies, and the like. Turning a caustic eye to the Bar Association's record of achievement in passing legislation and improving the quality of life of its members, President Royall chided the association for its ineffective organizational scheme and methods:

> We are doing nothing — in fact trying to do nothing — to solve our
> economic problem — to help the young lawyer and the average
> lawyer in his struggle to earn a fair living — a living that will give him
> a background for ethics and service. Our Bar Associations seem
> gripped by some terror that the great bogey of commercialism will
> seize upon the profession if economic questions are discussed above
> a whisper. The fact is that the law has rapidly been commercialized,
> but from the outside — and just because we have stood in the
> background and permitted it to be done.

For Royall — like President MacRae eight years earlier — the solution lay in organizing effective local associations throughout the state and allying them with the state association:

> A local association reaches a much larger proportion of lawyers in its
> community than the State Association reaches in the State — reaches
> them not only in membership but also in attendance at meetings and
> in discussion and consideration of the matters undertaken by the
> Bar.... The legislature or the public or other vocations may ignore the

Kenneth C. Royall of Goldsboro, youngest person ever to serve as president of the Bar Association (1929-1930).

The University of North Carolina at Chapel Hill law class of 1925. Daisy Strong Cooper served as the first female student editor of the Law Review that year.

pronouncements of this gathering — but they would find it more difficult to ignore the requests of an organized bar with local units interested in those requests....

In 1931, the Bar Association gathered in Chapel Hill for the first time, at the University of North Carolina, where the state's first university law school was founded. In an address titled "The Lawyer: His Privileges and Responsibilities," President Charles G. Rose of Fayetteville invited the membership to return to the fundamental principles of the profession and the association's original ideals in that time of social and business upheaval:

> Why a lawyer? What useful purpose does he serve? The legal profession, as it now exists, has no hereditary or exclusive rights in handling the business of the public within the bounds of what is now called the practice of law.... If the public is seeking other and more expeditious means of settling disputes by arbitration, by industrial commissions and by insurance adjusters, we lawyers can have no just cause to complain, and we are forced to admit that, in many instances, there is cause for proper complaint.... [But] if we as a bar and as individual lawyers render a real service in the administration of justice, both in the courtroom and in the office, and actually aid and assist to bring about this desirable end, we need have no fear of the so-called 'unlawful' practices by laymen.... Brethren of the Bar, I call you back to the high purposes and to the great privileges of our beloved profession, that each member may become and remain a minister of Justice.

This Charlotte street scene in the early 1920s shows the mayoral campaign headquarters of Julia M. Alexander, 1876-1957. She joined the Bar Association in 1915. Although an unsuccessful mayoral candidate, she served in the North Carolina House of Representatives from 1925-1927, and was later elected vice president of the Mecklenburg County Bar and the American Bar Association.

Licensing Standards: Another Try

The issues that came before the annual meetings of the Bar Association in the 1920s were similar to those which had been considered in previous years. One of the pressing issues that reappeared on a frequent basis was standards for admission to the bar. The association had addressed these issues almost from its beginning. A number of lawyers who had pressed for a written examination in 1898 were instrumental in the founding of the association a year later. By 1900, it was generally required that candidates for admission should have studied law for at least two years, but there was no effective way to enforce this mandate.

Not only was the length of study required for admission to the bar an issue but also the matter of the course of study which candidates should pursue—whether in a school of law or under the tutelage of a practicing lawyer. Discussion of the course of study, including debates over specific texts, had occurred in 1903 and again in 1910. From the comments made during the debates over the issues, private squabbles outside the regular meetings occasionally grew heated and created much animosity between supporters of rival proposals. The 1910 report of Wake Forest Law School Dean N. Y. Gulley on the length and course of study discussed in Chapter Five indicates the frustration of some of those who sought to enhance the educational level of those entering the profession.

The Committee on Legal Education and Admission to the Bar had reported in 1921 on its draft proposal to the state Legislature that "each applicant for admission to practice law in the future should have a high school education or its equivalent." Several legislators, including some who favored this requirement, suggested that since the Supreme Court could prescribe the course of study to be pursued by applicants, it was the appropriate body to issue such a ruling, rather than the General Assembly.

The Court failed to respond to this suggestion, just as it had failed to
respond to Dean Gulley's proposals in 1910. In 1925, the annual meeting heard
again the familiar complaint that neither the Legislature nor the Supreme Court
had acted, and that North Carolina still had no educational prerequisite for
admission to the bar. Only in 1926 did the Supreme Court confirm the neces-
sity of evidence of good character in order to obtain a license to practice law.

The Committee on Legal Education and Admission to the Bar submitted
a careful report for the year 1927, once again lamenting the Legislature's refusal
to require completion of a high school course before admission to the bar. The
report also provided a convenient account of the changes in licensing laws from
the colonial era to the present, as well as charts on the numbers of lawyers in the
state. Statistics on total applicants, nonresident applicants, women applicants
and black applicants were also provided. At the committee's suggestion, the
association adopted a resolution urging the Supreme Court to review and revise
the requirements of study for admission to the bar.

New Laws for a New Society

In many ways, the work of the legal profession in North Carolina was
changing and the Bar Association was regularly involved in that process. Calls
for increasing the requirements for admission to the bar came in part because
the difficulties in practicing law were increasing. In 1928, North Carolina adopted its first Workmen's Compensation Act, joining the majority of the other states
in the country who already had legislation requiring employers to carry insurance for workers injured on the job. At the 1929 annual meeting, Matt H. Allen,
chairman of the North Carolina Industrial Commission, the state agency
charged with enforcing the law, addressed the members:

We in North Carolina have found ourselves confronted not only with new industrial conditions and problems, but also with new social problems, than which none is more important than the labor problem with its many delicate relations.... The principle of social justice which underlies and is the foundation of the Workmen's Compensation idea recognizes that accidents due to the ordinary hazards of industry are inevitable, and that industry, therefore, should bear the burden of such accidents, and that the cost of such accidents should be added to the selling price of the product.

Allen gave a primer on the history of workmen's compensation laws, their intent, and how the act would be implemented in North Carolina. The association then created a committee to work with the Industrial Commission to set the fees which attorneys could charge clients for representing them in workmen's compensation cases. Well before the New Deal and even before the Great Depression, association members were dealing with regulatory laws and their own role in helping them work properly.

A Last Stand on Admissions Standards

Also in 1929, President Alexander B. Andrews, longtime leader of the association, presented an address on "Legal Education and Admission to the Bar." Andrews was well known as a supporter of increased educational requirements for admission to the bar and of the creation of an independent state bar organization which would control the admission process. In his address, Andrews pointed out that the state's standards for admission to the practice of law were so low that North Carolina had become a haven for out-of-state candidates, many of whom were poorly trained.

The Supreme Court of North Carolina in 1929. The Stacy Court heard arguments regarding legal education standards and bar admission requirements.

GEORGE W. CONNOR   WILLIAM J. ADAMS   WALTER P. STACY
CHIEF JUSTICE   HERIOT CLARKSON   WILLIS J. BROGDE

Andrews felt that many of the nonresident candidates came to North Carolina because they wished to "be eligible for advancement in civil service positions in the government or else be eligible for admission to practice before the departments of the United States, especially tax matters, as well as admission to the United States Supreme Court and all other Federal courts." The state Legislature soon responded by denying nonresidents admission to bar examinations unless they had studied law in a recognized North Carolina law school.

In 1929, noting that the Supreme Court had as yet to act on strengthening requirements for admission to the bar, the association passed a resolution calling for a "public presentation of the matter of legal education and admission to the bar by any residents and citizens of the State of North Carolina, particularly members of the legal profession, and that due notice of the same should be given to the press." The Supreme Court at last responded, and a hearing was held by the Court on April 16, 1930.

The hearing began by recognizing recommendations made by a special committee of the North Carolina Bar Association, based on a set of standards adopted by the American Bar Association in 1921. The committee's chief proposals were: (1) that the course of study of law be increased from two years to three years; (2) that students should register at the time of beginning their study; and (3) that two years of college preparatory work be required.

Representatives of the three major law schools in North Carolina spoke to the proposal. Dean C. T. McCormick of the University of North Carolina School of Law urged the adoption of the ABA standards. Acting Dean T. D. Bryson of the Duke University School of Law also supported the proposal. Dean N. Y. Gulley of the Wake Forest College School of Law supported portions of the proposal but expressed concern about the cost of two years of college and three years of law school for the state's

This view of Greensboro around 1930 shows Gaston Street, now Friendly Street.

students. Other attorneys spoke at the hearing, and a large body of information was presented to the Court showing that North Carolina's standards for admission to the practice of law were among the lowest in the nation.

Toward the Incorporation of a State Bar

Despite the wealth of information gathered at the 1930 hearing before the Supreme Court, over the next two years the Court did nothing to increase admission standards. Perhaps in frustration, the leaders of the North Carolina Bar Association returned to President Thomas W. Davis' 1921 proposal to incorporate the bar, for the purpose of having effective control of licensing, examining and disbarring attorneys.

In 1926, the association had appointed a Special Committee on Incorporating the Bar. Four presidents of the association served on the committee — Lycurgus R. Varser, W. M. Hendren, G.V. Cowper and J. Melville Broughton — as well as Henry Groves Connor Jr. Its chairman, Isaac Mayo Bailey of Jacksonville, general counsel for the North Carolina Corporation Commission, reported at the 1927 annual meeting that they had been gathering information and considering arguments for and against the proposal, and made the following recommendation:

Your committee, therefore, from its study of the proposition has reached the conclusion that the advantages to be obtained from an all-inclusive organization of the bar materially outweigh any disadvantages that might result therefrom, and, speaking from its experience as members of the bar and citizens of the State interested in the bar's welfare, seriously proposes and advocates the all-inclusive principle as the solution of the problems now confronting the profession in this State.

R. Gregg Cherry, a future governor, and Ruth Hobbs, his secretary, at his partner's desk, Gaston County, April 1930.

On a motion to adopt a resolution expressing these sentiments, Judge J. Crawford Biggs and others opposed approving what they termed "such a nebulous proposal." A substitute motion was approved asking that a concrete motion be brought before the committee for its consideration. But no action was taken that year nor at the 1928 annual meeting.

In his 1929 presidential address, "Legal Education and Admission to the Bar," Alexander B. Andrews had also commented on the examination process itself. He reported that of the 52 law licensing jurisdictions, 50 of them "have Boards of Bar Examiners." Only North Carolina and South Dakota retained their Supreme Courts as the Board of Bar Examiners. In South Dakota, graduates of the University of South Dakota Law School were admitted to practice after passing their law school exams, so the Supreme Court of South Dakota only examined 10 to 24 law applicants each year.

Andrews reported that in August 1928 and February 1929, 332 applicants had appeared before the North Carolina Supreme Court — a far greater number than that in South Dakota:

This means that the lack of a State Board of Bar Examiners oblige the Supreme Court to annually examine, read, grade and pass upon 332 law examination papers, consisting of sixty-seven questions each, 200,000 questions and answers. The valuable time of the Supreme Court is now being taken for two weeks each year, passing upon the papers of the law applicants, when it could be more expeditiously and advantageously done by a State Board of Bar Examiners, whose expenses could be financed out of the $20 license fee which each successful applicant has to pay.

In 1931, Andrews reported to the association for the Committee on Legal Education and Admission to the Bar presenting current information on the practice of law in North Carolina. He spoke particularly to the question of whether the profession was overcrowded, an issue being discussed on the local and national scene as the nation fell further into the Great Depression. He also noted that the Supreme Court appeared to be taking a long time in responding to the issues discussed before them in 1930.

On the last morning of the 1931 annual meeting, a motion was adopted calling for the incoming president to appoint a committee "to prepare a draft of a proposed bill for incorporating the Bar, or making it self governing." Although Chairman I. M. "Ike" Bailey had also wisely inserted a phrase in the motion specifying that "by so doing the Association is not committing itself to incorporation," momentum for a self-governing bar was building within the membership.

A Wave of Local Bar Association Activity

Admission standards was not the only issue before the bar, and the North Carolina Bar Association was not the only organization active on the legislative front. Local groups began to address the problem of unlicensed practitioners. Before the 1931 session of the General Assembly, the unauthorized practice of law in North Carolina was common in certain areas of the state. But, in December 1931, a bill sponsored by the Wake County Bar Association passed the Legislature. The new law, which proscribed many activities by nonlawyers and provided penalties for offenders, replaced an ineffectual and largely unenforceable provision in state law that stated that "no person may practice law without a license."

Another signal development in the area of unauthorized practice also occurred in 1931 when the Junior Bar Association of Buncombe County filed suit against the Carolina Motor Club. In the complaint the Buncombe Junior Bar charged the motor club with establishing an in-house legal department and using it to provide legal advice to club members and assist in the collection of claims, such acts thus constituting the practice of law by the defendant. The decision of the trial court to issue a restraining order against the Carolina Motor Club brought nationwide attention to the case in 1931. (The judgment was later affirmed on appeal by the North Carolina Supreme Court.)

Though the local bar associations seemed to be supplying the forward momentum, certain currents at last seemed to be running in the right direction for the North Carolina Bar Association, even in the midst of a deepening economic depression.

∝

In many small North Carolina towns, the courthouse was the center of legal, political and social activity. Here, several local citizens enjoy a game of cards on the grounds of the Caswell County Courthouse in Yanceyville in October 1940.

CHAPTER 7

"Depression and Regression" 1932-1940

T he stock market crash of 1929 was the beginning of the end of what had been a long period of commercial growth in North Carolina. Since the turn of the century, urban development had generated a host of wholesale enterprises and retail stores. Banks, savings and loan associations, insurance companies and other financial institutions multiplied in North Carolina, as did the professionals who served them, particularly lawyers. The per capita income of Tar Heels in the 1920s had increased at a rate more than triple that of the country as a whole.

But such statistics masked North Carolina's relatively weak financial and commercial position on the eve of the 1929 crash. For example, the state's total bank resources in 1929 were barely a third of the average in other states. When farm income dropped by two-thirds between 1929 and 1933, it was not only business but the economic heart of the state that was in danger.

Employment, wages, profits and property values began dropping, followed quickly by a decrease in tax revenues. Banks failed in droves. Jobless men roamed the streets and highways of the state, and hunger stalked the countryside.

After a national bank holiday was declared in early 1933, Congress passed an Emergency Banking Act, which helped restore confidence in the banking system. Helped by federal programs, most of North Carolina's financial institutions were soon stabilized.

This photo of a Shoofly, Granville County, farm home was taken on November 16, 1939, as part of a Farm Services Administration project to document the effects of the Great Depression on America.

But massive amounts of federal relief money were also needed to simply ward off starvation. Two of the most important New Deal relief programs in North Carolina were the Civilian Conservation Corps (CCC) and the Works Progress Administration (WPA). The CCC provided work, wages and board for thousands of unemployed young men, while the WPA — much broader in scope and enrollment — spent nearly $175 million in the state, employing thousands in building roads, bridges, schools, hospitals, airfields and other structures.

These and other programs helped stop the downward spiral of the early 1930s and brought about a slow recovery in the years following. By 1937, nearly all measures of business activity — including bank deposits, retail trade and construction contracts — were showing substantial gains. By the fall of 1939, with the war in Europe hurting cotton and tobacco exports but otherwise boosting the North Carolina economy and lawyer's incomes, the trauma of the depression was beginning to fade.

One Lawyer's Beginnings

Perhaps the year 1933 was not the most auspicious time to begin a solo law practice in North Carolina — and for that matter, to establish the first tax law firm in the state — but Richard E. Thigpen did just that. In his autobiography *90 Years Into the Twentieth Century*, Thigpen recounts his first few months of private practice in Charlotte:

> In April 1933, I found a suitable office...and some office furniture I could afford... The prior tenant sold me the 'French Design Walnut Desk, four walnut leather chairs' and several other items for a few $20 bills... Rent was only $30 a month, but for several months I didn't make the rent.... The first five months of practice produced many days 'without another dollar' — but in November and December collections were $398.58. When I started using a columnar journal, I posted the following quotation inside the front cover: 'This is a strenuous world and success in any field is won only by an intense application of whatever talent one may have.'

Richard E. Thigpen joined the North Carolina Bar Association that summer and attended the 1933 annual meeting at Wrightsville Beach. His practice would grow and prosper, as would the Bar Association, thanks in part to his leadership and many years of service to the profession.

A Self-Governing Profession

One common element of the depression years was underemployment in nearly every area of work. The response of professions throughout the nation, especially medicine and law, was to question whether or not there were too many individuals practicing in these areas. Often the next step was to raise the requirements for entry. Such trends coincided with movements in both professions to improve the education and skill levels of their members.

The American Bar Association had long been pressing for a greater length of study as well as more rigorous educational requirements for the practice of law. The North Carolina Bar Association had, early in its existence, made efforts along the same lines—some successful, some not. The creation of an independent state bar, with control over admission to practice, seemed to many outsiders a move to limit the number of lawyers practicing in North Carolina, even though it was a position which the association had been advocating for many years.

At the annual meeting in Asheville on July 15, 1932, the North Carolina Bar Association's Special Committee on Incorporating the Bar proposed a statute for consideration by the membership. The committee — whose members included I. M. Bailey, L. R. Varser and Kemp D. Battle — had worked diligently for more than four years in refining the legislation. As proposed, the bill

Charlotte's Richard Elton Thigpen, Bar Association president from 1948-1949, was also one of the first tax specialists in North Carolina. He was an advocate for the annual Tax Institutes which began in 1944.

was titled, "An Act to Provide for the Organization as an Agency of the State of North Carolina of the North Carolina State Bar, and for its Regulation, Powers, and Government, Including the Admission of Lawyers to Practice and Their Discipline and Disbarment."

Members discussed the proposed legislation at great length. While at many previous meetings the association had gone on record favoring the principle of a self-governing bar, this time proponents of the measure met considerable opposition. Some members of the Bar Association — and many members of the Legislature and the public — fought against the act to incorporate a state bar. Many resisted the idea of turning over the governance of the profession to a state board that would consist primarily of attorneys. Others feared that once attorneys were given authority to set requirements for acquiring a license to practice law, they would set unreasonably high standards as a means of reducing competition within the profession.

Some of those present at the meeting argued that because a number of attorneys were not members of the Bar Association, a period of education about the proposed legislation was needed, since membership would be compulsory in a new state bar organization. Many feared that the birth of a state bar would mean the death of the voluntary Bar Association.

The vote on the proposal was close. On the final motion to adopt the bill and authorize its presentation to the General Assembly, the proposal was carried by a vote of 46 to 30. Julius C. Smith of Greensboro, general counsel for the Jefferson Standard Life Insurance Company, called the legislation "a necessary and proper act, a step forward in legal procedure and progress." But it must have been disappointing to the leaders of the association that only 76 of the 175 members who attended the annual meeting chose to vote on an issue of such vital importance to the legal profession in North Carolina. Perhaps Kemp Battle spoke for many when he said, "The passage of the act means only that the public is restive under present conditions and is willing to try the experiment of permitting the lawyers to put their house in order and to regulate their professional destinies in harmony with the general welfare."

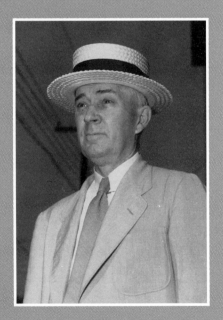

Elevating the Bar

On Saturday morning, July 16, President Kemp D. Battle was authorized to appoint a steering committee to present the bill and "endeavor to procure its passage by that body," and the executive committee instructed to "take such action as in its best judgement will promote the passage of the act." Both committees set to work and, with the assistance of Bar Association Secretary Henry M. London, began efforts to secure legislative approval. London was also legislative reference librarian. His knowledge of the legislative process and his contacts with lawyers and legislators certainly made timely passage of the legislation much more possible.

On April 3, 1933, Chapter 210 of the Public Laws of 1933, incorporating the North Carolina State Bar, would be ratified—a great milestone in the history of the legal profession in North Carolina and in the history of the North Carolina Bar Association.

Effective July 1, 1933, the North Carolina State Bar was incorporated, with full power to license, discipline and disbar lawyers. The act of incorporation created a seven-member Board of Law Examiners to be elected by the council of the State Bar. (The chief justice of the North Carolina Supreme Court was designated the chairman *ex officio* of the board of examiners, but was later relieved of this responsibility.) L. R. Varser and Charles W. Tillett Jr., active members of the North Carolina Bar Association and one-time presidents, were among those elected to the first Board of Law Examiners in the state's history.

The council of the State Bar — its governing body — consisted of one councilor elected by each of the 21 judicial districts, plus a president, vice president, and secretary-treasurer. I. M. Bailey, who shepherded the proposed state bar legislation past its political opponents, was chosen as the first president of the North Carolina State Bar, while Julius C. Smith, also a longtime proponent of a self-governing bar, was elected vice president. The redoubtable Henry M. London, secretary-treasurer of the Bar Association, was elected to serve in the same position with the State Bar.

At the 1933 meeting of the association, copies of the bar incorporation act were distributed and Bailey recommended a committee of five "to continue the sponsorship and advocacy of the act." This recommendation was approved and a committee appointed to furnish information about the law and its requirements and to defend any challenges to its constitutionality. President Kemp D. Battle, who had sponsored the act, asked members to support the State Bar and expressed concern about the future role of the North Carolina Bar Association.

Battle noted that the Bar Association's executive committee was proposing a reduction in dues from $4 to $2 and observed that "the ultimate functions of this Association, I presume, will have to be left for the future." The first meeting of the North Carolina State Bar was held in conjunction with the annual meeting of the Bar Association on June 29, 1934. Just as President Battle had challenged members of the Bar Association a year earlier, President Bailey challenged his fellow members of the bar to live up to the task set before them:

> This is an important point in the life of the legal profession in North Carolina.... There is now placed upon the profession a responsibility which makes each lawyer his brother's keeper.... Today we must recognize that the presence in our ranks of one unworthy member discolors our reputation throughout the State.... Let us together grasp the power that has been given us by the people of this State, and use it in the lifting of our profession to higher planes of usefulness. Let us do our full share in the building up in this State of a more perfect society...

Legal historian Edwin C. Bryson called the creation of the State Bar "the most important piece of work in the history of the North Carolina Bar Association." While there was considerable difference of opinion among the state's attorneys at the time and strained relations between the two organizations for a number of years, today most attorneys would no doubt agree with the opinion of William M. Storey, former executive vice president of the Bar Association:

> The creation of the State Bar and the retention of the Bar Association has resulted in a happy, logical, and efficient situation. The police functions of the profession are now vested, as they should be, in a state agency administered by lawyers (and to a limited extent by laymen), and our voluntary association has been freed from this burden and permitted to carry out its many and varied programs undiverted by these statutory responsibilities.

Main Street in Waynesville during the late 1930s.

Terra Incognita

With the creation of an independent state bar organization, to which all practicing lawyers in North Carolina would belong, issues such as admission to the bar (including the bar examination) and disciplining of lawyers were no longer the business of the North Carolina Bar Association. Individual members continued, of course, to have opinions on these matters and many of them participated in the work of the State Bar in supervising the profession. Occasionally, one of these topics would gather enough momentum that the Bar Association would debate the issue and adopt a resolution on the subject. But, for the most part, these matters were left to the State Bar.

The North Carolina Bar Association had prospered during the "Roaring '20s," and by 1932 boasted a membership of 1,249. But within three years, the number of members, annual expenditures and association assets had begun to decline. By 1940, all three figures had dropped substantially, as shown in the table below:

Richard M. Nixon was the only U.S. president to graduate from a North Carolina law school. This photo was taken while he attended the Duke University School of Law in the late 1930s.

Bar Association Membership & Finances, 1920-1940:			
Year	Members	Expenses	Assets
1920	805	$1,716	$ 805
1925	1,047	$2,900	$2,700
1930	1,151	$3,196	$2,949
1935	943	$1,808	$ 954
1940	713	$1,265	$ 522

While the Great Depression no doubt had a significant effect upon the drop in membership and revenues, association leaders at the time generally conceded that the major reason for the association's decline was the creation of the State Bar. The concurrent developments were something akin to a fighter's "combination punch," a double-blow to the body of the association.

It was a staggering series of developments for the Bar Association. From 1935 until 1940, the Bar Association was seriously hobbled. Some had argued that the formation of the State Bar would sound the death knell for the Bar Association. While the association did not sink into oblivion, nor fall into the "innocuous desuetude" which befell the "Old Bar Association," the organization struggled to gain momentum and a new sense of mission. In the words of former Executive Vice President Bill Storey, "the association retained its characteristic as a social debating society and contributed to its own regression."

A Mixed Report Card

Bryan Bolich of the Duke University School of Law addressed the association at the 1936 annual meeting on the "Activities of the North Carolina Bar Association, 1925-1935." In a generally negative assessment of the association's effectiveness, Bolich reported that from 1899 to 1929 the bar association had sponsored 28 measures before the state Legislature, but only 10 of them had been enacted into law. "Since 1929 the Association has actively sponsored passage of some four State measures, of which one, Bar Incorporation, went according to our wishes," he said. He also noted that the association had approved canons 33 through 45 of the Canons of Professional Ethics of the American Bar Association and had adopted that organization's Canons of Judicial Ethics as well.

Professor Bolich also declared that the Bar Association had failed in its efforts to limit the practice of law by justices of the peace and court reporters in

Bar Association President J. Melville Broughton presided at the 1936 annual meeting held at the Grove Park Inn, July 9-11, 1936. Broughton, association president in 1935-1936, later served as governor of North Carolina (1941-1945) and U.S. senator (1948-1949). This picture on the Sunset Terrace continued the tradition of the annual group photograph.

the state. On the other hand, a workmen's compensation law had been enacted and legal aid groups established in Charlotte, Asheville and Winston-Salem. Still, in many areas the resolutions and opinions of the association appeared to have been ignored by state government officials.

Despite the Duke law professor's report on the association's ineffectiveness, there were small signs of changes afoot in the organization and also in the profession as a whole in the mid-1930s. The election of Franklin D. Roosevelt as president and the beginning of the New Deal brought many changes to the legal profession, including an increase in special areas of practice—especially in administrative law. Over the next few years, members of the association would follow Richard E. Thigpen's lead into special areas of practice, such as tax law. Other hopeful notes for the association included initiatives on junior bar organizations and on legal assistance for the poor.

A Pivotal Year (1934)

In addition to its usual favorite meeting sites — Asheville, Wrightsville Beach, Pinehurst — the Bar Association in the 1930s embarked on a new series of convention adventures. In 1934, another university town hosted the association, three years after the annual meeting in Chapel Hill. Duke University and the city of Durham welcomed attorneys attending the first-ever joint meeting of the North Carolina Bar Association and the North Carolina State Bar.

The 1934 meeting appears to have marked a turning point in the association's history. The State Bar of North Carolina was now fully organized and at work, fulfilling a long-held dream of the Bar Association. Association committees such as Justices of the Peace, Legal Aid, Uniform State Laws, and A Proposed New State Constitution had made important progress in the past year. Speeches by Thomas J. Pearsall of Rocky Mount on "The Young Lawyer and Self Preservation" and by President J. Elmer Long of Durham on "The Relationship Between the Younger and Older Men of the Bar" had finally awakened some of the membership to the problems of young lawyers, so much so that Kemp D. Battle was moved to speak:

Clinical legal education was introduced into the curriculum with the establishment of the pioneer Duke Legal Aid Clinic in 1932, the first law school-connected program of its kind in the country.

> As one of the middle-aged generation, I feel that Mr. Pearsall's speech is a merited rebuke to the men of my generation in being so slow to take action to protect the young men from the competition which they have had to come into the last decade.... I, for one, feel a certain degree of shame that we have for so long delayed taking effective steps. I believe that we now have the machinery to do better... I feel that this junior-bar movement is bringing into the life of the profession a really energizing stream of new blood....

In the closing moments of the 1934 annual meeting, I.M. Bailey remarked, "I do not think that we have had anywhere a meeting of the North Carolina Bar Association where so much has been done to facilitate the work of the organization, or certainly not with the spirit in which it has been done here." But moments later Powell W. Glidewell, a Reidsville attorney, turned the association's attention back to social matters, an area of greater interest to the older and wealthier members:

This year the Bar Association of the State of Virginia has chartered a ship and they are going to Bermuda and hold their sessions on board ship. I make a motion, Mr. President, that a committee be appointed by the President to consider this Association's doing that next year. And I serve notice that if my motion is adopted I shall make another — that the dry members of the Association be required to go, and the wet members may go or not, as they like. That would ensure a good attendance.

Glidewell's original motion carried, and the executive committee was charged with considering the idea of a cruise ship meeting. In the midst of the Great Depression, the Bar Association would soon embark on a new level of convention adventures.

An Association at Sea

In 1935, the Bar Association sponsored its first convention boat cruise, ratifying the Glidewell motion of a year earlier. Nearly 300 lawyers, members of their families and friends sailed from Norfolk, Virginia, to Nova Scotia on the German cruise ship *S.S. Reliance* on August 16, 1935. Virtually all the leaders of the Bar Association made the cruise, and the Canadian excursion was apparently a great success. Allston Stubbs, former secretary-treasurer, recalls that three lawyers and their spouses were left behind in Nova Scotia when the luxury liner sailed, and that the *Reliance* often had to slow to a leisurely speed of four knots in the North Atlantic because of icebergs.

The group returned to Asheville the next year, but in 1937 the association booked passage once again on the *Reliance*. This time the destination was Bermuda, and the barristers' companions were newspapermen, as the North Carolina Press Association held its annual convention on board. The correspondent for the Greensboro *Daily News* reported that the quaint British colony provided a welcome respite from the modern economic and governmental problems back in the states:

> The North Carolina press and bar Saturday a week ago left their country worrying along with major industrial disturbances, increased taxes from unemployment, relief burdens, and other ailments common to the American public.... [On Bermuda] they found no unemployment, no traffic problem, scarcely any taxes, no race problem, no politics, [and] little crime.... Truly the North Carolinians were far from home!

Annual meetings were held in early May at The Carolina in Pinehurst in 1924, 1927, 1930, 1938 and 1942.

After trips to Pinehurst and Wrightsville Beach in the interim, the membership voted three-to-one in favor of having the 1940 annual meeting on board a cruise ship again. More than 200 members and their families indicated their interest, and the executive committee planned a trip to Bermuda and Cuba on board the Swedish liner *Kunshon*. But a travel warning issued by the U.S. State Department in April 1940 about the danger of German U-boat attacks on Allied vessels in the Atlantic led the travel agency, Thomas Cooke & Company, to cancel the cruise. The 1940 annual meeting was held at Mayview Manor in Blowing Rock, "a place clear away from all danger of German submarines," quipped W. Frank Taylor, chairman of the executive committee.

A 1930s era moot court in the Duke law school classroom of Professor T.D. Bryson. Note the female students in the foreground.

The Junior Bar Movement

Recognizing that their needs were not being adequately addressed by the North Carolina Bar Association, young lawyers in some of the state's larger cities had begun to form junior bar groups beginning in the early 1920s. Winston-Salem, for example, established a junior bar association in 1922. The North Carolina Bar Association was, as Kemp D. Battle indicated, slow to respond effectively to the needs of younger members.

The junior bar movement in North Carolina attained its greatest influence in the mid-1930s. At that time, junior bar groups were flourishing in Winston-Salem, Charlotte, Durham, Asheville and Greensboro. The constitution of the Junior Bar Association of Durham is representative of those of its sister groups:

> The mission of the Junior Bar Association of Durham is to help raise standards in the legal profession and to help correct abuses in connection therewith; to promote good citizenship and good government; to advance the professional and general education and interests of its members and to enrich their lives by affording a new avenue for social activity and encouragement of a spirit of brotherhood.

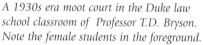

Due to the cancellation of the Bermuda-Havana convention cruise scheduled for June 1940, Mayview Manor in Blowing Rock served as the alternative annual meeting site.

93

Elizabeth Lupton Peterson, pictured, and Lee Smith McKeithen were the first female graduates of Duke University's law school in 1935. Women attorneys often practiced with their fathers upon graduation.

At the 1935 meeting of the North Carolina Bar Association, Edward L. Cannon, a young member of the Durham County Bar, chaired a round-table discussion on the junior bar movement. Cannon presented delegates from across the state representing either junior bar groups, barristers' clubs, or young lawyers associations. (In 1934, the American Bar Association had formed a special section for members under 36 years of age.)

During the program, Allston J. Stubbs Jr., another young attorney active in the Durham Junior Bar, urged the creation of young lawyers' groups as a way to curb the unauthorized practice of law. Stubbs noted that the Durham Junior Bar Association was more active than the Durham County Bar Association and added: "The fact that a Junior Bar Association exists in Durham has a tendency to curb the practices of certain justices of the peace and other laymen from practicing law as they know we have a constant eye on their activities." Following the American Bar Association's lead, the North Carolina Bar Association formed a Special Committee on Junior Bars.

Though the junior bar associations began to die out during and after World War II, young lawyers such as Cannon, Stubbs and others would provide strong leadership for the North Carolina Bar Association and the legal profession in North Carolina in years to come.

North Carolina's New Law School

Young black lawyers of the 1930s — and aspiring black attorneys — had far fewer options in North Carolina, and faced a less than receptive legal climate. No law school in the state admitted blacks; in fact, no law school serving black students had existed since Shaw University's law school closed in 1914. Black students trained at out-of-state law schools passed the North Carolina bar examination at a far lower rate than whites, and those that did were excluded from membership in the voluntary bar. (Black lawyers in the state would form their own organization, —The Old North State Bar Association— in 1935.)

But there were a few hopeful signs. A few blacks did begin an embryonic challenge to the state's exclusionary "Jim Crow" policies in higher education. In March 1933, three black men from Durham — Conrad O. Pearson, Cecil McCoy and S. C. Coleman — announced their intention to apply for admission to the University of North Carolina School of Law. "These men," wrote a reporter for the *Durham Morning Herald*, "are not radically inclined and have no connection with Communism or Socialism. They are going about their business in an orderly manner, basing their contentions on the Fourteenth amend-

The North Carolina College for Negroes School of Law Dean Albert L. Turner, first dean of the new law school at what is now known as N.C. Central University, welcomes Wake Forest School of Law Dean Carroll W. Weathers to Law Day observances. Pictured left to right are Dean Turner, Dean Weathers, N.C. Central law student and future state senator Frank W. Ballance Jr., and Hugo Payne of the Florida A&M School of Law.

African-Americans watch the proceedings of the Superior Court in Oxford in November 1939. Courtroom spectator seating was racially segregated.

ment of the federal constitution." Indeed they were, for Conrad O. Pearson, a graduate of the Howard University Law School, was the state general counsel for the National Association for the Advancement of Colored People (NAACP).

Even with the liberal reformer Frank Porter Graham at the helm of the University of North Carolina, the governor and Legislature were clearly not ready to allow black students at the law school at Chapel Hill. In short order, a law department was established at the North Carolina College for Negroes.

James E. Shepard, founder and president of the Durham college, announced that Maurice T. Van Hecke, dean of the University of North Carolina School of Law, would serve as acting dean of the new department for one year. Six professors from the law schools at North Carolina and Duke University would also serve as interim instructors for the first year of the new school.

The law school of the North Carolina College for Negroes formally opened on September 17, 1940, with seven students. President Shepard announced that the first-year law class was being selected under the same entrance requirements as at Duke and Chapel Hill. It was the only black law school in the South requiring three years of undergraduate work.

The new law school had been approved by the State Board of Law Examiners with a curriculum virtually identical to the first-year law course at Chapel Hill. A full three-year curriculum was to be implemented by 1942. Three full-time black instructors were added in 1941, and a black dean, Albert L. Turner, succeeded Dean Van Hecke in 1942. Two of the seven original students graduated in the Class of 1943.

North Carolina Supreme Court Chief
Justice Walter P. Stacy, North
Carolina Attorney General Harry
McMullan, and Gov. Clyde R. Hoey
participate in the laying of the Justice
Building cornerstone in Raleigh, on
June 9, 1939, a Works Progress
Administration project.

A New Generation of Leadership

In a resolution introduced at the 1940 annual meeting, Kemp D. Battle,
former president, memorialized the late Henry M. London, a man who had
done so much for the Bar Association:

> From his election in 1921 until his death in Raleigh on December 30,
> 1939, he practically ran the Association. Under the constant stimulus
> of his efforts, the Association outlived the ancient taunt that it was
> the affair of a small group of corporation lawyers and it became the
> instrument through which the legal profession, awakened from its
> apathy, faced the fact of public disesteem, and demanded of the
> Legislature the powers necessary to purge itself and start the long
> overdue task of fashioning itself into an effective instrument of
> public service.

Granville County court records,
in Oxford, November 1939.

96

Superior Court in session in Granville County, November 22, 1939.

The year 1940 marked the beginning of a new era for the association. For its entire existence and particularly for the previous 18 years, its secretary-treasurer, under the supervision of each year's elected president, had performed the work that made the organization function. Henry M. London's death at the end of 1939 brought young Durham attorney Allston J. Stubbs Jr. into the position.

Although the Great Depression may not have impacted North Carolina as significantly as it did other regions of the nation, as the economic plunge intensified, its consequences were felt in all areas of the state. The legal profession and the Bar Association were among those who faced the consequences of a declining economy.

Clearly, as the depression decade of the 1930s ended and the early rumblings of World War II posed concern for the future, the legal profession was going through a difficult time. Changes in the practice of law brought by the New Deal and the emergence of various federal agencies altered the practice of law in the nation and in parts of North Carolina. In much of the state and for most of its legal profession, the practice of law was still a small-town, "country-lawyer" occupation. That would alter drastically during the next several decades. The North Carolina Bar Association would change as well.

∽

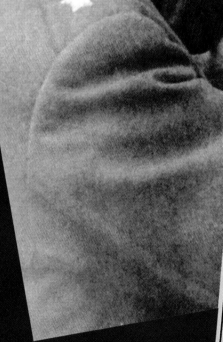

North Carolina lawyers left their profession to serve their country. Gen. J. Lawton Collins (a.k.a. "Lighting Joe") pins a service medal on U.S. Army Maj. James K. Dorsett Jr. Photo taken somewhere in France weeks after successful D-Day invasion (1944).

Dorsett's military record notes his occupation as 'lawyer' and lists the battles in which he fought.

MILITARY RECORD AND REPORT OF SEPARATION
CERTIFICATE OF SERVICE

1. LAST NAME · FIRST NAME · MIDDLE INITIAL		2. ARMY SERIAL NUMBER	3. AUS. GRADE	4. ARM OR SERVICE	5. COMPONENT
DORSETT JAMES K JR		O 362 283	Major	Inf	Res

6. ORGANIZATION
CIC Ctr Ft Geo G Meade Maryland

7. DATE OF RELIEF FROM ACTIVE DUTY
11 Dec 1945

8. PLACE OF SEPARATION
Separation Point Woodrow Wilson GH Staunton Virginia

9. PERMANENT ADDRESS FOR MAILING PURPOSES
108 N. Fulton Street Salisbury North Carolina

10. DATE OF BIRTH
15 Nov 1916

11. PLACE OF BIRTH
Spencer N C

12. ADDRESS FROM WHICH EMPLOYMENT WILL BE SOUGHT
See 9

13. COLOR EYES	14. COLOR HAIR	15. HEIGHT	16. WEIGHT	17. NO. OF DEPENDENTS
Hazel	Brown	5' 11"	165 LBS.	0

18. RACE			19. MARITAL STATUS			20. U.S. CITIZEN		21. CIVILIAN OCCUPATION AND NO.
WHITE X	NEGRO	OTHER (specify)	SINGLE	MARRIED X	OTHER (specify)	YES X	NO	Lawyer 68.500

MILITARY HISTORY

SELECTIVE SERVICE DATA	22. REGISTERED		23. LOCAL S.S. BOARD NUMBER	24. COUNTY AND STATE	25. HOME ADDRESS AT TIME OF ENTRY ON ACTIVE DUTY
	YES	NO X			See 9

26. DATE OF ENTRY ON ACTIVE DUTY
9 January 1942

27. MILITARY OCCUPATIONAL SPECIALTY AND NO.
Counter-Intelligence Officer 9302
Training and Operations Staff Officer 2162

28. BATTLES AND CAMPAIGNS
Ardennes   Rhineland   Central Europe   Normandy   Northern France

29. DECORATIONS AND CITATIONS
Bronze Star Medal   EAME Campaign Ribbon with Five Bz Sv Stars and One Bz Arrowhead
Croix de Guerre with Vermillian Star

30. WOUNDS RECEIVED IN ACTION
None

31. SERVICE SCHOOLS ATTENDED
Rifle and Heavy Weapons
Counter Intelligence School

32. SERVICE OUTSIDE CONTINENTAL U.S. AND RETURN		
DATE OF DEPARTURE	DESTINATION	DATE OF ARRIVAL
9 Oct 1943	England	14 Oct 1943
1 June 1944	France	6 June 1944
5 Sept 1944	Belgium	5 Sept 1944
15 Sept 1944	Germany	15 Sept 1944
22 Dec 1944	Belgium	22 Dec 1944
5 Feb 1945	Germany	5 Feb 1945

33. REASON AND AUTHORITY FOR SEPARATION
RR1-5 Demobilization and par 32 SO 240
Woodrow Wilson GH Staunton Va dtd 10/4/45

34. CURRENT TOUR OF ACTIVE DUTY

CONTINENTAL SERVICE			FOREIGN SERVICE			35. EDUCATION (years)		(See 43)
YEARS	MONTHS	DAYS	YEARS	MONTHS	DAYS	GRAMMAR SCHOOL	HIGH SCHOOL	COLLEGE
2	2	4	1	8	30	8	4	7

CHAPTER 8

"In the Arsenal of Democracy"
1940-1945

By the summer of 1940, the North Carolina Bar Association was already well aware of war conditions in Europe, the summer cruise to Bermuda having been canceled because of German U-boat attacks on American vessels. Like most North Carolinians, the Bar Association was solidly behind American involvement in the European conflict. As novelist James Boyd said about his fellow Tar Heels and their neighbors, "As France was stabbed and Britain abandoned, the Southerner grew deeply, even passionately concerned. From Dunkirk on, he was ready to fight.... To Southerners, then, Pearl Harbor was no shock; it was a relief."

Maj. Gen. Jacob L. Devers, Eleanor Roosevelt, Gov. and Mrs. J. Melville Broughton and President Franklin Delano Roosevelt visit Fort Bragg on March 31, 1941. North Carolina's population grew immensely during World War II due to the influx of soldiers and their families.

Mobilizing for War

Indeed, North Carolina was literally building up for war. When the first draft registration day was held in the state on October 16, 1940, more than 450,000 men were registered. In the latter half of 1940, the federal government began awarding contracts to North Carolina shipyards along the coast. Soon Fort Bragg, an Army post since 1918, would become the largest artillery post in the world, and the Marine Corps would establish major new bases at Camp Lejeune and Cherry Point.

With thousands of miles of coastline and a multitude of military installations and port facilities, defending North Carolina against attack by sea and air was a top priority. Civilian defense efforts were soon organized across the state.

Lincolnton's Charles R. Jonas, Bar Association president from 1946-1947, served as the leading lawyer for North Carolina's Selective Service.

Allston J. Stubbs Jr., a young Durham attorney, served as secretary-treasurer during most of World War II from 1940-1944.

Gov. J. Melville Broughton, one of the association's longtime leaders, was a step ahead of the national civil defense plans when, in 1941, he established the North Carolina State Council for National Defense, an organization later brought under the federal government's civilian defense plan. From Manteo to Murphy, local civilian defense volunteers — attorneys included — were trained as air raid wardens, auxiliary firemen and policemen, and first aid providers.

In 1940, another prominent member of the North Carolina Bar Association played a major role in helping the state mobilize for war. Charles R. Jonas of Lincolnton was one of a small group of North Carolina National Guard officers who directed the operation of the draft in the state during World War II. As the only lawyer on the staff, Capt. Jonas was assigned as chief of the appeals division, responsible for supervising and coordinating the work of the seven regional appeal boards in the state. Jonas' skill, effectiveness and integrity helped North Carolina avoid the draft corruption scandals that occurred in some states.

The Lawyer's Privilege in a Time of War

In May 1941, the annual meeting of the association convened at the Sedgefield Inn in Greensboro. In a response to the welcoming addresses from citizens of Greensboro and High Point, Vice President Emmett Bellamy of the Wilmington bar called on his fellow attorneys to make sacrifices for the sake of democracy:

> Now, more than ever, must the lawyer lead, or the civilization of this Nation and that of England, built up largely by lawyers, will perish from the face of the earth.... Each and every lawyer should attach himself to some patriotic group, should convey his ideas and impressions with force to our statesmen to aid them in their deliberations.... Never before have the extra curricular activities of the lawyer become so important as now. *It is indeed a time for sacrifice.*

Months before Pearl Harbor, the entire tone of the annual meeting reflected the crisis that faced the nation and the world.

Many of the committee chairmen and speakers addressed ways in which lawyers might assist in the mobilization effort. The Legal Aid Committee took on the task of organizing the state's attorneys so as to "help democracy endure on the important battle front at home." First, members were asked to serve on local draft and appeal boards across the state, helping to advise registrants on the provisions of the Selective Service Law.

Also, Charles R. Jonas of the Selective Service System and secretary Allston Stubbs invited members to help in the handling of the legal problems of servicemen and their families. Professor John S. Bradway of the Duke University School of Law, chairman of the association's Legal Aid Committee, described the problem:

> Men in the military forces of the United States have dependents at home. The morale of these men may be impaired if they are concerned about the welfare or business or financial difficulties of their families or themselves. Debts, landlord and tenant problems, and undischarged contractual obligations are merely examples of the legal situations which may give rise to distress. It is our privilege as lawyers to look after such matters. In a democracy it is the privilege of the lawyer to see that justice is a matter of right, not of grace.

Professor Bradway served as director of the Legal Aid Clinic at Duke. Established in 1932, the clinic was the first legal assistance program in the country administered by a law school, and a pioneering effort in clinical legal education. Lawyers affiliated with the Duke clinic had been instrumental in establishing the Bar Association's own Committee on Legal Aid.

Even those attorneys unable to serve in the military or on civilian boards could do their part for the war effort. President Hamilton C. Jones III called on C.R. Wharton of Greensboro near the end of the 1941 meeting to speak on defense bonds, a subject which had been emphasized throughout the convention. Wharton made a strong plea for all members to "buy a share in America." Many members did, and many — such as Kathrine R. Everett of Durham — were active in local war bond drives.

Ration books epitomized the hardships of the home front during World War II. Civil defense, scrap drives, victory gardens and other civilian war efforts affected all North Carolinians.

"Running Low on Gas, But High in Spirit" The 1942 Meeting

By the time of the association's next annual meeting in Pinehurst in May 1942, life in North Carolina had changed dramatically. Wartime activities and interests permeated both public and private life. Shortages of foods and consumer goods brought home the reality of war to lawyers and other civilians, and soon rationing became necessary to distribute equitably those supplies available. A few months earlier, the federal Office of Price Administration had issued books of ration stamps to every civilian.

Gasoline and rubber tires were particularly scarce, so much so that far fewer automobiles cruised the state's roads, and the rural filling station became something of an endangered species in the state. R. Gregg Cherry, who served as governor during the last months of the war, called the country's gas stations "a sad sight with their windows boarded up and grass growing around the door."

The country was clearly on a war footing during the Pinehurst meeting. Attendance was down significantly from the previous year, and executive committee member Linville K. Martin may have stated the reason in his welcoming remarks: "It is quite evident that Mr. [Harold] Ickes and the Rationing Board has done something to our Bar meeting."

Wartime annual meeting sites were held at central locations such as the Sandhills and the Piedmont region to minimize the travel burden for members. One such site was The Carolina in Pinehurst.

Willis Smith of Raleigh, left, Bar Association president in 1941-1942 and future U.S. senator, talks with U.S. Attorney General Tom Clark at a Bar Association function.

Even the music which preceded the sessions reflected a wartime flavor. To begin the Friday evening session, the audience joined in singing "God Bless America," then "Give Me That Old Time Religion" before concluding with "The Star-Spangled Banner." It was a time of unabashed patriotism in North Carolina, and the state's lawyers were right in tune, from the governor on down. School children wrote patriotic poems; radio stations played patriotic songs; churches sang patriotic hymns and observed special days of prayer. Gov. Broughton later asked every North Carolinian for their "earnest prayers" in the days prior to the Allied invasion of Europe in 1944, and decreed D-Day to be a special "Dedication Day" in North Carolina.

Also during the 1942 meeting, President Willis Smith delivered an address on "Citizenship and the Bill of Rights in Wartime;" Charles R. Jonas, a major, spoke on the "1940 Soldier's and Sailor's Civil Relief Act." Professor John Bradway of Duke's law school spoke again to the membership on "The Bar's Contribution to the War Effort."

Willis Smith would go on to serve as president of the American Bar Association (the only member of the North Carolina Bar Association to do so) and as a U.S. senator.

"Staying the Course Until Victory" *The 1943 Meeting*

The annual meeting for 1943 convened in Winston-Salem, in part to reduce transportation difficulties from the far reaches of the state. Still, attendance was down from the previous year. In welcoming the attendees, Winston-Salem's Fred S. Hutchins, past president of the association, said:

> We meet today without fear of criticism. Approximately twenty-five percent of our profession are engaged in the active military service of our country. Practically all the remaining practicing lawyers are

Walter L. Hannah of Greensboro arrived in Manila, The Philippines, after a 45-day voyage from France via the Panama Canal on August 5, 1945. This photo was taken shortly after his arrival. "We were told that we would be in Manila for four weeks, then go to San Fernando on northern Luzon for six weeks of training, then go aboard ship for the invasion of Japan. The atomic bomb was dropped the next day."

engaged in the war effort in one form or another.... Lawyers are serving on draft boards and have in most cases acted as appeal agents with the responsibility of reviewing the drafting of each selectee and of appealing such cases as appear to have merit. Lawyers are serving on War Price and Rationing Boards. A considerable number are actively enrolled in Civilian Defense and speaker's bureaus of every sort.

Secretary Stubbs reported that he had names of 140 members in active service out of a total membership of 701. He further reported that many members of committees and even the president-elect of the Bar Association had volunteered for military duties and been unable to continue their work with the association. Stubbs had voluntarily reduced his own salary from $400 to $200 annually because of the diminished financial state of the organization.

A good portion of the 1943 meeting addressed issues that were related to the war. The work of members in rendering legal aid to servicemen and their families was reported to the convention, and copies of state and federal legislation relating to those in service were distributed and included in the annual *Reports.*

Other attorneys were indeed hard at work on the home front. In May 1943, Albert Coates, director of the university's Institute of Government and a longtime member of the association, published a guidebook for "The Victory Speakers Corps" program of the North Carolina Office of Civilian Defense. The governor and the State Defense Council had asked the institute staff to organize and conduct training schools to help local communities protect the state in the event of air raids, sabotage or sneak attacks. Coates called on his lawyer-instructors and fellow citizens to keep morale high, and to stay the course until victory:

> The war is not yet won. We must work and fight our way through many months of suffering and blood on the roads to Rome, Berlin and Tokyo. On these roads we must not fail or falter, we must not weaken or tire, neither the sudden shock of battle nor the long drawn trials of vigilance and exertion must wear us down. The state of this nation is good. The heart of this nation is sound. The spirit of this nation is strong. The faith of this nation is eternal.

Gov. J. Melville Broughton, one of the state's finest orators, spoke to the association on the responsibilities of the lawyer in a time of war. In an address titled "The State's Responsibilities—Now and After the War," Broughton gave a morale boost to those assembled:

Greensboro's John A. "Jack" Kleemeier Jr., lieutenant commander, U.S. Navy, served as an officer on the USS Quincy, the ship that transported President Franklin D. Roosevelt to meet with Churchill and Stalin at Yalta in 1945.

Gov. Broughton enters the House Chamber to address the General Assembly on February 16, 1942.

It is not an easy thing to hold a meeting under these trying circumstances. We live under many difficulties. Someone has wittily said that everything in America is either illegal, immoral or rationed; or, to put it another way, we have to try to keep sweet without sugar, buoyant without rubber, and to maintain high spirits under low ceilings.... We need, my friends, even in war with its grimmest aspects, we need the exchange of ideas, the freedom of debate, the fellowship of association. Indeed, the greatest contribution of America to this war is not simply ships and tanks and guns and planes...[it] is in the spirit, the unconquerable spirit of the American people and of its soldiers.

Also in 1943, a publishing project that the Bar Association had assisted in, *The North Carolina Code of 1943*, came to fruition. Funded by the 1939 Legislature and directed by the attorney general's office, it was the first recodification of the state's general statutes since 1919. Bar Association members Bennett H. Perry, H.G. Hedrick, H. Gardner Hudson, C. Clifford Frazier and Bryan Grimes worked as advisers on the project. The association would again lead efforts to recodify the general statutes at the 1976 annual meeting.

A Quiet Beginning

Also in 1943, the state's newest law school, the North Carolina College for Negroes School of Law, graduated its first two students: Robert Richard Bond and John Willis Langford. Six new students enrolled that year — because of the war, the school opened up night classes to local businessmen — including two who would become prominent members of the Durham bar. The first, C. C. Spaulding Jr., son of the founder of the famed North Carolina Mutual Life Insurance Company, would go on to serve as vice president of his father's company and as a director of the Mechanics and Farmers Bank.

The second student, John Hervey Wheeler, would become a nationally known civil rights leader and mentor to a generation of black lawyers in North Carolina. Appointed to the United States Equal Employment Opportunity Commission by President John F. Kennedy in 1961, Wheeler became the first black delegate from North Carolina to the 1964 Democratic National Convention. He was also president of Durham's Mechanics and Farmers Bank for a number of years, and a former chairman of the influential Durham Committee on the Affairs of Black People.

North Carolina College for Negroes School of Law Dean Albert L. Turner (left) visits with John Hervey Wheeler, JD '47, and North Carolina College for Negroes President Alfonso Elder (right) in the late 1940s.

"Working Together for a Better World"
The 1944 Meeting

In mid-June 1944, the Bar Association gathered in Raleigh for the first time since its 1899 organizational meeting. The "D-Day" invasion of Normandy by allied forces had occurred less than two weeks earlier on June 6.

In his opening remarks, Charlotte's Fred B. Helms, a longtime association member and leader, lamented that "for all of these succeeding centuries humankind has borne its greatest curse, that of war, because of the fact that humankind has not been able to evolve and put into practice any workable law in the realm of international affairs." He told the assembled members of the association that "our voice should be raised here in no uncertain tones and in no uncertain terms toward the formation and adoption of some system of law in international affairs which will give the people of the earth peace and security under law."

The 1944 annual meeting included the presentation of certificates of appreciation from the secretary of war and the secretary of the Navy commending the association and its members for "the splendid legal assistance that the members of the bar of North Carolina have rendered to servicemen and their families and dependents."

In his second consecutive address to the Bar Association, "Social Progress Under Constitutional Law," Gov. J. Melville Broughton outlined the tension between the need for laws responsive to the social conditions of an advancing civilization — such as North Carolina's Workmen's Compensation Act of 1929 — and the threat that some provisions of those same laws posed to constitutional liberties:

> We have got to strive under our constitutional system of government, without violating those well-separated rights between the Federal and State governments, somehow to improve the justified needs of the people for health, progress, for social security and for protection against unemployment and to do it without tearing down these institutions of law and government which we hold dear.... Labor and management have got to learn how to work together. Racially, we have to learn to work together, and we have got to do it within the constitutional limits of our established government. I believe we can do it.

The Birth of Continuing Legal
Education (CLE) in N.C.

When Allston Stubbs resigned as secretary-treasurer in 1944, Edward L. Cannon was chosen as his replacement. Ed Cannon, who had been secretary of the State Bar since 1938, knew Stubbs well from their work together with the Durham Junior Bar. Cannon operated both the State Bar and the Bar Association out of a one-room office in the Justice Building. He served as secretary-treasurer of the Bar Association until 1953, and as secretary of the State Bar until his retirement in 1967.

Cannon's responsibilities included making arrangements for a tax institute for attorneys which the association had voted to sponsor in 1943. The tax institute was held prior to the 1944 annual meeting and proved popular with attorneys who were members of the association and with those who were not. One hundred three lawyers attended the three-day institute coordinated by

FUNDAMENTALS OF FEDERAL TAXATION

•

A COURSE OF 12 LECTURES
FOR PRACTISING LAWYERS

conducted by

NORTH CAROLINA BAR ASSOCIATION

in cooperation with

THE AMERICAN BAR ASSOCIATION

SECTION OF TAXATION

AND

PRACTISING LAW INSTITUTE

•

JUNE 13-16, 1944
SIR WALTER HOTEL
RALEIGH, NORTH CAROLINA

This is the program cover for the first-ever North Carolina Tax Institute, the predecessor of the modern continuing legal education seminars.

*Senior law students at Duke University
in September 1942.*

*Linville K. Martin of Winston-
Salem, who was elected president of
the Bar Association in May 1942,
resigned his office later that year
when called to active duty
during World War II.*

Richard E. Thigpen. The popularity of the institute was such that it was continued on an annual basis, marking the beginning of the association's continuing legal education (CLE) program. The popular and successful CLE series would be recognized with the American Bar Association's Award of Merit in 1958.

These CLE institutes — advanced legal education programs — were seminars on technical subjects made available and accessible to lawyers at minimal expense. Association leaders saw them as a way of bringing bar organization activity to those small-town lawyers unable to attend the annual meetings.

Wartime Legal Education in North Carolina

Other items of business considered at the 1944 meeting included a variety of issues concerning wartime legal education. In 1942, many faculty and students left the state's four law schools to enter military service. The number of entering law students declined drastically, so Wake Forest joined with the Duke University School of Law in a "Wartime Joint Program." In this collaborative effort, students met on the Duke campus for three semesters each year in joint classes taught by the remaining faculty of both institutions. A version of this accelerated program was also instituted at the University of North Carolina School of Law.

Early in the war, the North Carolina Board of Law Examiners had decided to allow a shortening of the law school course of study from three to two and a half years. Still, these accelerated courses had not attracted a large number of students; moreover, those who completed the shortened course had not fared well on the bar examination. When presented with these facts, those present at the 1944 annual meeting of the association passed a resolution against such "speed-up" programs.

"When Johnny Comes Marching Home"
Veterans and the Law

The Bar Association also looked into the question of how many returning veterans would study law and apply for law licenses. The association resolved that in North Carolina "government money expended for legal education of a veteran in law schools shall be only in those schools approved by the North Carolina Board of Law Examiners." The association also went on record as opposing any reduction of the existing standards of legal education and bar admission.

Just as the association was considering the potential needs of returning veterans, so too were the state and federal governments. After his inauguration in January 1945, Gov. R. Gregg Cherry continued the state's plans for demobilization and veterans' assistance, particularly as it became apparent that Germany was nearing defeat. As early as February 1943, Gov. Broughton had spoken of the need for the state to reconvert from a wartime footing to one of peace. By March 1944, veterans were already returning to North Carolina at the rate of 1,500 per month.

The federal government had already passed the Servicemen's Readjustment Act ("G.I. Bill of Rights") in June 1944, but North Carolina sought ways to offer other educational, training and readjustment services. The State Department of Labor added veterans' service divisions in Asheville, Charlotte, Greensboro, Raleigh and Greenville. And with unemployment a major concern during the difficult process of industry reconversion, Gov. Cherry turned to the State Planning Board, in which lawyers from Albert Coates' Institute of Government played a prominent role.

A Whole New World

Leading North Carolina lawyers also began to turn their attention to the shape of the postwar world. As the war in the Pacific neared an end, and as representatives from around the world gathered in San Francisco in June 1945 to adopt a charter for the United Nations, Gov. Cherry noted:

> In a universe of nations so closely integrated by the marvels of
> transportation and communication, and so constantly threatened
> by bigger and better engines of destruction, our only alternative is
> international law, openly arrived at and collectively enforced.

As World War II wound down, the North Carolina Bar Association was beginning to take on a new personality. A new generation of attorneys — many of them veterans, many from different walks of life — would soon get down to work confronting a changing practice of law in an increasingly complex society.

President Harry S. Truman, Secretary of the Army Kenneth C. Royall, and lawyer Gov. R. Gregg Cherry
dedicate the "Three Presidents" monument on Capital Square in Raleigh on October 19, 1948.
Royall served as Bar Association president from 1929-1930.

CHAPTER 9

"Forging Ahead"
1945-1955

The G.I. Bill of Rights probably did more to change the postwar practice of law in North Carolina — and in the United States as a whole — than any other single event. The veterans who were able to attend law school under provisions of the G.I. Bill would do much to change the North Carolina Bar Association during the next decade. They came to the bar in great numbers, and they came from circumstances quite different from their prewar predecessors. As historian H.G. Jones has noted, "These veterans occupied a special status among a grateful people, and many of them were soon thrust into leadership roles."

The 1944 and 1945 annual meetings, both at the Sir Walter Hotel in Raleigh, held abbreviated sessions due to wartime conditions.

Providing a Sharp Mind:
The 1945 Annual Meeting

The first postwar meeting of the North Carolina Bar Association was held at the Sir Walter Hotel in Raleigh on September 7, 1945, just after the end of the war in the Pacific. Another tax institute, larger than the previous year's, preceded the 1945 meeting, marking the second year of the association's fledgling continuing legal education program.

The founder of the institutes, Richard E. Thigpen of Charlotte, also served as chairman of the North Carolina Bar Association Executive Committee and, according to custom, presided over the opening session. Thigpen introduced "a gracious lady of the Reidsville Bar, Miss Susie Sharp" to respond to Ike Bailey's welcome to Raleigh. Sharp began the convention on a light note with comments that could have applied to many Bar Association sessions over the years:

> It is said that with some people you spend a day, while with others you invest it. All lawyers know that there is no better investment than the contacts and associations which they make with other lawyers in North Carolina. Aunt Het once said to Pa that a certain boy and girl

John J. Parker Award

John J. Parker was a Bar Association member for 44 years and the chief judge of the U.S. Court of Appeals for the Fourth Circuit for 27 years.

For years Judge James B. McMillan of Charlotte kept a framed quotation from Edmund Burke that read, "The only thing necessary for the triumph of evil is for good men to do nothing."

Since 1959, 24 good men and women, including Judge McMillan, have been honored for doing much to improve the administration of justice in North Carolina.

The Judge John J. Parker Memorial Award is given to honor the memory and accomplishments of Judge Parker and to encourage the emulation of his devotion and enduring contribution to the law and to the administration of justice. The award is not awarded annually but is reserved for presentation only to those who truly capture and sustain the spirit and quality of Judge Parker's career and ideals.

John Johnston Parker (1885-1958) was a member of the North Carolina Bar Association for 44 years. He served for 32 years as a judge on the United States Court of Appeals for the Fourth Circuit, including 27 years as the chief judge of that court.

Judge Parker, who was one of two American judges on the Nuremberg International Military Tribunal following World War II, practiced law in Monroe, Greensboro and Charlotte. He was known as a profound and eloquent advocate of the improvement of the law and the legal profession.

The award recognizes "conspicuous service" by members of the bar to the cause of jurisprudence in North Carolina.

RECIPIENTS OF THE JUDGE JOHN J. PARKER MEMORIAL AWARD

J. Spencer Bell (1959) served as chair of the NCBA's Committee on Improving and Expediting the Administration of Justice. Judge Parker and Bell outlined the committee's work and chose the name. Later, the committee became known as the Bell Commission and led to court reform in the state.

Hoyt Patrick Taylor Jr. (1961) was recognized for his unswerving efforts in securing the passage by the General Assembly of a constitutional amendment to judicial article IV.

Robert Franklin Moseley (1962) was honored for his work in the creation of the General Statutes Commission and for the 15 years that he served as its chairman.

Judge J. Will Pless Jr. (1963) was especially honored for his work as chairman of the North Carolina Bar Association Committee on the Judicial Amendment.

Albert Coates (1964) created the Institute of Government and served as its director for more than 30 years, becoming an important figure in state and local government.

Rep. **David Maxwell Britt** and Sen. **Lindsay C. Warren Jr.**, (1966) during the 1965 General Assembly, spearheaded the drive to improve the administration of justice and the courts by enactment of legislation creating a new District Court System.

Chief Judge **Raymond B. Mallard** (1969) of the North Carolina Court of Appeals, in 1967, breathed life into the newly authorized Court of Appeals. He helped organize the new court, designed its rules of practice and prepared for the onslaught of appellate cases that followed.

William Marion Storey (1971) served as executive vice-president and treasurer of the North Carolina Bar Association during a time of great growth and accomplishment from the '50s to the '70s.

Carroll Wayland Weathers (1972), honored, in part, for his "integrity and devotion to the profession's highest ethical concepts," was dean of the Wake Forest School of Law during a time of rapid growth from 1950-70. He served as a professor at the school for several years afterward.

J. Dickson Phillips Jr. (1975) served as a chairman of the North Carolina Courts Commission and was a member of several committees of the association including the Penal System Study and Appellate Rules Study committees.

Superior Court Judge **Hamilton H. Hobgood** (1977) presided over several high-profile cases with an "even hand and a judicial temperament." He was president of the Conference of Superior Court Judges and served on the Penal System Study Committee and the N.C. Judicial Council.

Chief Justice **Susie M. Sharp** (1978) was North Carolina's first female city attorney and its first female judge. She became a member of the N.C. Supreme Court in 1962 and was elected Chief Justice in 1974.

Sam J. Ervin Jr. (1981) served three terms in the North Carolina State Assembly and was a member of the North Carolina Supreme Court from 1948-1954. He is best known as a country lawyer who became a U.S. senator for more than 20 years and served as chairman of the Senate Watergate Committee.

William F. Womble (1984) is a past president of the North Carolina Bar Association and a member of the ABA Board of Governors. A senior partner in the Womble, Carlyle, Sandridge & Rice firm, he served three terms in the N.C. House of Representatives.

Harry E. Groves (1986) served as dean of the North Carolina Central Law School and was a professor at the UNC-Chapel Hill School of Law. In addition, he served as president of Legal Services of North Carolina, Inc.

Chief Justice **Joseph Branch** (1987) served in the N.C. House of Representatives for four terms and served as an associate justice of the N.C. Supreme Court for 13 years prior to becoming Chief Justice. He is known for his role in the creation of IOLTA, in the creation of a client security fund and in sanctioning the use of cameras in the courtroom.

James B. McMillan (1989) was best known for his decision in the *Swann v. Board of Education* case in 1970 which imposed court-ordered busing in Charlotte. He made a number of significant rulings involving such issues as job discrimination and free speech. He served as president of the N.C. Bar Association and was a member of the North Carolina Courts Commission.

Judge **Franklin T. Dupree Jr.** (1991) was the U.S. District Judge for the Eastern District of North Carolina for eight years prior to becoming Chief Judge in 1979. He presided over the highly publicized murder trial of Jeffrey MacDonald. His district's case disposition ranking rose from 76th place to first place during his first year and remained there throughout his tenure.

Carmon J. Stuart (1992) served on the NCBA's Dispute Resolution Task Force and was a moving force as chairman of the subcommittee which recommended court-ordered arbitration. He helped draft legislation that established the pilot program and he helped draft the rules for court-ordered arbitration.

Russell M. Robinson II (1993), founder of the firm Robinson, Bradshaw & Hinson, was instrumental in drafting the original North Carolina Business Corporation Act and twice chaired the Business Corporation Act Drafting Committee of the N.C. General Statutes Commission.

Julius L. Chambers (1994) became chancellor of North Carolina Central University in 1993. He previously served as director of the NAACP Legal Defense and Educational Fund. He was a founding partner in the state's first integrated law firm.

William L. Thorp (1996), the first attorney to win a $1 million verdict in North Carolina, is known more for being a pioneer in pro bono legal services to the poor and for his devotion to improving the quality of life of lawyers.

Chief Justice **James G. Exum Jr.** (1997) was an associate justice of the N.C. Supreme Court for 12 years and was chief justice for eight years. He established the N.C. Judicial Conference, persuaded the General Assembly to finance the Courts Commission, and started the Commission on the Future of Justice in North Carolina.

Dr. **Norman A. Wiggins** (1999) has been president of Campbell University since 1967. He was instrumental in establishing and developing the law school at Campbell in 1976 and oversaw a $3.5 million expansion to the school in the early '90s. In 1988, the university's school of law was named the Norman A. Wiggins School of Law in his honor.

they both knew evidently had up a case of true love. Pa wanted to know how Aunt Het knew that and she said, 'Well, she is trying to improve his morals and he is trying to improve her mind.' The Bar Association improved our morals a number of years ago and they are now working very hard on our minds with this institute and program which it has prepared for us.

The relaxed tone of the session was also reflected in Thigpen's version of the treasurer's report: "The treasurer says he still has a balance in the bank and the hotel is going to get most of the money. Do you want to hear a detailed report or do you want to dispense with it?" The members voted to move on to the evening's entertainment.

Not all was sweetness and light at the 1945 meeting. In his autobiography, Richard E. Thigpen recounts an incident at the closing banquet which shows his own character and devotion to the law:

> In the course of the evening I was chatting with a young lawyer who was not fully committed to the profession who said something about just using the law as a stepping stone. I replied: 'The law is a noble profession and success requires the intense application of all our talents at all times. Furthermore, the law is a jealous mistress and will not tolerate for long a half-hearted service.'

Other addresses on the program of the 1945 annual meeting dealt with more practical issues of law and matters of public debate. Judge L.R. Varser of Lumberton spoke to the delegates on "Trial Practice." L.P. McLendon of Greensboro spoke on "Federal Practice" and John M. Robinson of Charlotte spoke on "Appellate Practice."

Judge John J. Parker, at the time being promoted as a potential U. S. Supreme Court appointee, presented an address on "World Government By Law." The Union County native gave a forceful, eloquent and passionate argument on the controversial question of establishing an international system of law and justice:

> Brother lawyers, the responsibility for the future rests very heavily upon us. It is written in the stars that the life of the world is to be unified; and you can rest assured that, if it is not unified on the basis of law and reason, it will be unified on the basis of force and self-interest.... This is a time for greatness.... It is a time to rise above ourselves, and, laying aside ambition and every other sin that may beset us, to grasp firmly the opportunity which has come to us in the providence of God. We stand humbled and appalled in the presence of the sacrifice that literally millions have made for our civilization to live. We owe it to them.

Irving E. Carlyle of Winston-Salem, Bar Association president from 1944-1945, chaired the commission that resulted in the consolidation of the university system in North Carolina.

High Standards at the Bar: Irving E. Carlyle

Irving E. Carlyle of Winston-Salem reviewed the association's work in raising the standards for legal education and admission to the bar in his 1945 presidential address, "The Bar and Legal Education." Carlyle began with a tribute to some of the century's leading legal educators:

> We in North Carolina have been fortunate in the high quality of legal education available in our three [sic] law schools to the young men

seeking admission to the bar. Under the guidance of men like Mordecai, McIntosh, Gulley and others, a solid foundation was laid, upon which their successors have built wisely by the use of scientific methods of instruction.

President Carlyle went on to support the association's new legal institutes; suggested that the membership work with the state's law schools to promote a "progressive" legal education program; and urged a united front against all "shortcuts" to admission to the bar. He reserved special praise for those association leaders who had helped to create the independent State Bar.

Irving Carlyle became one of the state's ablest and most respected lawyers of the postwar period, remembered for his keynote speech at the 1954 North Carolina Democratic Convention, and for his leadership on the Governor's Commission on Education Beyond the High School, which came to be known as "The Carlyle Commission." In his speech before the state's Democrats, made just days after the Supreme Court's decision in *Brown v. Board of Education of Topeka, Kansas*, Carlyle boldly backed the Court's decision, in the face of widespread opposition from the state's political leaders:

> The Supreme Court of the United States has spoken. As good citizens we have no choice but to obey the law as laid down by the Court. To do otherwise would cost us our respect for law and order, and if we lose that in these critical times, we will have lost that quality which is the source of our strength as a State and as a nation.

A fellow member of the North Carolina Bar Association, Judge John J. Parker, would head a three-judge panel which issued the first lower court injunction implementing the *Brown* decision.

Irving Carlyle's principled stand cost him an appointment to the U.S. Senate to fill the unexpired term of Sen. Clyde Hoey, but he went on to serve his state in other ways. It was Carlyle who spearheaded efforts to establish a four-year medical school at Chapel Hill and who chaired the committee that raised funds to relocate Wake Forest College to Winston-Salem. Ever a Wake Forest man, he once said: "The great loves in my life are my family, the law and its supremacy, Wake Forest College and the Democratic Party...in that order."

Instituting Refresher Courses: The 1946 Annual Meeting

The 1946 annual meeting was held at the Robert E. Lee Hotel in Winston-Salem, with Louis J. Poisson of Wilmington — a former law partner of Thomas W. Davis — presiding as president. A third "Annual Institute for Attorneys" preceded the meeting on Wednesday and Thursday, sponsored by the Institute of Government in conjunction with the Bar Association. Topics of the Institute included "Labor Law and Administrative Procedures as Illustrated in Labor Law" and "Modern Loan Transactions."

North Carolina Bar Association

•

Forty-Eighth

ANNUAL MEETING

and

3rd Institute For Attorneys

•

WINSTON-SALEM, NORTH CAROLINA

August 29-31, 1946

(Institute August 28-29)

•

HEADQUARTERS

ROBERT E. LEE HOTEL

Top: The Robert E. Lee Hotel was the site of the 1946 annual meeting and the third annual Institute for Attorneys.

Bottom: 1946 annual meeting brochure.

The Institute of Government was an early co-sponsor of legal "refresher courses" with the Bar Association.

During the previous year, the Institute of Government at Chapel Hill had worked with the association to provide courses, mostly on weekends, on topics of interest to returning lawyers. Some 25 association members, a few from law schools but most from private practice, had presented institutes on topics ranging from "State Income Taxes" to "Statutory Changes, 1941-45." Institute director Albert Coates spoke of plans to sponsor more refresher courses with the help of the Bar Association.

The report of the association's executive committee dealt with another issue related to the transition from war to peace. During the war, many attorneys had provided legal services free to individuals in military service and their families. The committee suggested that this should be done only in cases where the client was unable to pay.

Motion pictures of the war crime trials at Nuremberg, Germany, were shown at a local theater and Willis Smith, president of the American Bar Association and a future senator from North Carolina, spoke of his experiences as an official observer at Nuremberg. Members of the association debated at length a resolution in support of international law and U. S. participation in the International Court of Justice (World Court). After much discussion, action was deferred until the next annual meeting.

Smith, a Duke law school graduate and longtime member of its board of trustees, was one of the most highly regarded and well-known lawyers of his day. In a light and informative "travelogue" talk about his trip across Europe, Smith stopped to praise the state's barristers:

> By and large, I haven't seen any bar the size comparable to the bar of North Carolina that I thought had any more ability or any more character and intelligence than the lawyers of North Carolina. These big-city fellows have sort of outsmarted us in mechanics and appearance in offices and that sort of thing, but when it comes down to understanding legal principles and being able to try law suits, I believe I'd rather take my chance in trying with these North Carolina lawyers.

Willis Smith is the only North Carolina Bar Association member to serve as president of the American Bar Association. He was ABA president from 1945-1946, becoming the first North Carolinian to hold that position.

Two of the North Carolina Bar Association's own also played leading roles at the Nuremberg trials. Richard D. Dixon of Edenton was appointed as an alternate member of the International Military Tribunal and presided over four of the trials. Judge John J. Parker also served as an alternate to Francis S. Biddle, the U. S. representative on the tribunal.

Simple wood-frame structures often served as law offices for many small-town lawyers. The Finley-Jordan law office was located in Wilkesboro.

Standing Up for the Constitution

T. Lamar Caudle, originally of Anson County, then serving as assistant attorney general of the United States and president of the Federal Bar Association, provided the principal address by a visiting dignitary. With a keen insight into the future, Caudle spoke on "Our Federally Secured Rights." He discussed the history of civil rights legislation in the United States and outlined the abuses of civil rights that had come to the attention of the federal justice department. He explained that the attorney general's office was working with the 80th Congress on legislation that would allow the federal government to take action when rights of citizens were abridged. He concluded:

> Mob violence, or any attack upon basic rights should be a local problem of primary concern to local citizens, to be handled in the community in which it occurs by local officers. But where a local authority neglects or fails to act your Federal government should have the power and authority to act vigorously in the district in which the offense is committed. The disrespect for law, it is true, is the concern of the community in which it breaks out, but it is also a threat to all Americans everywhere and an attack on our established institutions — an attack upon your constitutional guarantees and mine.

These were courageous words for 1946, and foreshadowed civil rights actions that the U.S. Justice Department would take in the South in the 1960s.

Taking bold stands in defense of citizen rights has been something of a tradition among North Carolinians. Albert Coates addressed the topic in his book, *Three North Carolinians Who Have Stood Up to Be Counted for the Bill of Rights.*

North Carolina College at Durham law school students demonstrate for better facilities at the State Capitol in Raleigh, 1949.

Samuel Spencer, a colonel in the Anson County militia during the American Revolution, defended the rights of citizens when he stood up in the Constitutional Convention in Hillsborough in 1788 and refused to vote to ratify the United States Constitution, because it lacked a Bill of Rights, such as he had helped to write into the North Carolina Constitution of 1776:

> There is no declaration of rights, to secure every member of society those unalienable rights, which ought not to be given up to any government.... There ought to be something to confine the power of this government within its proper boundaries.... The government is proposed for individuals.... The expression 'We the People of the United States' shows that this government is intended for individuals. There ought therefore to be a Bill of Rights.

Zebulon B. Vance, governor of North Carolina, stood up for civil rights in 1862 when he learned that 40 North Carolina citizens had been taken from their homes and put into a military prison on suspicion of disloyalty. He wrote to President Jefferson Davis:

> As Governor, it is my duty to see that the citizens of this state are protected in whatever rights pertain to them, and, if necessary, I will call out the State Militia to protect them and uphold the principles of Anglo-Saxon liberty — trial by jury; liberty of speech; freedom of the press; the privileges of Parliament *habeas corpus*; the right to petition and bear arms; subordination of military to civil authority; prohibition of *ex post facto* laws.

The Green Park Hotel in Blowing Rock was the idyllic site of the 1947 annual meeting. The mountain resort town of Blowing Rock hosted seven annual meetings.

Sam J. Ervin Jr., chairman of the Senate Select Committee on Presidential Campaign Activities, would stand up for the rule of law and the Bill of Rights in his dealings with President Richard M. Nixon and his aides in 1973-74. In a speech to the student body of the University of North Carolina at Chapel Hill in 1973, Ervin said:

> So long as I have a mind to think, a tongue to speak, and a heart to love my country, I shall deny that the Constitution confers any arbitrary power on any President, or empowers any President to convert George Washington's America into Caesar's Rome.

President Charles R. Jonas and the 1947 Annual Meeting

The 1947 annual meeting was at Blowing Rock, which had last hosted the Bar Association in the prewar year of 1940. Adjustments to the postwar world were evident in the expanded committee reports of the association.

Former Bar Association President Charles R. Jonas meets with President Dwight D. Eisenhower in the Oval Office at the White House.

"Charlie" Jonas went on from his leading role in the Bar Association to serve as vice president of the North Carolina Good Health Association — a citizens' group dedicated to improving the state's health care and medical facilities — before beginning a career in politics. He was elected as a Republican to the U.S. Congress from North Carolina's 10th congressional district in 1952, defeating first-term congressman Hamilton C. Jones III, another former president of the North Carolina Bar Association. Known for his integrity, dignity and decency throughout his two decades in the House of Representatives, Jonas came to be known as the father of the two-party political system in North Carolina.

The North Carolina Bar Association Executive Committee reported that the expansion of the secretary's responsibilities and an increase in membership with the return of attorneys to civilian life merited an increase in the secretary's salary from $50 per month to $100 per month with up to $25 per month in expenses. The secretary reported 897 active members and 53 honorary members for a total membership of 950.

A proposal that would ultimately result in changes in the manner in which the association kept in contact with its members came from the Committee on Publications. Ed Cannon, then serving as secretary to both the North Carolina Bar Association and the State Bar, had proposed to the committee "some periodic method of reporting to the membership of the bar of the state on legal matters." The State Bar had been considering the matter of a periodical publication as well.

116

The last annual issue of the Bar Association's *Reports* had been published in 1943 —a very meager volume without much of the usual detail. The *Reports* were confined to matters dealing with the annual meeting and had not addressed current legal issues in a timely manner. No decision for change was reached in 1947 but many options were raised and discussed.

The 1947 session also adopted a revised constitution and bylaws of the Bar Association, primarily adjusting the old constitution to conform with current practices. And in response to Gov. R. Gregg Cherry's appointment of the North Carolina Commission for the Improvement of the Administration of Justice, President John C. Rodman appointed an association advisory committee to work with the commission. Members included Charles R. Jonas, John H. Anderson, Fred B. Helms, Albert Coates, I. M. Bailey, W. Frank Taylor, Kingsland Van Winkle, Norman C. Shepard and D. L. Ward.

"Cruising Along"
The 1948 Annual Meeting
in Bermuda

The 50th annual meeting of the North Carolina Bar Association was held on board the *SS Evangeline* en route to Bermuda in June 1948. Actual sessions were held on the high seas so that the members and their families could have a full day of leisure in the capital city of Hamilton. Attendance was limited but the vision of the members present was broad. Recognizing that judges in North Carolina were underpaid, a resolution was passed urging that Supreme Court justices be paid $15,000 and Superior Court judges $10,000 per year. An insurance program for members was introduced for consideration, a special section for the junior bar was created, and much time was devoted to debate over a uniform state code of laws. Richard E. Thigpen, who had initiated the early CLE "institutes," was elected president of the association.

Law schools at the University of North Carolina, Wake Forest and Duke cooperated in the first jointly sponsored North Carolina Bar Association Tax Institute, held on the Duke University campus on September 10, 1948. This was a logical extension of the refresher courses for returning veteran lawyers and a part of the beginning of the association's continuing legal education (CLE) program. Within a few years, the association was sponsoring three institutes each year, one on each law school campus.

Also in the summer of 1948, a young naval veteran from Dallas, N.C., passed the State Bar exam. Although he would soon set aside a legal career for the job of assistant dean of students at the University of North Carolina, he would become perhaps the best-known lawyer in the state: William C. Friday, the long-serving president of the University of North Carolina system.

This list of attorneys who were licensed in 1947 was certified by Edward L. Cannon, who was also the secretary-treasurer of the Bar Association. Elreta Melton Alexander of Greensboro was the first African-American woman licensed in North Carolina.

"Winds of Change"
Presidents and Meetings, 1949-1955

Edward L. Cannon served concurrently as the secretary-treasurer of the North Carolina Bar Association and the North Carolina State Bar, and also served at the same time as the secretary of the Board of Law Examiners.

In another action concerning communication between the association and its members, at the 1949 annual meeting in Blowing Rock, leading members of the association expressed dismay at the fact that no annual report had been published since 1943. The secretary was promptly instructed to publish in one volume the reports for 1944-1948. Secretary Cannon did so, but noted that many of the records from the war years and immediately afterward were not in the association files and that he had not been able to locate them. That was the last volume of the *Records* to be published. Not until 1953 would *BarNotes*, a pamphlet-sized publication, begin publishing minutes from board meetings and annual meetings.

In his presidential address at the 1949 meeting, Richard E. Thigpen invited the Bar Association to return to the core mission outlined by the first president Platt D. Walker some 50 years earlier: "to cultivate the science of jurisprudence; promote reform in the law, and facilitate the administration of justice." His eight-point program was a virtual road map of where the Bar Association would go in the coming years:

1. Increase revenues to support expanded programs;
2. Cooperate more closely with the North Carolina State Bar, Inc.;
3. Coordinate association programs more closely with those of local bar groups;
4. Sponsor institutes for continuing legal education opportunities;
5. Sponsor public forums to explain America's democratic institutions;
6. Transform the annual meeting into a session for "inspiration and fellowship;"
7. Eradicate "archaic concepts of rugged individualism" in the profession;
8. Increase cooperation with the state's judiciary toward a better system of justice.

Losing an Advocate and a Friend

A few months before the Blowing Rock meeting, on March 6, 1949, the association lost a great friend with the death of U.S. Sen. J. Melville Broughton. Broughton, who graduated and attended law school at Wake Forest College, was admitted to the Bar in 1910. He attended Harvard's law school in 1912-13 and began practicing law in Raleigh in 1914. He built a strong civil legal practice and served in a variety of legislative and other elective and appointive offices. He was president of the North Carolina Bar Association in 1936.

A strong supporter of Franklin Roosevelt and the New Deal, Broughton was particularly proud of the North Carolina legal profession and the Bar Association's support of the state's workmen's compensation law "despite the fact that many attorneys lost clients because of it."

In a history-making event, Elizabeth O. Rollins, who was licensed in 1949, administered the oath to her husband, Clyde T. Rollins, the following year.

WOMEN IN THE PROFESSION

In 1970, women comprised only 3 percent of the legal profession nationally. By the early 1990s, women comprised 21 percent of the legal population (a 600-percent growth rate in just 20 years). About 80 percent of female attorneys licensed have entered the profession since 1980. It is estimated that soon women will comprise 40 percent of all attorneys in North Carolina.

Attempts to organize women attorneys in the state began in March 1978, when some 125 of the state's 350 licensed women lawyers gathered at the UNC School of Law to establish the North Carolina Association of Women Attorneys (NCAWA).

In June 1990, the North Carolina Bar Association, in cooperation with NCAWA, established a Commission on the Status of Women in the Legal Profession in North Carolina to examine the role that gender plays in the practice of law. The commission, which was composed of 19 women and 16 men, represented the judiciary, the legislature, law faculties, large law firms, public interest law firms, small law firms, sole practitioners, corporate counsel and state government.

The commission, co-chaired by Dorothy C. Bernholz and Sharon L. Parker, was charged to examine issues including leadership roles and opportunities in the bar; participation in the judiciary; delayed entry into the profession; interrupted careers; migration from the field of law; compensation and other benefits; pregnancy, child care and family dynamics; societal perceptions of female attorneys and their impact on rainmaking, community, and professional environments; and other issues regarding inappropriate recognition of gender differences.

After an intense study of gender differences identified by a 1989 survey conducted by the NCAWA [with funding by the NCBA] of 1,800 male and female attorneys and statistical analysis of survey data collected in 1990 by the NCBA Quality of Life Task Force, and after thoughtful consideration of the changes in the legal profession resulting from the increasing numbers of women entering the profession, the commission issued its final report in January 1993.

The Committee on Women in the Legal Profession in North Carolina was created by the NCBA Board of Governors on January 14, 1993, and has carried on the work of the commission. The work of the association was made possible due to the long tradition of distinguished practice by groundbreaking female attorneys in North Carolina.

Ann Marwood Durant, who moved to Perquimans County between 1661 and 1662 when she married, has been honored with a state historical marker as North Carolina's first female attorney. Historians believe that Durant, a mother of nine children, who often managed her household while her husband was away on business, was the first female to act on behalf of someone else in a North Carolina court. Ironically, when Durant appeared in court asking that money owed her from an estate be paid, the court ordered the money to be paid to her husband under the laws then in existence.

Tabitha Anne Holton was the first woman in a Southern state to be officially licensed to practice law. North Carolina became the sixth state to admit a female lawyer to the bar when Holton passed the bar exam without missing a single question.

In 1915, Margaret Berry Street became the first female graduate of the UNC School of Law. The 1915 issue of the school yearbook, the *Yackety Yack*, described her in these terms: "A rare combination of high aspirations, keen intellect, and 'just girl.' A suffragette, of course, and proves her right to the ballot by standing among the first in the class. But she is too full of the joy of living to sacrifice her girlhood to her theories. She excels in arguing a case, but is more at home in a drawing room. We predict her ready smile will captivate one as well as 12 men."

A graduate of the University of North Carolina School of Law in 1920, Kathrine R. Everett was licensed to practice law in the same year the 19th Amendment gave women the right to vote. Just out of law school and working with her father's firm in Fayetteville, she became the first woman to argue and win a case in the North Carolina Supreme Court. She remained active in the practice of law for 72 years, which included 20 years in elective office as a member of the Durham City Council. As evidence of her commitment to both law and family, she even took notes for her son, Robinson, at his Harvard law school classes when he became ill with hepatitis.

Admitted to practice in 1928, Susie Marshall Sharp was appointed as the first woman Superior Court judge in 1949. After distinguished service as an associate justice of the Supreme Court of North Carolina, in 1975, she became the first woman elected to the office of chief justice in any state supreme court. In an interview, Justice Sharp astutely commented, "(n)o, I did not object to being distinguished as a 'woman attorney.' I thought it was obvious from the beginning."

A graduate of Columbia Law School in 1947, Elreta Alexander-Ralston was the first black woman to be licensed to practice law in North Carolina. In 1966, she formed the South's first integrated law firm in Greensboro, and two years later became the first black elected judge in North Carolina. Known as "Judge A" to all, she was noted for her willingness to give first offenders a chance to avoid a criminal record.

"I try not to be too critical knowing what the system has done, but I get angry at people who are in a position to take risks but don't," Annie Brown Kennedy said. Events in Kennedy's life have demonstrated her willingness to take risks. In 1952, the year she was admitted to the Georgia State Bar after receiving her law degree from Howard University, Kennedy gave birth to twin sons, who today are partners in the firm started by Mrs. Kennedy and her husband, Harold L. Kennedy Jr.

In 1957, Kennedy and her husband won the right for black golfers to play on the segregated Gillespie Park Golf Course in *Simkins v. City of Greensboro*. Always active in politics, Kennedy was appointed to the state Legislature in 1979, becoming the first black female to "serve" in the Legislature. In addition, Kennedy has been a delegate to numerous Democratic National Conventions and served on the NCBA Board of Governors.

A graduate of Wake Forest's law school and now a member of its faculty, Rhoda B. Billings became the first female president of the North Carolina Bar Association in June 1991. A district court judge from 1968 to 1972, she was noted for her work on the North Carolina Criminal Code Commission, which reviewed and updated criminal procedures and statutes. Billings, who served as associate justice of the North Carolina Supreme Court, was appointed chief justice by Gov. James G. Martin in 1986.

B.C. Allen Jr. of Raleigh (right), a lieutenant, served aboard the USS Mount McKinley off the coast of Korea in 1950. Allen was the staff legal officer for the ship which led the Inchon invasion during the Korean War.

Attorney John H. Zollicoffer Sr. and his secretary Esther Brown temporarily occupied the old City of Henderson jail while his next-door law offices underwent major renovations in 1949.

A Raleigh native but also a Wake Forest fan, for many years Broughton proudly led a delegation of state legislators and leaders of the bar on an Easter Monday train ride from Raleigh to Wake Forest for the traditional Wake Forest vs. North Carolina State baseball game, and for many years had the honor of throwing out the first ball. His death, shortly after he entered the Senate, deprived North Carolina and the legal profession of a strong and experienced voice in the national government.

Getting the Word Out

In the early 1950s, a radio series describing the work of attorneys and their role in society was developed and broadcast on radio stations across the state. About the same time Dean Robert E. Lee of the Wake Forest School of Law, with support from the association, began a popular newspaper series titled "This is the Law." Lee, a Kinston native, had been a member of the law faculty at Temple University in Philadelphia, where he wrote a regular legal column for the *Philadelphia Enquirer*.

Throughout the '50s, these and other association efforts to communicate with the public were moderately successful, as were the efforts of the association's leaders to communicate with the state Legislature, which was still mostly composed of lawyers. Efforts to communicate with the members of the association outside the annual meetings apparently stalled however. One apparent

problem was that while the North Carolina Bar Association was increasing its activities, so was the State Bar. Ed Cannon continued to serve as secretary-treasurer for the Bar Association, as secretary-treasurer of the State Bar and secretary of the Board of Law Examiners.

Leadership from the Top, 1950-1955

Presidents in the early 1950s included Francis J. Heazel (1950-1951), an Asheville attorney and civic leader, formerly secretary of the Madison Square Garden Corporation; W.A. Leland McKeithen (1951-1952), a Moore County native who was later appointed a special judge of the state Superior Court by Govs. Umstead and Hodges; and William L. Thorp (1953-1954), a Rocky Mount attorney whose son and namesake, Bill, later would be recognized for his work on legal aid and his *Thorp's North Carolina Trial Practice Forms* (1975).

Under J. Spencer Bell's presidency (1952-1953) the association began to consider a comprehensive reform of the state's judicial system. Bell soon began to make speeches across the state, pointing out that the delays, inefficiencies and expense of justice under the non-unified court system were leading citizens to

Judge H.E. Phillips presides in his courtroom at the Duplin County Courthouse, Kenansville, September 1954.

The Capital Club building in downtown Raleigh was the location of the first permanent North Carolina Bar Association offices from the early 1950s until the first Bar Center was built in 1962 on Wade Avenue.

turn to compulsory arbitration, quasi-judicial administrative agencies and other makeshift devices for settling differences.

In the words of Albert Coates, J. Spencer Bell turned the North Carolina Bar Association "from a social organization with annual meetings and sideline activities into a positive working force." It was Bell who led the drive for a full-time staff and budget adequate to the needs of a growing professional association offering services to its members. In his 1953 address to the Bar Association meeting at Blowing Rock, Bell gave a tough-minded talk to his fellow attorneys:

> Let us look frankly at the organization we have.... We meet once a year — about one-tenth of the practicing lawyers of the State — we pass high sounding resolutions — we appoint committees — we mouth platitudes about justice and citizenship and the Constitution and our great profession — then we go our several ways and forget these problems, doing absolutely nothing to implement our resolutions and pledges, leaving it up to our officers and committees to perform miracles....
> We must make up our minds that we are going to take definite concrete action here and now to put into effect a plan of action which will solve these problems.... I say, in all earnestness, if we are not going to do the job with this organization, let us quit deceiving ourselves. Then we can turn our efforts to the Incorporated Bar, broaden the statute to include these functions, and levy a license fee collectible by law, which will properly finance them.

In 1953, Cannon and the leadership — probably in response to J. Spencer Bell's comments — agreed that the job of part-time secretary-treasurer had become too difficult for one person to manage. Cannon resigned his positions with the association, though he retained his positions as secretary of the State Bar and the North Carolina Board of Law Examiners until his retirement in 1967. In 1954, the association honored Ed Cannon with a life membership in recognition of his meritorious services. Perhaps one of the great tributes to Cannon was the establishment in 1954 of the Young Lawyers Division, initially called the Junior Bar Section, with Charles F. Blanchard of Raleigh as its first

Duke law students argued against Wake Forest law students in this November 1950 moot court competition.

leader. Cannon had begun his membership in the association as a spokesman for the Durham Junior Bar, and was an active member of the association's junior bar section.

On November 14, 1953, following Cannon's resignation, the association's executive committee announced the appointment of Charles W. Daniel of Fuquay Springs to fill the newly created post of executive secretary. The appointment was part of a developing public relations effort by the Bar Association, designed to "create a closer liaison and better understanding between the members of the bar and the people of North Carolina," said William L. Thorp, president of the association in 1953-1954. The executive committee charged Daniels with the task of establishing a new office for the association, and increasing and improving services to members.

In many ways Charles Daniel seemed to be the ideal person for the job, with a promising combination of experiences. He had served in the U. S. Navy during World War II. After receiving a degree in journalism from the University of North Carolina, he worked for newspapers in several North Carolina towns. He had been active in the state's veterans groups and had just received a law degree from the Wake Forest School of Law.

Daniel used his journalistic background and a close relationship with Ed Cannon — who continued as secretary of the State Bar — to publicize the work of the association, both to the membership and the public. He began the membership publication *BarNotes* and used his journalistic contacts to garner coverage of the association's activities in the state's newspapers.

After serving as executive secretary for two years, Daniel resigned and opened his own practice in his native Fuquay Springs, where he practiced until his death in 1967. President James K. Dorsett Jr. asked Wright Dixon to supervise the Bar Association office until a replacement could be found.

With Daniel's resignation in 1955, the leadership of the North Carolina Bar Association began a search for a full-time executive who could devote his entire time to administration and planning. The association's goals and objectives were clear, but strong leadership was necessary for progress and development. To accomplish this, the association appointed William M. Storey executive secretary. The progress of the association over the next three decades would demonstrate the wisdom of this decision.

∞

The significant growth of the North Carolina Bar Association during the '50s, '60s and '70s required a larger staff and expanded facilities. Shown here, the first Bar Center building at 1025 Wade Avenue in Raleigh, which was occupied from 1962 until 1983, and the second Bar Center on Annapolis Drive in Raleigh, which was occupied from 1983 until 1994.

∞

CHAPTER 10

"Soaring Higher"
1955-1974

The mid-1950s was the heyday of the political moderate in North Carolina, at a time when moderation was sorely needed. The U. S. Supreme Court's 1954 decision in *Brown v. Board of Education* had ignited racial tensions in the state. Leading moderates such as the association's own Irving Carlyle had attempted to calm racial feelings, but feelings remained high a year later. In 1955, North Carolinians were fortunate to have a moderate, progressive businessman, Luther H. Hodges, as their chief executive. In the same year, the association's executive committee wisely chose a moderate, business-minded progressive, William M. Storey, to be the association's new executive secretary and treasurer. Both men would provide strong leadership and establish firm foundations for future growth.

New Constitution, New Committees

The major event in the association's first year with Storey at the helm was the implementation of a new constitution. The 1955 constitution attempted to put a system in place that would assure progress for the association. Sixteen new standing committees were established: Administrative Law, Courts and Civil Litigation, Commercial Banking and Business Law, Continuing Legal Education, Criminal Law and Procedure, Finance, Insurance, Labor Law, Legal Aid, Legislation and Law Reform, Memorials, Office Management and Fees, Public Relations, Real Property, Probate and Fiduciary Law, and Taxation.

The Committee on Office Management and Fees was one of the first of the new committees to show results. Under the leadership of Rocky Mount attorney Herman S. Merrell, the committee undertook a complete economic survey of the legal profession in North Carolina. The study demonstrated that the state's lawyers generally had not kept pace with the improving economic condition of most other professions.

The Merrell committee then drafted and the association published an *Advisory Handbook on Office Management and Fees* in 1956, despite the concerns of some that it might appear that the profession was attempting to "fix fees." Nonetheless, attorneys could point to the fee schedule in the book to justify fees charged for basic services. One attorney reported that within two weeks of receiving the book he recouped the $5 cost by more than 10 times in only two transactions. Merrell became recognized as an authority in the field of office management and fees and the association published revised editions of the handbook in 1962 and 1972.

ECONOMICS OF THE BAR
SURVEY

The North Carolina
Bar Association

With the Cooperation of
The American Bar Association
Committee on Economics of Law Practice
and
The American Bar Foundation

1965

By answering this short questionnaire you will be helping the legal profession to gain an understanding of its economic status, and that knowledge will be of interest and benefit to all lawyers.

CONFIDENTIAL
NO SIGNATURES PLEASE—THANK YOU

RETURN IN ENVELOPE PROVIDED

The Economics of the Bar Survey was a successful annual project begun in 1956. Programs such as this helped change the Bar Association into an organization dedicated to serving its members and the public in concrete ways.

Law Office Management

WAKE FOREST COLLEGE LAW SCHOOL

April 17 and 18

Sponsored by
NORTH CAROLINA BAR ASSOCIATION
ITS COMMITTEES ON
CONTINUING LEGAL EDUCATION AND
OFFICE MANAGEMENT

And

The Law Schools of
WAKE FOREST COLLEGE
UNIVERSITY OF NORTH CAROLINA
DUKE UNIVERSITY

This 1959 continuing legal education (CLE) seminar was one of an increasing number of programs sponsored by the NCBA. Early CLE programs were most often co-sponsored by the Bar Association and the law schools, with seminar locations rotating between their campuses.

Carroll Wayland Weathers was a man who had an enormous and positive impact on the lives of many law students and lawyers.

Weathers, who served as a professor and as dean of the law school of Wake Forest College from 1950-1970, was known as a highly principled man who instilled in his students a lofty respect for the law and diligent obedience to ethics. He continued to serve as a professor at Wake Forest until 1972.

He held a sincere interest in each of his students after they departed law school and entered into what he would call, "the honored profession of law." In fact, he had the ability to recall the names, addresses, spouses and firms of many former students.

Weathers was born in Shelby on October 18, 1901. He grew up in Raleigh and received a B.A. degree in 1922 and an LL.B. degree in 1923 from Wake Forest College. He practiced law in Raleigh for 27 years with the firm of Weathers and Young (now Young, Moore & Henderson).

He served one term in the North Carolina Senate, worked on the General Statutes Commission and was on the Wake Forest University Board of Trustees. Weathers was active in civic work throughout his career. In Raleigh he was a longtime member of the board of trustees of both the State School for the Blind and Deaf and the Olivia Raney Library.

He was also active in the First Baptist Church of Raleigh, where he was a member of the board of deacons for 27 years. He was also a deacon at the First Baptist Church in Winston-Salem.

An active member of the North Carolina Bar Association, Weathers was vice president of the NCBA in 1953 and received the association's highest honor, the John J. Parker Award, in 1972. In 1979, the Wake Forest University School of Law established the Carroll Wayland Weathers Distinguished Alumnus Award in his honor.

Weathers, who lost his sight in the late 1970s, was a member of the board of directors of Industries for the Blind of Winston-Salem from 1981 until his death in February of 1983.

Weathers and his first wife, Sarah, who died in 1938, had two children. He and his second wife, Mary Parks, whom he married in 1946, had two children. His and Mary Parks' daughter Jane has been director of section activities of the North Carolina Bar Association since 1985.

The Bar Center's library is named after Weathers. In addition, a North Carolina Bar Association Justice Fund was established in honor of Carroll Wayland Weathers. In the description of his life, it reads: "Weathers was a truly inspirational man. He was the epitome of an educated, Southern gentleman and served as an esteemed example to all who had the privilege of knowing him."

Carroll W. Weathers was dean of the Wake Forest University School of Law from 1950-1970.

Doctors and Lawyers Working Together

Also in 1956, a "Medico-Legal Interprofessional Code" formalized relationships between lawyers and doctors in North Carolina. The code, approved by both the North Carolina Bar Association and the North Carolina Medical Society, set forth a "declaration of principles as standards of conduct for attorneys and physicians in interrelated practice." The code began by recognizing that "a substantial part of the practice of law and medicine is concerned with the problems of persons who are in need of the combined services of a lawyer and doctor."

This guide to interprofessional relations included sections on medical reports requested by attorneys, medical testimony and compensation for services of physicians in litigation matters. The code included a section on interprofessional courtesy and tolerance that stated:

> It is recognized that both legal and medical professions are essential to society; and their aims are essentially parallel. This necessitates at all times full understanding and cooperation. Each has the duty to develop an enlightened and tolerant understanding of the other in the best interests of the public, as well as the reputations of the two professions.

This agreement by no means eliminated all friction between the two professions, but it did set standards that eased their working relationship and improved their relations with the public. After the American Bar Association and American Medical Association adopted their own codes, a revised medico-legal code for North Carolina was adopted in 1962.

"Seeking a Better System of Justice"
The Bell Commission

One of the most far reaching projects ever undertaken by the North Carolina Bar Association was a comprehensive study of the state judicial system, which led to a thorough revision of the state court system and the administration of justice in North Carolina. In July 1955, Gov. Luther H. Hodges expressed his conviction that the courts of North Carolina "no longer held the high place in the minds of our citizens that they once held," and he urged the Bar Association to do something about it. The association promptly established the Committee on Improving and Expediting the Administration of Justice. J. Spencer Bell accepted the chairmanship of the committee, after consulting with Judge John J. Parker about its mission and work.

Charlotte attorney Spencer Bell served as president of the association in 1953-54 and was active in the revision of the association's constitution and in the decision to employ a full-time executive secretary. He became so associated in the mind of the public with the Committee on Improving and Expediting the Administration of Justice and its successors that the committee became generally known as "the Bell Commission." He continued to chair the committee even after he was appointed a judge of the U.S. Court of Appeals for the Fourth Circuit.

Bell's committee initially recommended a thorough study of the system for administering justice in North Carolina in order to determine the needs and possible solutions. They made their case so persuasively that three North Carolina foundations contributed a total of $85,000 to finance the work. The money was given to the association to be used only for the work of the committee.

The study took three years to complete and included a thorough investigation into all aspects of the state court system from the magistrates and justices of the peace to the North Carolina Supreme Court. The committee assembled the results of this extensive research and provided an exhaustive interpretation of the facts revealed. During the process of fact gathering and interpretation, a continuous program of public information and education was implemented. The material was designed to create and maintain the interest of the people in their courts.

The Bell Commission and the
North Carolina Courts Commission

Following the study, a series of tentative recommendations were prepared for improving and expediting the administration of justice in North Carolina. Recommendations included significant proposals for changes to court structure and jurisdiction, the jury system, judges and solicitors, practice and procedure, and court administration.

The committee was expanded to include laymen as well as lawyers and the recommendations were discussed openly and publicly. Copies of the recommendations were mailed to each member of the North Carolina Bar Association. Full and heated discussions resulted at the annual meetings. As a result of this thorough discussion, the original recommendations were revised and revamped in many ways. The revised proposals were included in a draft amendment to the North Carolina Constitution that was submitted to the 1959 General Assembly.

J. SPENCER BELL

J. Spencer Bell was the first recipient of the Judge John J. Parker Award.

Jesse Spencer Bell was born in Charlotte on April 1, 1906. He graduated from Duke University with an A.B. degree in 1927. Bell attended Harvard law school for one year, but transferred to the University of North Carolina at Chapel Hill and received his LL.B. in 1930.

He began work with his father, James A. Bell, whose partner was state Sen. H.N. Pharr. Pharr's son Neal also practiced in the firm.

In 1941, Spencer Bell enlisted as a private in the Army field artillery branch. He rose to the rank of major and was honorably discharged in 1946. After his discharge, he returned to Charlotte and resumed law practice. In 1951, he formed the law firm of Shannonhouse, Bell and Horn. He served as a state senator from 1954 to 1960. At the time of his appointment to the Fourth Circuit, he was senior partner in the Charlotte firm of Bell, Bradley, Gebhardt & Millette.

On May 8, 1953, he married Catherine (Kitty) Castellett. Although they had no children, he and his wife treated his law clerks as his children. Harry "Buck" Griffin, his law clerk during the 1963-1964 term of the Fourth Circuit Court of Appeals, later observed:

> Childless, he and Mrs. Bell adopted and welcomed as family his law clerks and their wives. There were traditions we all enjoyed during one year with him. Lunch once a week at his club. More frequent lunches at the S&W Cafeteria, where his favorite entree was "Georgia t-bone" (better known as hamburger patty). And most memorably, the daily ritual of afternoon tea and English biscuits. Judge Bell was one of the few people I have known to always see the best in life and to enjoy it to the fullest. Balance exemplified his life.

From September 29, 1961 until his death on March 19, 1967, Bell served as judge of the Fourth Circuit Court of Appeals. His judicial opinions demonstrated his strong convictions and his plain speaking. For example, in one opinion involving a condemnation case where the defendant was denied severance damages, he distinguished a case cited by the appellant saying that it "did not get Defendant home safe." *U.S. v. Mattox,* 375 F.2d 461 (4th Cir. 1967).

Judge Bell's contribution to the North Carolina Bar Association was extensive. He served as a member and on its various committees from early in his career until his death. He served as president in 1952-1953. In 1958, he was the first recipient of the John J. Parker Award, the association's highest honor.

But his most significant contribution was in the area of judicial reform. In 1953, he was named chairman of a 15-member committee to study the judicial system and recommend improvements. That committee met regularly and made annual progress reports to the N.C. Bar Association. In 1955, the N.C. Bar Association, at the request of Gov. Luther H. Hodges, created the Committee on Improving and Expediting the Administration of Justice in North Carolina. But, everyone came to refer to it as "the Bell Commission." The previous committee membership was expanded to include nonlawyers and prominent citizens such as Shearon Harris, Fred Fletcher and Ashley Futrell. The committee met every other Friday afternoon at the Bar Association.

On Friday, June 13, 1957, he made a report to the N.C. Bar Association as chairman of the Committee on Improving and Expediting the Administration of Justice. In his comments, he summarized the efforts of several subcommittees, challenging the association to take up the issue of judicial reform. His remarks so impressed the leadership that its entire contents were included in the minutes of the association. He emphasized the committee's philosophical approach:

> As the committee has proceeded with its works, two general propositions have been constantly kept in mind. First is the proposition that courts exist for the people of the state and not for the lawyers. ... The second general proposition ... is that the judicial department of the government should be non-political. This means the judicial office should not be a reward for political service. It means that the courts should not be so organized, staffed and conducted that the political views or activities of a person should not be a factor in any decision concerning him....

And so, in conclusion, your committee offers you the biggest case you'll ever have, for the best client you'll ever serve, for the finest feel you'll ever get—the respect, the admiration and the gratitude of the people of North Carolina.

This challenge led to the Bell Commission report in December 1958, which in turn led to the introduction of legislation in the 1959 General Assembly. Most significantly, the report promoted the concept of an independent judiciary. A Constitutional Commission had authored another alternative to judicial reform which proposed greater legislative authority over the courts.

The debate on these two bills was not resolved in the 1959 General Assembly and continued through the General Assembly of 1961. The Bar Association proposal prevailed by receiving approval of H.B. 104, enacted as Chapter 313, 1961 Session Laws. A Constitutional amendment was approved by the voters in 1962. This legislation created a unified and uniform general court of justice for the state. It has become a model system for other states which have copied its organization and emphasis on judicial independence. While the N.C. Bar Association receives much credit for this work, it is truly a monument to the dedication and efforts of J. Spencer Bell.

When the draft amendment became entangled with legislative reapportionment and a number of other highly controversial issues, the association recalled its proposed amendment. Substantially the same bill was re-introduced in 1961, when it was passed by the General Assembly and submitted to the people in the 1962 general election. Approval of the constitutional amendment provided authority for most of the recommended improvements.

For five years the Bell Commission and the North Carolina Courts Commission met every other Friday at the North Carolina Bar Center. By 1970, most of the recommendations were implemented. The association, with the leadership of Spencer Bell and his committee, had secured major reforms in the judicial system including a uniform system of district courts under the state supreme court. The Greensboro *Daily News* editors' praised the association's "active program of judicial improvement through the years."

The continuing legal education series, the *Handbook on Office Management and Fees,* and the study of the North Carolina judicial system were all recognized in an award of merit conferred by the American Bar Association in 1956. This was the first of many such awards to follow from the national organization.

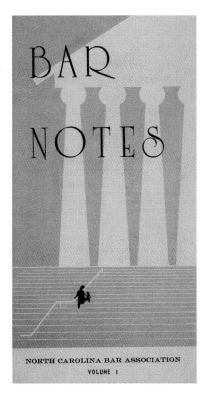

The cover of the first volume of BarNotes, 1953. This publication, now known as North Carolina Lawyer, became the vehicle for regular communication with the membership.

Public Relations and Public Service Efforts

Another activity identified with Bill Storey's early years with the North Carolina Bar Association is the development of *BarNotes,* a well-respected quarterly journal sent to all members of the association. Richard E. Thigpen had called for such a publication in 1949, and the first pamphlet-sized issue appeared in 1953. Storey realized the importance of communicating regularly with association members and moved quickly to publishing quarterly issues in a booklet-sized format. The journal contained articles of current and lasting interest to the legal profession as well as reports of annual meetings. It thus served as a replacement for the old annual *Reports* along with keeping the membership informed.

In 1959, the association strengthened its public relations program. Building on an earlier radio series and Dr. Robert E. Lee's "This is the Law" newspaper column, a series of 15-minute television films were produced. The 13 television programs, titled "Out of Court," sought to educate the public on normal day-to-day legal problems and encouraged people to seek professional advice promptly.

HERB TAYLOR
THE SMALL-TOWN LAWYER

Every small town in North Carolina has its "pillars of the community"—the doctor, the minister, the teacher, the lawyer. As an attorney and counselor at law, Herbert H. Taylor Jr. has fulfilled that role in Tarboro for more than 64 years. His role as Tarboro High School class president and valedictorian in 1928 was a harbinger of future achievements.

Armed with a law degree from Chapel Hill, he returned to Tarboro in 1935 and served his community through seven decades. His first public position was service as a town trial justice, only four years out of law school, and later as a county recorder's court judge. The only interruption in local service was active duty military service overseas during World War II.

Both city and county schools benefitted from his counsel as school board attorney over six decades. He served as attorney for the town of Tarboro from 1947-92 and for Edgecombe County from 1958-93. Carolina Telephone and Telegraph Company relied on his legal counsel from 1958-79, as did hundreds of local families and businesses from the 1930s through the 1990s.

As a member of the Bell Commission and the N.C. Courts Commission, he helped fashion the current state court system. He also served as a member and chair of the N.C. Veterans Commission under four governors. The capstone of Herb Taylor's professional career was his election as president of the North Carolina Bar Association in 1977.

Taylor was also inducted into the North Carolina Bar Association General Practice Hall of Fame in 1990. In 1997 he received the NCBA Young Lawyers Division's Liberty Bell Award, presented to those who have "strengthened the American system of freedom under law."

Although he retired in 1993, Taylor continued to be a great and respected counselor of the law and a dedicated public servant. A colleague has said that "he has been and continues to be a kind, friendly, warm, caring and affable man, as well as a courteous, courtly and gracious gentleman of the old school."

Herbert H. Taylor Jr. is a lifelong resident of Tarboro.

The association also published a brochure titled "With this Ring." Distributed to the registrar of deeds in each county to be given to couples when they obtained a marriage license, the brochure discussed how the law looks at property and the like in the context of a married couple.

Another activity of the association that began in 1957 provided a great service to the state of North Carolina while at the same time enhanced the public image of the association and its membership. About 300 attorneys, nearly 15 percent of the membership of the association, worked to provide an inventory of North Carolina's state-owned property. For the first time, the state had an accurate list of its property in each of the 100 counties. More than 4,500 hours were contributed to the project at no cost to the state. One news commentary estimated that this was the equivalent of a $90,000 gift to the state by the North Carolina Bar Association. The American Bar Association recognized the worth of the project with an award of merit in 1960.

In 1957, the association succeeded in its efforts to persuade the state Legislature that the Supreme Court needed relief from its workload. A study had demonstrated that Supreme Court justices in North Carolina were individually writing 55 percent more opinions than justices in other states. The association persuaded the Legislature that this was a misuse of court officials' time, preventing full, thorough and complete study of pending cases. The General Assembly provided for seven research assistants, one for each justice. Not only did this provide relief to the court, it provided many young attorneys, generally recent law school graduates, a year or more of practical training in appellate work.

Mr. and Mrs. Grainger Pierce and Mr. and Mrs. James O. Moore en route from New York to London aboard the Queen Elizabeth I in 1957, to attend the ABA's annual meeting in London.

In 1959, the Judge John J. Parker Award for "conspicuous service to the cause of jurisprudence" was established to commemorate the life and memory of one of the association's most prestigious members, who had died the previous year. It is the highest award presented by the North Carolina Bar Association.

A Foundation for Greater Service

In 1960, the North Carolina Bar Association Foundation was chartered. The purposes of the foundation were outlined in the charter:

    a. To foster and maintain the honor and integrity of the law;

    b. To study, improve and facilitate the administration of justice;

    c. To promote the study of law and research therein, the diffusion of knowledge thereof, and the continuing education of lawyers;

    d. To cause to be published and to distribute addresses, reports, treatises and other literary works on legal subjects;

    e. To maintain a law library and research center.

Secretary-Treasurer Storey, always a careful manager of funds, had managed to accumulate small amounts of money from such sources as unspent proceeds from CLE institutes and wanted a secure place to invest such funds for future use. He envisioned continued growth for the association as it sought to meet the needs of the membership and the legal profession. The foundation would become an outstanding vehicle for providing public service, education, research and information to the profession.

Into the '60s

At the 1960 annual meeting, James M. Poyner, chairman of the membership committee, announced a membership of 2,000. This was a growth of more than 1,100 members since 1955. More than 400 of the total membership were "sustaining members," who provided additional support for the association by paying double their normal dues. The surge in membership in all categories coincided with the increased activity of the association in all areas.

The North Carolina governor's race in 1960 pitted two prominent members of the North Carolina Bar Association against each other in the all-important Democratic primary: I. Beverly Lake, a Raleigh attorney and former professor of law at Wake Forest; and Terry Sanford, a Fayetteville attorney active in the political organization of former Gov. Kerr Scott. Sanford defeated Lake in a closely contested second primary by some 75,000 votes and went on to win the general election. After losing again in the first primary in the 1964 gubernatorial race, Lake threw his support to Daniel K. Moore, also an NCBA member, who went on to win the governorship. I. Beverly Lake had a distinguished 13-year career as a justice of the N.C. Supreme Court, where he came to be known for his razor-sharp legal mind, his lucid writing, and his hard work. Dr. Lake's son, I. Beverly Lake Jr., was appointed to the N.C. Supreme Court in 1992 and elected in 1994.

A rare photo of proceedings of the North Carolina Supreme Court in 1963. Although judicial robes are now commonplace, North Carolina's justices first donned robes in January 1958.

In April 1963, the Bar Association, in cooperation with a special committee of the State Bar, drafted a bill to provide for the appointment of counsel for indigent defendants in criminal trials. The General Assembly adopted the legislation in June 1963 and appropriated one-half million dollars for the indigent counsel program.

The Bill Storey Years

Many individual members and leaders were responsible for the growing level of services provided by the North Carolina Bar Association during the late 1950s, the 1960s and 1970s. Each area of activity had one or more attorneys who saw a need in the profession and worked to meet it. But the person who orchestrated the entire movement was William M. Storey, executive secretary of the association.

William Marion Storey was born in Savannah, Ga. in 1924, and his family moved to Raleigh when he was five. He entered the University of North Carolina and completed his freshman year before entering the Navy where he served for three years. He returned to UNC to receive his bachelor of arts degree in 1947 and his bachelor of laws in 1950. He showed a strong personality and leadership aptitude as a student, serving as president of his freshman class, of Pi Kappa Alpha, and of the Phi Alpha Delta legal fraternity. He served in the Pacific during World War II reaching the rank of lieutenant commander, which he continued to hold in the Naval Reserve. Storey was admitted to the North Carolina Bar in March 1950, and was in private practice in Raleigh from 1950 until 1955.

William M. "Bill" Storey led the association from 1955-1981

In 1955, Storey was chosen as executive secretary and treasurer of the North Carolina Bar Association. In the 1960s, the association changed his title to executive vice president and treasurer and provided an executive secretary to

*The North Carolina Bar Association's
Practical Skills Course for newly licensed
attorneys is the nation's longest running
seminar of its type. During the 1963
course, attendees ate in the Student Dining
Hall and stayed in the Burgaw Dormitory
at what is now North Carolina State
University.*

assist him. When the North Carolina Bar Association Foundation was formed, Storey became its secretary-treasurer and served the association in both capacities until his death in 1981.

Known as the "dean of continuing legal education" in North Carolina, Storey was a forceful figure who had big dreams for the association and the legal profession. He was active in professional organizations and represented North Carolina well on the national level. In 1958, after only two years in his position, Storey saw the association win an award of merit from the ABA. In 1971, the NCBA won its 10th such award presented during Storey's tenure.

For these and other activities, Storey received the John J. Parker Award in 1971. Storey's activities were summarized in *BarNotes*:

> Ten times in the past 15 years this Association has been accorded the distinction of receiving the Award of Merit from the American Bar Association. The programs of this Association in Continuing Legal Education, Practical Skills Training, Court Improvement, Legislation and Law Reform, Penal System Study and Bar Center Development are but a part of the truly remarkable work which has been undertaken, carried to success and continued on a high level of excellence during these years. Throughout this period, the North Carolina Bar Association has grown in strength and ability as it has grown in service to the Bar, to the Courts and to the people of North Carolina.

Many able lawyers have enlisted in these programs; many have served and labored to make them succeed but in all of them, and with all of us, there has been the ever present guidance and encouragement of one man, whose complete commitment to the law and the improvement of the administration of justice has moved the Bar of North Carolina to even greater achievements.

A Permanent Home for the Association

One of the great events in the career of Bill Storey, and in the history of the North Carolina Bar Association, was the dedication of the Bar Center at 1025 Wade Avenue on October 26, 1962. The association had begun operations out of the offices of the first secretaries. In 1919, President E. F. Aydlett of Elizabeth City had called for a permanent home for the association. In the 1920s, records had been moved to the Supreme Court Building and then in the 1950s to a suite in the Capital Club Building, first on the second floor and then to larger space on the seventh floor. The idea of a permanent home of its own remained only a dream until the upsurge in association membership and activity made larger quarters necessary.

Beginning in 1960, work toward a building proceeded. A steering committee with James M. Poyner as chairman was appointed. A lot on Wade Avenue

*Numerous American Bar
Association Awards of Merit were
received by the NCBA. Pictured left
to right are Executive Secretary-
Treasurer Bill Storey, President
James B. McMillan and President-
Elect Isaac T. "Pete" Avery Jr.
receiving the 1961 award.*

was contributed by an anonymous donor on the condition that a bar center be built there within three years. Lawyers in the state pledged more than $150,000 within six months, and construction began. The nearly 5,000-square-foot building would include staff offices, a library and room for expansion. The "Dedication Issue" of *BarNotes* (October 1962) included photos of past presidents and secretary-treasurers and a brief history of the association compiled by Storey. As usual, the Bar Association looked to its past to find guidance for the future.

The 1962 Bar Exam Controversy

A less favorable news event for the legal profession in North Carolina in 1962 was the record failure rate of 51 percent of the applicants who took the State Bar examination. The results of the 1962 exam gained widespread press attention across the state, and both the North Carolina State Bar and the North Carolina Bar Association came under intense pressure to lobby the State Board of Law Examiners to make changes. Association member L.P. McLendon of Greensboro said the exam results were "shocking," and Dean Henry P. Brandis Jr., also a member of the association, called the 1962 exam "indefensible and inexcusable." At the urging of the North Carolina State Bar Council the State Board of Law Examiners undertook an in-depth study of the examination process and made significant changes by the time of the next exam.

The 1962-1963 NCBA Board of Governors at the dedication of the new North Carolina Bar Center on October 26, 1962. First row (left to right): G.E. Miller, Ralph N. Strayhorn*, J. Dickson Phillips Jr., John R. Haworth*, Isaac T. "Pete" Avery Jr.*, J. Will Pless Jr., C. Woodrow Teague, Sam J. Ervin III, Joseph W. Grier Jr., Landon H. Roberts. Second row: William M. Storey, James M. Poyner*, Wallace C. Murchison, R. Kennedy Harris, Henry L. Anderson*, John R. Ingram, David M. Britt, George A. Long*, H. P. Taylor Jr., William L. Mills Jr. Third Row: Louis J. Poisson Jr.*, Jerome Clark, Larry Johnson, Don Evans, Norman Block, Marshall Cline, James E. "Bill" Walker*, Dean Robert E. Lee. Eight of these (marked with an *) eventually served as president of the Bar Association.

AFRICAN-AMERICANS IN THE PROFESSION

While James Edward O'Hara, a black lawyer trained at Howard University, was admitted to the North Carolina Bar in 1868, it wasn't until the civil rights movement of the 1960s that black lawyers were admitted into the voluntary North Carolina Bar Association. The NCBA became the first state bar association in the South to integrate its membership when Julius L. Chambers and Henry E. Frye were admitted to the NCBA in April 1967. Brothers Mickey and Eric Michaux were rejected for membership at that meeting, and again at the annual meeting in June before finally being admitted. (Mickey later became the first black U.S. attorney in North Carolina and a state legislator, while Eric would later serve as chairman of the N.C. Board of Law Examiners.)

Black lawyers had previously responded to the need for their own professional organization by forming the Old North State Bar Association in 1935 and then the North Carolina Lawyers Association in 1954, which later became the North Carolina Association of Black Lawyers.

In recent years, the North Carolina Bar Association has worked with the N.C. Association of Black Lawyers, providing space in the N.C. Bar Center for administrative purposes and even having a joint board meeting.

In 1993, the NCBA joined with the NCABL to form a Commission on Race Relations in the Legal Profession, which issued its final report and recommendations in 1996. The work of this commission continues with a standing Race Relations Implementation Committee of the N.C. Bar Association.

A decade earlier, in 1985, future NCBA President Charles Burgin chaired a Minorities in the Profession Task Force which became an NCBA committee in 1987.

Today, the committee provides Bar Exam writing clinics aimed at minority law students and law career conferences targeting minority high school students across the state. A minority clerkship program matches students with law firms and other organizations for summer intern programs.

In the late 1980s, the Minorities in the Profession Committee attracted statewide press coverage with a news conference unveiling a public service announcement featuring lawyer Len Elmore, a former University of Maryland basketball player who went on to play professional basketball. The PSAs, urging students to stay in school and consider law as a career, ran on a dozen television stations from the coast to the mountains.

That change in attitude must have seemed like an impossibility more than 50 years earlier in 1933 when Conrad O. Pearson, a black pioneer civil rights lawyer, successfully attacked the systematic exclusion of blacks from North Carolina juries.

Subsequent suits filed by Pearson and other black lawyers in the 1950s led to the desegregation of the UNC School of Law, graduate schools and undergraduate school. Under court order, J. Kenneth Lee, Harvey E. Beech Jr., Floyd McKissick Sr. and James Lassiter were admitted to UNC in June 1951. Harvey Beech of Kinston became the first black graduate of the UNC's law school in June 1952. In 1956, Henry E. Frye would become the first black student to enter the first-year class at the UNC law school.

In the 1960s and 1970s, Pearson and Julius Chambers attacked institutional racism, filing school desegregation cases, employment discrimination cases and public facilities discrimination cases. It was Chambers who filed the complaint in *Swann v. Charlotte-Mecklenburg School Board*, which led to the landmark 1971 U. S. Supreme Court decision on busing to achieve school integration.

Chambers' law partner James E. Ferguson II of Charlotte was a leader in the struggle for equal justice in North Carolina trial courts. Ferguson and Chambers joined with Adam Stein to form one of the earliest interracial law partnerships in the state in 1967. By 1973, the firm had 11 lawyers—six blacks and five whites.

In 1999, Ferguson led the NCBA's Race Relations Implementation Committee along with Durham native Allyson Duncan. Duncan was the first black woman to sit on the N.C. Court of Appeals, to serve as a commissioner on the N.C. Utilities Commission and to be appointed a law professor at N.C. Central University.

Duncan was aided in reaching these milestones by the previous generation of pioneer black women. In 1947, Elreta Alexander-Ralston became the first black woman to practice law in the courts of North Carolina, and in 1968, she became the first black woman in the United States to be elected as a District Court judge. In 1954, Annie Brown Kennedy became the second black woman to pass the North Carolina Bar exam and, in 1955, she and her husband, Harold, co-founded the Winston-Salem firm of Kennedy & Kennedy. Their twin sons are now partners in that firm. In 1982, Kennedy became the first black female elected to the N.C. General Assembly.

The first African-American elected to the General Assembly in the 20th century was Henry E. Frye, who was elected to the House in 1968 and to the Senate in 1980. He was also the first black justice on the N.C. Supreme Court. He became the first black chief justice in September 1999. Although he had graduated *summa cum laude* from N.C. A&T University in 1953, the Ellerbe native was not allowed to vote because a registrar claimed he did not pass the literacy test. Years later, Frye's first act as a legislator was to sponsor a bill to abolish the literacy test.

The first black to serve on an N.C. appellate court was Winston-Salem's Richard Erwin, who also was the first black U.S. District Court judge in the state. James A. Wynn Jr. of Raleigh was the first black to serve on both N.C. appellate courts. Clifton Johnson of Charlotte was the state's first black Chief District Court judge, the first black resident Superior Court judge, and the third black N.C. Court of Appeals judge.

Charles Becton, the second black N.C. Court of Appeals judge, is considered one of the nation's best trial advocacy skills teachers. During the last quarter century, Becton, as a lecturer at the UNC School of Law and the Duke University School of Law, has taught trial advocacy skills to more lawyers than any other person in the state.

Two legal scholars who each served as dean of N.C. Central University law school were Harry E. Groves and Charles Daye. Groves, the 1986 recipient of the N.C. Bar Association's John J. Parker Award, authored five books and more than 30 law review articles, including three influential articles on the "separate but equal" doctrine published before the Supreme Court's decision in *Brown v. Board of Education*. Both Groves and Daye also taught at the UNC School of Law. In 1972, Daye became the first black full-time law professor at UNC. Daye, who taught at UNC for 22 years, has authored two books and numerous law articles.

Many black attorneys have become dedicated public servants over the years and no one better fits that mold than Raleigh's Victor Boone, who won the NCBA's Outstanding Legal Services Attorney Award in 1986. A winner of numerous community service awards over the years, Boone has dedicated his entire career of more than 25 years to legal services for the poor.

While initially slow to admit blacks into membership, the North Carolina Bar Association now is an inclusive, umbrella organization for all attorneys in the state. Of the attorneys mentioned in this section, nine—Becton, Boone, Duncan, Erwin, Ferguson, Frye, Groves, Kennedy and Wynn—have served as a board member or a vice president of the North Carolina Bar Association.

A New Constitution for North Carolina

At the request of Gov. Daniel K. Moore, the North Carolina Bar Association joined with the North Carolina State Bar Council in appointing a 25-member commission to study the state Constitution and make recommendations to the Legislature and the Executive Department. Under the leadership of Justice Emery B. Denny, the commission — widely known as "the Denny Commission" — recommended a number of amendments to the Constitution, which were adopted by the voters in 1970.

Admitting African-Americans

One struggle within the North Carolina Bar Association during this period, which reflected the larger struggles of the civil rights movement at the time, was the admission of African-American members. Until a revision of its constitution in June 1966, the association limited membership to "any white person" who was a member of the State Bar in good standing.

African-Americans were not admitted to the law schools at Duke, the University of North Carolina or Wake Forest until the early 1950s and, even then, their numbers were few. Present-day North Carolina Central University began teaching law courses in 1939 and its law school was accredited by the American Bar Association in 1950. In the November 1958 issue, *BarNotes* had begun listing reports from the law schools at the University of North Carolina, Duke and Wake Forest. It was not until February 1972 that this section included a report from the North Carolina Central University's law school. Black attorneys from North Carolina Central, and from schools elsewhere who passed the State Bar examination, could practice law but were frequently not welcomed by the profession.

In the 1950s, J. Kenneth Lee of Greensboro and other black lawyers began applying for membership in the association but were always denied. In 1954, African-American attorneys formed the North Carolina Lawyers Association

Negro Gets Acceptance Of N.C. Bar

DURHAM (AP) — H. M. Michaux, the Negro attorney from Durham who has fought for 18 months to gain membership in the North Carolina Bar Association, won that acceptance Thursday, but his brother will still be excluded from the organization.

"It comes as much of a surprise to me as everybody else," Michaux said. "I'm very pleased and highly gratified that we are able to make some progress."

Michaux said he received the notification by mail. "I received a membership certificate and card, and a letter of acceptance," he said. "At the same time, I received a rejection for my brother."

The brother, Eric C. Michaux, is a captain in the Air Force judge advocate general corps, the legal branch of the military. Both men are licensed attorneys.

Michaux' acceptance would apparently bring the number of Negroes in the bar association to four. "As of now, I only know of three others," he said.

No reason has ever been given for the refusal of the bar association to accept the brothers, Michaux said. Eric Michaux' Air Force status has nothing to do with his rejection, his brother said.

Eric Michaux is a graduate of the Duke University Law School. And when the Bar Association refused to admit him, it sparked the withdrawal of the school from the organization.

H. M. Michaux is a North Carolina College law graduate, but Duke took up his cause along with his brother's and has urged the admittance of both to the association.

The racial integration of the North Carolina Bar Association warranted media attention in the mid-1960s.

The civil rights movement of the '50s and '60s affected the legal profession in profound ways. Shown here are anti-busing demonstrators in front of the home of Judge James B. McMillan in Charlotte in the mid-1960s. McMillan was president of the Bar Association in 1960-1961.

JULIUS CHAMBERS

Julius L. Chambers, pictured here during law school at the University of North Carolina at Chapel Hill.

An attorney of the highest caliber and one of North Carolina's most devoted public servants, Julius Chambers represents the best of the legal profession. He grew up in Mount Gilead, and graduated from high school the same month the U.S. Supreme Court decided *Brown v. Board of Education*, the landmark decision mandating racial desegregation of public schools.

Chambers served as student government president and graduated *summa cum laude* from North Carolina Central University. After obtaining a master's degree in history from Michigan State University, he entered law school at the University of North Carolina as one of the few black students, graduating in 1962 ranked first in his class. He continued his legal education at Columbia University, obtaining a master's in law degree, and thereafter worked briefly for the NAACP Legal Defense and Education Fund in New York. Within a year, he was back in North Carolina, opening a one-person office in a cold-water walk-up in Charlotte, and beginning a legal career that would lead him to become one of North Carolina's greatest lawyers.

The complexity of the cases Julius Chambers undertook when he came to Charlotte is astounding for a lawyer so new to practice. Within his first year, he filed the complaint in *Swann v. Charlotte-Mecklenburg School Board*, which led to the landmark 1971 U. S. Supreme Court decision on busing to achieve school integration. The filing of the *Swann* complaint was followed by numerous

ground-breaking, high-profile civil rights cases, including *Griggs v. Duke Power* (1971) and *Albemarle Paper Co. v. Moody* (1974), two of the leading, early Supreme Court cases setting standards for interpreting employment discrimination provisions under Title VII of the Civil Rights Act.

Chambers' work required not only exceptional legal ability, but tremendous courage. He received numerous threats to his life. His car, home and office were all either bombed or burned. By 1967, he had joined with two other attorneys to form one of the state's earliest racially integrated law firms. Their work soon expanded to many other parts of the state, and by the time Julius Chambers left the firm to become director-counsel of the NAACP Legal Defense and Education Fund in 1984, the firm had attained national prominence as a leading force for civil rights and social justice.

Julius Chambers stayed as director-counsel of the Legal Defense Fund for eight years, during which he continued his work as an advocate for civil rights of racial minorities and expanded his reputation as an attorney of national stature. In 1992, he was persuaded to return to North Carolina to accept the chancellorship of his alma mater, North Carolina Central University, where he has served as an educational leader of great tenacity and vision.

Chambers has received numerous honors and has been prominently promoted as a candidate for appointment to the U.S. Supreme Court. In his work as an advocate, a civic and professional leader, and as a public servant, Chambers has epitomized the professionalism of the lawyer. In addition to his other public accolades, the North Carolina Bar Association has awarded him the prestigious John J. Parker Award, inducted him into the General Practice Hall of Fame, and chosen him as a Justice Fund honoree.

(later named the North Carolina Association of Black Lawyers). Continued rejection of black applicants brought increasingly unfavorable public comment and pressure from more liberal members of the association and its board of governors.

The struggle over integrating the association received much attention in the press when the "liberal" faction of the Duke University School of Law began to apply pressure to admit qualified black applicants to membership. In December 1966, a majority of the Duke law faculty voted to discontinue support of the association's activities "until such time as all applicants are accepted for membership in the North Carolina Bar Association without discrimination based on race." In a statement to the N.C. Press Association, President William F. Womble responded to the Duke vote:

N.C. Rep. Henry M. Michaux Jr., left, and NCCU School of Law Dean Harry E. Groves, right, welcome Judge Leon Higginbotham to a late 1970s' event at Central.

I agree with the proposition that applications for membership in the North Carolina Bar Association should be considered and voted on without regard to race. On the other hand, I regret that the Duke Law Faculty has seen fit to withdraw its support of our Continuing Legal Education program.... I hope that we shall be able to work things out so that the cordial relationship heretofore existing between the North Carolina Bar Association and Duke Law School may be resumed.

By early 1966, liberal and moderate leaders of the North Carolina Bar Association had already concluded that the time had come to take positive action on the race issue. First, a majority of the board and then the membership concluded that the time had come to remove racial restrictions on membership. In June, the NCBA's constitution was amended to remove the "white only" clause. Even then, in October 1966, brothers Eric C. and Henry M. Michaux Jr. were interviewed by the membership committee but denied membership, apparently because they were African-Americans. "Getting out front" on the integration issue was a difficult step for some of the board members to take.

Not until April 1967 did the board of governors admit Julius Chambers and Henry Frye as the first African-American members of the North Carolina Bar Association (after denying them membership at an earlier meeting). To many, both inside and outside the legal profession, the NCBA appeared slow to integrate, but its action in April made it the first state bar association in the South to admit a "Negro." Black membership in the association grew slowly at first, with most black attorneys continuing to find membership in the North Carolina Association of Black Lawyers.

"Tabitha's Daughters"
Women in the Profession

Another area of concern among membership, although one fought more quietly and without attendant controversy, was gender-based. A few women had practiced law in North Carolina since Tabitha Anne Holton began practicing in Guilford County, but the number of women attorneys remained small. Although Lillian Rowe Frye was admitted to the North Carolina Bar Association in 1913, women members remained few when considered as a percentage of those who were practicing law in the state.

During the 1950s and 1960s, the number of women in the legal profession in North Carolina gradually increased. While some women found a hostile environment in certain localities, others began to make significant roles for themselves not only in the practice of law but also in the various legal organizations. Beginning in local organizations, women served in various offices. In 1958, Mrs. Winifred T. Wells was president of the Duplin County Bar Association and continued serving in that capacity throughout the 1960s. In 1962, Mrs. Arch H. Schoch was president of the High Point Bar Association.

The number of women members of the North Carolina Bar Association gradually increased in the 1950s and 1960s as well. By the mid-1950s, a few women were serving on association committees on calendar control. In the same year, Ann Llewllyn Green of Concord and Judge Susie Sharp of Reidsville were members of a committee on family law. Judge Sharp was also a sustaining member of the association in that and subsequent years. By the late 1950s, several women served on local committees on membership and on the committees doing research on state-owned real property.

North Carolina Supreme Court Chief Justice Henry E. Frye has been a member of the North Carolina Bar Association for more than 30 years.

SUSIE M. SHARP

When Susie Marshall Sharp launched her career in law, women were not allowed to serve on juries in North Carolina. In 1926, she was the only woman in her law class at the University of North Carolina. Afterward, as an appellate lawyer, she was the sole woman in a courtroom full of men.

Legend has it that she was such a curiosity in Rockingham County where she practiced for 20 years, that an old native of the area creakily climbed the stairs to her office just to see what a "lady lawyer" looked like. Sharp took the attention in stride, just as she took in stride all the challenges and opportunities life offered.

The oldest of 10 children, and despite obligations at home, Sharp still managed to graduate from high school in 1924 as salutatorian of her class. After two years at the North Carolina College for Women (now UNC-Greensboro), she entered law school at the University of North Carolina in 1926 where she became an editor of the *North Carolina Law Review*, a member of the Order of the Coif and, in 1929, a law graduate (LL. B. with honors).

After graduation, she returned to Reidsville where she had been raised since age seven when she and her family moved from Rocky Mount. She began a two decade-long practice with her father, James Merritt Sharp, in the firm of Sharp and Sharp. In 1939, she was appointed Reidsville's city attorney, the first town attorney in the state's history. In 1948, Kerr Scott, in his gubernatorial bid, appointed Sharp his campaign manager for Rockingham County.

After he was elected governor, Kerr Scott appointed Susie Sharp to the Superior Court—the first woman judge in the then 364-year history of the state. It was the beginning of a 30-year career on the bench. For the next 13 years, Judge Sharp served as Special Judge of the Superior Court of North Carolina. During that time, she traveled the state, holding court in 64 counties from Currituck to Cherokee, returning home only on the weekends to be with her family.

In 1962, Susie Sharp was appointed associate justice of the North Carolina Supreme Court. Later that year, she was elected to complete an unexpired term and, in 1966, she was elected to serve a full eight-year term.

In 1974, Sharp again made history when she became the first woman in the United States to be elected chief justice of a state supreme court, garnering 74 percent of the vote, the highest percentage of any statewide candidate that year.

She was known for setting and keeping high standards of moral and judicial conduct in the state's judiciary and successfully advocated for a 1980 constitutional amendment requiring that all judges be lawyers.

During her long and distinguished career, Justice Sharp received many accolades. In 1976 she won a special award for Outstanding Legal Achievement from the New York Women's Bar Association. That same year, she was named in a *Time* magazine cover story as one of the 12 women of the year for 1975. The magazine called her a "trail blazer" with a "reputation as both a compassionate jurist and an incisive legal scholar."

Sharp died in 1996 at the age of 88.

Susie M. Sharp served as the first female chief justice of the North Carolina Supreme Court from 1975-1979.

In the early 1960s, women assumed leadership roles in executive posts in the North Carolina Bar Association. Judge Susie Sharp was elected vice president for 1962-63 and again in 1967-68. Winifred T. Wells served a three-year term on the board of governors beginning in 1971. Progress was slow, but the number of women in the association was increasing and their leadership roles were growing. In 1970, women attorneys comprised only 3 percent of the lawyers practicing in the United States. If projections are accurate, women will comprise 40 percent of all attorneys in North Carolina as the Bar Association enters its second century.

Recent efforts to make the NCBA more broadly based have succeeded in increasing female and minority membership and participation. The newly organized Hispanic Lawyers Committee and the location of the offices of the North Carolina Association of Black Lawyers in the new Bar Center are points of pride for association leadership.

The Early '70s: Expanding Membership and Services

Storey continued to lead the expansion of the activities of the association through the 1970s. Efforts to expand membership and services followed patterns set in his earlier years with an occasional outstanding accomplishment. Efforts to get merit selection of judges continued. Salary increases were sought for trial and appellate judges.

In 1972, the Bar Association and State Bar, working together under the name "The Lawyers of North Carolina, Inc." began a joint public relations project designed to foster a better understanding of the law, the courts and the legal profession. Television and radio stations were furnished with 30-second and one-minute public service "spots," some of them adapted from Dr. Robert E. Lee's earlier "This Is the Law" newspaper column, which later became the namesake for a series of pamphlets distributed free to the public. The voluntary project, funded by contributions from the state's attorneys, proved very successful in informing the public about the profession.

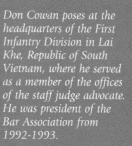

Don Cowan poses at the headquarters of the First Infantry Division in Lai Khe, Republic of South Vietnam, where he served as a member of the offices of the staff judge advocate. He was president of the Bar Association from 1992-1993.

A New Law School for North Carolina

In the early 1970s Norman A. Wiggins, president of Campbell College, began to discuss the possibility of establishing a law school at the college. Wiggins, a former Wake Forest University law professor, felt that there was a genuine need for another law school in the state. The Baptist State Convention's Council on Christian Higher Education began studying the proposal in October 1974, and the General Board of the Baptist State Convention authorized the Campbell College Board of Trustees to establish the program in July 1975. The school opened in the fall of 1976.

In 1967, Richard Vinroot of Charlotte enlisted in the United States Army after graduating from UNC's law school. He received a Bronze Star for distinguished service in Vietnam on October 23, 1968.

Throughout the Vietnam era, North Carolina lawyers continued to answer the nation's call to service in the armed forces.

From its inception the law school at Campbell University envisioned a mission for itself different from those of other law schools in the state. The school identified itself as a distinctly Christian institution which seeks to reflect the Judeo-Christian tradition and communicate a Christian world view. Dr. Wiggins and many of the early proponents saw the law school as attracting students who wished to practice in North Carolina's rural areas and small towns.

Within a few years, the new law school in Buies Creek would become a significant contributor to the legal community in North Carolina and establish itself as a major player in the delivery of legal services to the citizens of the state.

Heading into the Fourth Quarter of the 20th Century

Storey was constantly planning for the future in many ways. He ran a tight organization with a limited staff, but he hired people who were devoted to the law and the aims of the association. Perhaps one of his greatest gifts to the future of the Bar Association was the hiring of Allan B. Head in 1973. Head came to a staff of only six but was immediately charged with adding sections to meet needs of particular groups of members. He also helped identify the space needs

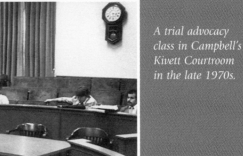
A trial advocacy class in Campbell's Kivett Courtroom in the late 1970s.

On November 5, 1975, a press conference announced the founding of the Campbell College School of Law. Pictured left to right are Board Chairman Dr. J. Leon Rumley, University President Dr. Norman A. Wiggins, Founding Law School Dean F. Leary Davis and contributor Roger Page.

that led to planning a move from the NCBA's headquarters on Wade Avenue. It is said that one test of a good executive is the provision of a competent and devoted successor. Whether or not he knew that he was doing so, Bill Storey passed this examination with high marks. Head would become executive director in 1981 following Storey's death.

The mid-1970s were a time of development and expansion for the North Carolina Bar Association. Many of the extensive programs of the association began or expanded during this period. The practice of law had changed greatly. Not only could applicants no longer substitute the "reading of law" under an attorney for a law school education; they were now required to update their training with CLE courses. While North Carolina still had one of the lowest per capita ratios of lawyers of any state, it had one of the more active and progressive bar associations.

Senator Sam hangs his shingle in Morganton after his retirement from the U.S. Senate in 1975.

PROFESSIONALISM

One of the highest goals of the North Carolina Bar Association since its inception has been the promotion of professionalism, a term which most lawyers revere, but which often seems to defy definition. Perhaps professionalism is best understood by example, and historically it has been through example that our heritage of professionalism has been maintained. There are many North Carolina lawyers who have served their fellow lawyers as models of the ideals of professionalism. Those mentioned below are but a few examples.

The Ideal of Service

Samuel J. Ervin Jr. of Morganton exemplified the professional ideal of public service to a high degree. He served his country in the U.S. Army in World War I, receiving the Distinguished Service Cross, Purple Heart with Oak Leaf Cluster, Silver Star and French Fourrage. After admission to the bar in 1919, he served as a member of the North Carolina General Assembly and in 1937 became a North Carolina Superior Court judge.

In 1946, he was appointed to the U.S. Congress and in 1948 became a member of the North Carolina Supreme Court. From 1954 until he retired in 1975, he served as U.S. senator from North Carolina, distinguishing himself in 1973-74 as chair of the Senate Select Committee on Presidential Campaign Activities investigating President Richard Nixon's involvement in the cover-up of the Watergate burglary. In that capacity and in his retirement, he became a national model of wit, wisdom and professional service.

The Ideal of Integrity

Judge James B. McMillan of Charlotte was known throughout his career as a lawyer of consummate skill and intelligence and a wise and courageous judge, who decided some of the most difficult cases of his day. But above all, for those who practiced with him and against him, and who appeared before him in federal court, he was admired as a man of the highest integrity. One of his law clerks stated simply, "I can say without reservation that he truly is the finest person I have ever known." Judge McMillan's integrity was not based upon a complex philosophy but upon simple principle. With characteristic wit, he once summed up that principle in a paraphrase from statesman Chancey Depew: "Always do right; it will gratify a few people and astonish the rest. Sometimes, it's hard to tell what's right, but if you're trying, you're going to do right more often than otherwise."

The Ideal of Commitment

Charles Becton of Durham, former judge on the North Carolina Court of Appeals and one of the state's leading trial attorneys, has served as a model of professional commitment to excellence for countless lawyers who have practiced with him or against him, or attended one of his many practical skills classes.

He is committed to the profession, to his clients and to the law, and he practices his commitment by giving, as he says, 150 percent. "[I] realize that few lawyers ... will cross as many T's and dot as many I's in preparation as I do. ... I do that so I can sleep at night," he said.

But commitment for Charles Becton is more than a work ethic. It is a commitment to the law itself, to jurisprudence, which includes a vision of the future of the law. To be the best, Becton warns, lawyers and judges must be able "to realize the evolving nature of the law. ... [Success] is not ... how much money you make, but how people respect you as a lawyer."

The Ideal of Civility

James K. Dorsett Jr. of Raleigh is recognized among fellow members of the Wake County bar as a gentleman in his treatment of judges, other lawyers and members of the public. For Dorsett, courtesy is not merely an obligation owed to the court and fellow lawyers or a tool for success as an advocate. It is a personal commitment and a way of life. And it includes a sense of honor in one's behavior toward others as well as courtesy. Where civility is practiced, Dorsett says:

> [There is] a very high level of trust between lawyers. ... [T]here is still the strong sense of being a good adversary to your fellow lawyer. That is, ... you go to the courtroom and contest a case strongly, but without rancor or dislike and without spoiling a friendship. ... So long as the lawyers [are] not uncivil, that [makes] a great deal of difference.

The Ideal of Competence

Since her entry into the UNC School of Law, where she was the first female editor of the law review, Doris R. Bray of Greensboro has been a model of competence as a lawyer because she consistently brings a high degree of skill, attention and judgment to her work. For her, these are not abstract virtues. They relate to her duties as a professional, first among which are her duties to her clients.

Lawyers owe their very best efforts to clients, Bray says, because at its deepest level, the lawyer-client relationship is based on a sacred trust. And lawyers earn that trust by placing the interests of the client first and using their skills in the client's behalf to the best of their ability. "My clients always come first," she says. "If it's a choice of what's good for the law firm and what's good for the client, the client always wins. That's my philosophy."

Pride in the Profession

Wade Smith of Raleigh views the law as a calling of the highest order and sees his life's work as a sacred commitment to that calling. It is, he says, "a great honor to be a lawyer." The lawyers of his generation had high ideals, he said. "They went to law school because it was a way to make the world better," he said. "The lawyers I work with in my firm and this region of the world are the best group of people. They're the most fun. They're the most intelligent. And I think it's still true that probably the best young women and men we produce aspire to be lawyers. It is a great profession."

Hundreds of conventioneers participated in the 5K road race at the Grove Park Inn in June 1979.

∞

"In Full Stride"
1974-1999

At times in 1974, all of North Carolina seemed to hold its collective breath, as a constitutional crisis gripped the nation. One of the state's finest, Samuel J. Ervin Jr., presided over the Senate Select Committee on Presidential Campaign Activities' investigation of abuses of power by President Richard M. Nixon. In June 1974, when former presidential counsel John Dean told the Ervin Watergate committee that the president and his aides were deeply involved in an illegal cover-up of the Watergate crimes, the tide began to turn against the Nixon administration. On August 9, 1974, Nixon resigned the office of the presidency. Gerald R. Ford, whom Nixon had chosen as his vice president in October 1973, was sworn in as the new president. The nation was secure. The Constitution was preserved. On several occasions, Sam Ervin described our national charter in these terms:

Justices William Bobbitt and Susie Sharp enjoy the formality of the 80th annual meeting banquet at the Myrtle Beach Hilton.

> The Founding Fathers dreamed the Earth's most magnificent dream. They dreamed they could enshrine a government of laws conforming to the eternal truths taught by history in a written Constitution, [a document] they intended to last for the ages and to constitute 'a law for rulers and people alike' at all times and under all circumstances.

The year 1974 also saw the North Carolina Bar Association "taking a deep breath" and moving forward. The association looked back at all that it had done over the past two decades, took stock of what remained to be done, and began a new era of professional and public service, with Allan B. Head in his first full year as executive secretary under Executive Director William Storey. Building on an already strong foundation, the leadership of the association continued to expand current programs, develop new services, and improve communication with the membership, the public and the legal profession. If any inspiration were needed, the NCBA's leaders needed only to look a couple of miles to the east, where one of the association's own, Judge Susie Marshall Sharp, was about to be sworn in as chief justice of the North Carolina Supreme Court, the first popularly elected female chief justice in the nation. In her acceptance speech, she reminded members of the bar and all citizens that they must "defend the rule of law, without which there can be no freedom."

Charlie Younce, Woody Harrison and future president Tony Hornthal were active tennis tournament participants in 1976.

Fun, food and recreation were common ingredients for all annual meetings during the '70s.

Future Chief Justice Joseph Branch presided at this Bar Center meeting where the new legal services of North Carolina structure was under discussion in 1976.

Closing a Breach in the Bar

The year 1974 also marked a turning point in improved relations between the North Carolina Bar Association and the North Carolina State Bar. NCBA President Walter F. Brinkley joined Executive Secretary William Storey in working with North Carolina State Bar President Ralph Ramsey Jr. to further cooperation and collaborative efforts between the two organizations.

The groups' relationship had begun to deteriorate after the hiring of Charles W. Daniel as executive secretary in 1953. Cannon, of course, remained as secretary-treasurer of the State Bar, but the Bar Association's files — which had been kept by Cannon in the Justice Building — were removed to Daniel's new office in the Capital Club Building in Raleigh. Relations became so bad that in January 1956 the State Bar Council adopted a resolution that the secretary of the State Bar would no longer be an *ex officio* member of the NCBA Executive Committee, as provided for in the association bylaws.

As a gesture of good will toward the association, Ramsey, the 1974 State Bar president, authorized the NCBA to use one of four American Bar Association delegate appointments allotted to the incorporated bar. Ramsey and the State Bar Council also endorsed the association's legal services report, which eventually led to the creation of Legal Services of North Carolina, Inc.

For its part, the leadership of the Bar Association extended a hand of friendship several years earlier. In 1967, William F. Womble, outgoing president of the Bar Association, had extended an invitation to the officers of the State Bar to attend the NCBA's board meetings. The State Bar Council responded by extending an invitation to the association president and president-elect to attend all meetings of the bar council. The jointly sponsored "Lawyers of North Carolina" public information program, begun in 1972, was another confidence-building measure on the way toward healing the rift between the two organizations.

NCBA President Walter Brinkley (1974-75), who did so much to build that relationship, described the organizations' missions in these terms:

> The North Carolina State Bar, as a governmental agency with mandatory membership, financed by license fees which are imposed by law, should perform the governmental functions which are prescribed by statute and which relate to the regulation of the bar and its members. By leaving the non-regulatory functions to the voluntary membership of the North Carolina Bar Association, a greater flexibility can be achieved without the danger of imposing itself upon members who may not agree with the position taken by the organization, and are not free to terminate their membership in it.

A "boyish" Allan B. Head, NCBA executive director, meets with President Robert F. Baker of Durham, left, and President-Elect Charles L. Fulton of Raleigh in 1983. The president, president-elect and executive director serve as the senior leadership of the association.

Throughout the '70s and '80s, attendance at the annual Practical Skills Course skyrocketed as more lawyers joined the profession. Hundreds of lawyers attended this session at the North Carolina State University McKimmon Center in Raleigh in the early 1980s.

Since membership in the North Carolina Bar Association is voluntary and tax money is not involved in its support, the organization is free to act politically and programmatically. Other states which now have "unified" bar organizations are looking to the North Carolina model because of the problems inherit when mandatory dues are used to pay for charitable endeavors and other "non-regulatory related projects" in a unitary bar organization.

Expanding Membership Services

If the North Carolina Bar Association started to "take off" in the mid-1950s, it was in "full stride" by the mid-1970s. Energy that had been focused on the preparation, publication and distribution of the three volumes of *North Carolina Pattern Jury Instructions* (in cooperation with the N.C. Conference of Superior Court Judges), substantial salary increases for North Carolina's trial and appellate judges, and the *North Carolina Rules of Appellate Procedure*, now shifted to the expansion of member services.

The N.C. Bar Association, through its Bar Foundation, quietly but quickly moved from four live continuing legal education programs in 1975 to more than 40 live programs in 1985. Having utilized video as a CLE distribution technique since 1969, the association, in 1983, was the first CLE provider in North Carolina to utilize a teleconferencing network, and, in 1984, joined two national networks by satellite for the distribution of CLE.

In March 1988, a national attendance record of more than 2,800 North Carolina lawyers attending one program at the same time in 26 different sites was set via a new Community College Satellite Network. More recently, CLE publications on CD-ROM are being introduced, as are plans for online CLE. The association's longtime commitment to provide convenient, high-quality programs at the lowest possible cost is still as real as it has always been.

A constant during this period was thousands of volunteer speakers, all willing to share their time and talents with other North Carolina practitioners. An impressive line of CLE Committee chairs provided leaders to a flagship that knew no course other than "full steam ahead." Leaders such as Jim Craighill, Frank Wyatt, Bob Elster, Jasper Cummings, Edgar Love, Don Cowan, Alfred Adams, John Doyle, Clark Brewer and Tom Waldrep helped establish the association as the major (and preferred, based on market share statistics provided by the North Carolina State Bar) provider of CLE in North Carolina in 1999.

A membership survey conducted in the 1980s ranked the publication *BarNotes* as the second most valued membership service behind only CLE. Since its inception in 1953, *BarNotes* has changed its size, shape, scope, frequency and finally its name to *North Carolina Lawyer*. The publication, which won more than 20 national and regional awards in the 1990s, is distributed as a membership service seven times a year.

President E. James Moore of North Wilkesboro waits for his cues, kicking off what was to be the nation's largest legal telecast in history. The statewide live satellite CLE program, held on March 4, 1988, drew 2,850 attorneys from 26 sites. Louis Bledsoe, left, and John Lunsford, right, assisted with the presentation on professional responsibility.

Allan B. Head, born in 1944 to E. Putnam and "Skip" Head, began his career as executive secretary with the North Carolina Bar Association in 1973 and has served as executive director since 1981.

Prior to coming to the NCBA, Head, an Atlanta native, served as an officer for nearly four years with the U.S. Army Security Agency in Kassel and Augsburg, Germany. He received his undergraduate degree from Wake Forest University in 1966 and his law degree from Wake Forest in 1969.

Since coming to the NCBA, Head has led the association through its greatest period of growth in the more than 100-year history of the NCBA. Membership has grown from 3,500 to more than 11,500 members while the budget has grown from less than $200,000 to more than $6 million. The staff has grown from six full-time employees to more than 50.

"It's amazing when you look at how far this association has come since Allan arrived," said Greensboro attorney Larry Sitton, who served as president of the NCBA in 1998-99. "It is Allan that keeps the association running smoothly, and motivates and encourages the great staff he has helped bring on board. Allan is the glue that holds it all together."

Head was the major force behind the addition of sections in the late '70s while still the executive secretary (what is now called assistant executive director). In 1981, the year he became executive director following the death of Bill Storey, there were eight sections. There were 25 at the close of the century. The number of divisions went from one (Young Lawyers) to four with the addition of Law Students, Senior Lawyers and Legal Assistants.

Head was the impetus for establishing the NCBA's statewide Lawyer Referral Service in 1975. The service assisted about 2,000 callers a year at the beginning but now receives more than 50,000 calls a year.

In addition, Head pushed continuing legal education advancements. There were four live NCBA-sponsored CLE programs in 1973 compared to 370 live and video programs in 1998. Aided by technology, the association maintains its position as the major provider of CLE to North Carolina lawyers.

Head was instrumental in the building process which resulted in the association's third Bar Center, which many recognize as "the best bar center in the country." The 50,000-square-foot building on Weston Parkway in Cary was a three-year project for Head from concept to completion. Each year, the Bar Center gets more than 10,000 visits from lawyers who attend CLE programs and other division, section and committee meetings.

Improvements to the NCBA Annual Meeting, including making it more family-oriented, are due to Head's input. He and his wife, Patti, have three children—David, Darryl and Jayme—born from 1969 to 1976. The three children joked as adults about how their memories of family vacations were always bar conventions.

Head's volunteer service is a driving force in his life. An elder at White Memorial Presbyterian Church in Raleigh, Head spent a week of his vacation each year from 1989-1999 leading senior high school students from the church on a home repair ministry in the Appalachian Mountains. In addition, he is an active volunteer for the YMCA on the local, regional and national levels. He became involved with the organization through its Y-Indian Guides and Y-Indian Princesses programs. He was a board member of the Capital Area YMCA from 1981 to 1992 and served as president from 1992 to 1995. He chaired the statewide organization for two years and served as a member of the national board of directors for four years. He serves as a member of the national YMCA's Legal Affairs Committee.

Head has been the field announcer for Raleigh's Broughton High School football games for many years. Prior to that, while both sons played, he moved the chains on the sidelines. In addition, he served as a spotter for legendary field announcer C.A. Dillon at N.C. State University football games and later he became field announcer for Wake Forest football.

An athlete in college himself, Head held a school record for many years at Wake Forest as a hurdler. He enjoys jogging and water skiing, and spends as much time as possible at the family's vacation home, "HeadQuarters," at Lake Gaston.

Known as an efficient and effective leader, Head has developed an interest and expertise in "meeting management and leadership for lawyers." Besides speaking annually on this topic for the association's Bar Leadership Institute, he has developed an energetic presentation that he has delivered upon request around the country.

Always emphasizing service to the members, Head is also an effective manager of volunteer resources. His commitment to the legal profession is perhaps best exemplified by the following well-known quote:

"It is only through the power of association that those of any calling exercise due influence in their community."

According to many, it is only through the leadership of Allan Head that the N.C. Bar Association has been able to accomplish all that it has for the legal community.

Allan B. Head has served as executive director since 1981.

A 21st Century Home

The original home of the Bar Association, constructed in 1962 at 1025 Wade Avenue, was a two-story custom-built, 5,000-square-foot Bar Center. By 1983, in the midst of enormous membership demand for increased services, the association outgrew this building and purchased the 1312 Annapolis Drive building (directly across the street) which became the second Bar Center. This home had as its centerpiece a huge atrium with offices and meeting rooms opening on to the atrium, which was frequently used as a reception and hospitality area. This Bar Center served the association well, until again the demand for increased services (program and administrative staff required) overcame the capacity of the 20,000 square-foot facility. Limited meeting rooms, offices, storage space and parking caused the Bar Association to search for yet another new home in 1991.

NCBA President Rhoda Bryan Billings appointed a site selection committee, chaired by Jim Talley, to search for the ideal location for a new Bar Center to accommodate the anticipated growth of the North Carolina Bar Association and Foundation well into the next century. The ultimate decision, recommended to and adopted by the board, was to move to a nine-acre site in Cary on the edge of Lake Crabtree and near Interstate 40 and the Raleigh-Durham International Airport. The decision to leave Raleigh and move "out-of-town" was controversial. There were those who suggested strongly that leaving a close proximity to state government was a mistake. The board, however, was committed to a more convenient and easily accessible location for the majority of the association's membership, which was located west of Raleigh.

The new site would comfortably accommodate a 50,000-square-foot building with more than 260 parking spaces. Talley, and later Gerald Thornton, chaired the Building Committee which, with tremendous vision by the then NCBA Officers and Board of Governors, brought into being a state-of-the-art building with the finest instructional facility (200-seat auditorium) for lawyers and judges in the state. The $6.5 million project on Weston Parkway was completed and occupied in August 1994. United States Supreme Court Chief Justice William Rehnquist presided at the dedication of the building on October 21, 1994, and remarked, "This is more than just a nice building. It is the cornerstone for the 21st century upon which the North Carolina Bar will build."

For the next five years, the new Bar Center was the newest and most modern bar facility in America, serving each year more than 10,000 lawyers and judges attending CLE programs, and division, section or committee meetings. The association, which has leased up to 30 percent of the building, has had room to grow. Notable tenants have included Lawyers Mutual Liability Insurance Company and its Lawyers Insurance Agency, the Wake County and Tenth Judicial District Bar Associations, the North Carolina Association of Black Lawyers and the North Carolina Association of Defense Attorneys. The location of these professional colleagues has added to the spirit of cooperation, mutual support and respect within the profession.

Important to note is the fact that all three NCBA buildings have been owned by the North Carolina Bar Foundation, with the association as a tenant, thus allowing charitable gifts to the foundation. Another interesting fact is staff size relative to growth, and the need for additional space. When originally occupied in 1962, the Wade Avenue Bar Center housed five staff members; when originally occupied in 1983, the Annapolis Drive Bar Center housed 20 staff members, and when originally occupied in 1994, the Weston Parkway Bar Center housed more than 45 staff members. By the end of the century, the association and its foundation had 55 permanent employees.

Periodic long-range planning efforts have helped the association maintain a steady course. President Elizabeth L. Quick (1997-98) led the most recent effort prior to being named president-elect. The final draft of the association's new mission statement is shown on the flip chart.

U.S. Supreme Court Chief Justice William Rehnquist was the keynote speaker at the dedication of the new N.C. Bar Center on October 21, 1994. Rehnquist congratulates NCBA Executive Director Allan B. Head on this major accomplishment.

The North Carolina Bar Center has been the home of the North Carolina Bar Association and the North Carolina Bar Foundation since 1994.

Social gatherings such as this oyster roast are part of the quarterly NCBA Board of Governors meetings which are held at various locations. Bar leaders Chuck Neely, Norfleet Pruden, Eddie Poe and Jack Lewis enjoyed the waterfront setting at the Spring 1996 meeting in Charleston.

Outgoing President James M. Talley Jr. of Charlotte passes the gavel to President John S. Stevens of Asheville in 1995. Passing the gavel is an annual tradition among bar presidents.

Providing Legal Services for North Carolinians

"Need a lawyer and don't know one?" was the motto for Jim Earnhardt's Lawyer Referral Committee in 1974-75. Thousands of middle-income North Carolinians did not know how to find a lawyer. Opposition to the concept came primarily from those who thought this was "just another opportunity for lawyers to advertise." A divided NCBA Board of Governors nonetheless authorized a statewide toll-free referral service "to help make quality legal services more readily available to greater numbers of people."

Sponsored by the Bar Association in cooperation with the North Carolina Department of Human Resources, the program began in January 1976. In its first year of operation, this nationally recognized public service referred more than 2,000 cases. In 1998, staff counselors received more than 52,000 telephone calls and made nearly 50,000 referrals to North Carolina lawyers in every corner of the state.

Equal access to justice has been more than a goal for the North Carolina Bar Association. It has been, and is, a passion. Ensuring that adequate legal services are delivered to North Carolina's poor is one of the issues that requires and receives constant recommitment by the leadership and membership of the association.

Down through the years, lawyers have always helped those less fortunate with their legal problems — it's a part of "the calling." However, in the '50s and '60s, staffed legal services offices began to appear in a few metropolitan areas. Although many lawyers recognized that the legal needs of North Carolina's poorer citizens were not being met, there were those who did not support a more centralized, government-funded delivery system for North Carolina. In 1974, NCBA President Walter Brinkley appointed a Legal Aid Study Committee, chaired by William "Bill" Thorp, to "find out where the poor are, what their legal problems are and the type of legal aid that would best meet their needs."

By 1976, with significant leadership provided by Thorp and soon-to-be Chief Justice Joseph Branch, a comprehensive study and report by the association resulted in the creation of a new, consolidated system for the delivery of legal services in North Carolina. It became known as Legal Services of North Carolina — a confederation of offices that ultimately served, with the help of three independent programs, the poor in all 100 counties. Major funding for the establishment and work of Legal Services of North Carolina came from the federal government.

In recent years additional funding sources (notably IOLTA and the North Carolina Legislature) have helped supplement the federal funds for a total in 1999 of more than $8 million per year. The funding was never enough, however. In 1983, the Bar Association organized the pro bono efforts of North Carolina lawyers via the highly successful Pro Bono Project, which recruits and activates individual North Carolina lawyers, law firms and local bars to give more free time to assist North Carolina's less fortunate. By 1999, this effort had

ABA President Roberta C. Ramo (1995-1996) came to North Carolina in late 1995. Here she visits with, left to right, Past President James K. Dorsett Jr., President John S. Stevens and later ABA House of Delegates Chair A.P. Carlton Jr.

resulted in an organized panel of more than 3,000 lawyers voluntarily donating thousands of hours of service each year. Leaders in establishing the success of Legal Services of North Carolina were Joe Moore, Walt Brinkley, Oz Ayscue, Jim Talley and Don Cowan — all presidents of the Bar Association — to mention only a few. The continued concern and support for legal services by the association was shown in 1995 by the appointment of a joint North Carolina State Bar/North Carolina Bar Association Commission on the Delivery of Civil Legal Services. The initial report of this commission resulted in the reorganization of Legal Services of North Carolina and an ongoing oversight initiative to ensure an effective and economical delivery of legal services to North Carolina's poor.

Meeting the Need for Liability Insurance

In a voluntary membership organization, the challenge is always to provide meaningful member service, and the agenda is not always clear. But when the needs of members were known, the association responded. Never was the need more obvious than in the mid-'70s, when the lack of available and affordable professional liability insurance for lawyers caused a national crisis. North Carolina lawyers turned to their association, and the Bar Association responded in what was one of its finest hours. The goal was to establish a North Carolina lawyer-owned, operated and controlled professional liability insurance company. The project was initiated on October 14, 1977 with a capitalization drive that had to raise $1 million in guaranty certificate sales—no small sum in those days. A statewide network of leaders was recruited.

Under the able leadership of John Q. Beard and the strong support of Executive Vice President Bill Storey, the campaign asked for $400 from every young lawyer (36 years of age or younger) and $700 from all other lawyers. The members quickly responded, and within six months the goal was met. Lawyers Mutual Liability Insurance Company of North Carolina was the first lawyers' captive insurance company in the nation. Authorized by the NCBA Board of Governors in 1978, the company began issuing policies on May 1, 1978. LMLIC, with assets of more than $39 million, by 1999 insured more than 70 percent of North Carolina lawyers in private practice. The company's aggressive risk management and claims prevention program has helped to contain insurance costs for North Carolina lawyers.

"Under One Big Umbrella"
The Formation of NCBA Sections

Responding to the efforts of lawyers to specialize, it was not a surprise in 1979 when the NCBA Board of Governors authorized the creation of the association's first "section." The decision by the board was not unanimous and was opposed by those who thought sections would "splinter" and divide what had been an "all-for-one and one-for-all" organization. Bankruptcy lawyers had for years been considering the need for specialized services, and after contemplating their own separate organization, chose to petition the association for a new status. Thus, sections were born.

The obvious advantages of being under the umbrella of the state's bar association far outweighed any advantages from independence. The N.C. Bar Association again accommodated members' needs, and in this instance avoided

Nominated by the Bar Association, Marlin Chee of Greensboro received the ABA Pro Bono Publico Award in 1991 from U.S. Supreme Court Justice Sandra Day O'Connor.

seeing the organization divide into separate organizations, as had the medical profession. It soon became clear that section members were indeed willing to pay more (section dues) for additional services (workshops, newsletters and lobbying staff support).

Sections in Real Property, Estate Planning, Tax and Business Law quickly followed. Additional staff was hired, and by 1999 more than 25 sections met the specialized needs of North Carolina practitioners. Each section allowed a greater opportunity for member participation and leadership. Combined section membership at the close of the century was nearly 16,500, with many lawyers belonging to two or more sections.

Gov. James B. Hunt Jr. signs into law Senate Bill 801, the North Carolina Planned Community Act (1998-99). This legislation was drafted by the NCBA's Real Property Section. From left to right are: John L. Jernigan, president-elect; Gov. Hunt; NCBA member Sen. Allen H. Wellons (D-Johnston); William G. Scoggin, NCBA director of governmental affairs; and Kevin D. Howell, NCBA assistant director of governmental affairs.

Responding to Public and Professional Needs in the 1980s and 1990s

Another example of responding to a need, this time an urgent request from North Carolina law school deans and law students, was the association's establishment, in 1981, of the North Carolina Bar Review Course to help North Carolina law schools and students prepare for the bar examination. This non-profit venture was successful in ensuring the availability of a reliable, high-quality, low-cost course of instruction. Once its purpose was accomplished and competition met the challenge, the course was ended in 1986.

In 1989, responding to renewed interest in local bar activities, the association reactivated its Local Bar Services Committee, began publishing a newsletter known as *N.C. Bar Leader*, and redoubled its efforts to provide the finest North Carolina Bar Leadership Institute available. At the institutes, rising local bar leaders receive practical management and leadership training focusing on current issues of concern.

As the length of legislative sessions grew longer and longer in the 1980s, fewer and fewer lawyers were able to leave their practices to serve. Lawyer membership in the Legislature, once "dominated" by lawyers, dropped from a high of 50 percent in the 1950s to a low of 20 percent in the 1990s. As a response to this phenomenon and in response to significant increases in North Carolina Bar Association-sponsored legislation (mainly coming from very active sections), the association employed a full-time legislative counsel in 1983 to ensure that all lawyers were represented in the Legislature. A second lawyer-lobbyist was added to the staff in 1998. By 1999, the association was drafting and sponsoring more than 30 bills annually and monitoring hundreds of others. The association was also serving as a valuable technical resource on many bills, providing advice to individual legislators and legislative committees.

Hundreds of minority students have attended the annual High School Law Career Conference sponsored by the Minorities in the Profession Committee. As a result, many have decided to pursue the law as a career. In the Fall of 1990, this standing room only crowd gathered at the Annapolis Drive Bar Center.

In the mid-'80s, the profession was reacting to public concerns that justice was "taking too long and costing too much." With the aid of NCBA Foundation grants from 1984-86, the Dispute Resolution Task Force studied alternatives to litigation and rendered a final report, which eventually became a national model and an inspiration to other state and local bars. As a result of this project, court-ordered arbitration and mediated settlement conferences are commonplace in North Carolina.

Space does not permit a full discussion of the association's public information projects and activities during the 1980s and 1990s, which have served the public well. Some of the more visible and successful programs are the *This is the Law* library and courthouse pamphlet series that provides the public free legal advice on any one of more than 15 topics — this program alone distributes more than a quarter of a million pamphlets each year with topics ranging from how to deal with landlord-tenant problems to drafting your will or serving on a jury. Law Day celebrations annually focus the attention of the state and its citizens on the importance of the rule of law and the role of lawyers. Call-in legal hotlines on television have been popular ways for citizens to connect with volunteer lawyers, and pre-election voter's guides have been helpful to the electorate with regard to the qualifications and background of judicial candidates. In 1998, the public gained further access to the Bar Association's public service information by way of its Web page at *www.barlinc.org* or *www.ncbar.org*.

"A Heritage for the Future"
The North Carolina Bar
Foundation Endowment

Operational revenues could no longer support the numerous public and professional services and projects which the N.C. Bar Association and its Bar Foundation wanted to undertake each year. Raising dues and CLE registration fees was not the longterm answer. The association's leadership appointed an endowment committee and, in 1985, set out to establish the North Carolina Bar Foundation Endowment. This ambitious undertaking, if successful, would help fund worthy projects for years to come. The Founders Campaign in 1987, under the leadership of former President William F. Womble, was a huge success, exceeding its goal and raising more than $1.5 million from 416 contributors.

The NCBA Development Committee was established in 1988. In 1991, the Builder's Campaign, under the leadership of Richard E. Thigpen Jr., another former president and son of a former president, added to the endowment. By May 1996, $2 million had been given or pledged by almost 1,000 contributors. On the basis of its fund-raising successes, and recognizing the need for an increased emphasis on contributions, the N.C. Bar Foundation hired its first, permanent full-time director of development in 1995 to better coordinate annual and deferred giving. The NCBF Endowment Committee was formed to receive grant requests.

To encourage and recognize deferred and planned giving, a group was formed to recognize those individuals who supported the NCBF Endowment with a gift from their personal estate plan. The NCBF Endowment chose "The Platt D. Walker Society" as the name for this select group of members, in honor of the association's first president. As of 1999, more than 30 individuals had chosen this opportunity to show their continued support "with a gift that will live forever."

William F. Womble of Winston-Salem is a longtime Bar Association leader and chair of the Endowment Founders Campaign.

In June 1999, the N.C. Bar Foundation Endowment proudly reported an endowment fund of more than $3.5 million with a 10-year grant total of more than $1 million. Critical to the success of the endowment has not only been continued contributions but also the wise investment of endowment funds. The NCBA's Investment Committee, under the longtime leadership of Gene McDonald (president of Duke University's Management Investment Corporation), has successfully guided the investment strategies of the association, its foundation and endowment. The endowment continues to grow — the beneficiary of enthusiastic support from lawyers and their families.

The establishment of "Justice Funds" has become a means by which families, firms and friends can honor the careers of North Carolina lawyers and judges. An endowment gift of at least $25,000 is required in order to establish a justice fund, which honors those lawyers "who have demonstrated dedication to the pursuit of justice and outstanding service to the profession and the public." Once established, a bronze plaque is commissioned and placed in a prominent location on the main level of the Bar Center.

University of North Carolina President Emeritus William Friday and former U.S. senator and Duke University President Terry Sanford attend the August 16, 1996, dedication of artwork honoring Judge J. Dickson Phillips in the Bar Center Galleria.

A Heritage of Professionalism

Professionalism, not surprisingly, has been a recurring theme of the association since its founding. Constantly of concern, the issue has been addressed in many ways. A Professionalism Committee appointed in the late 1980s has encouraged annual CLE programs in this area, provided professionalism speakers to the law schools and encouraged professionalism speakers at all annual meetings. Funding for speakers was made possible by the $100,000 Willis Smith and Willis Smith Jr. Justice Fund, which supported this important goal through the endowment. Beginning in 1988, the North Carolina Supreme Court and State Bar required two hours of ethics and professionalism courses as a part of its mandatory CLE requirement, and a three-hour ethics and professionalism block once every three years. The association and its CLE and Professionalism committees rose to the challenge, providing annually a three-hour professionalism CLE program that was creative, entertaining and informative.

The annual Law Week ceremony is the high point of year-round efforts by the Young Lawyers Division to educate young North Carolinians about the law and our legal system. The May 1999 ceremony was held in the Old House Chamber in the State Capitol. Here, President John L. Jernigan (1999-2000) and the crowd pay respects to the colors displayed by the honor guard.

Lawyers Young and Lawyers Senior

By 1990, the NCBA's Young Lawyers Division had a track record of service to the profession of more than 37 years, and a membership of almost 4,000. Recognized by the American Bar Association with awards for excellence on numerous occasions, the association's YLD had a history of its own in terms of service to the profession and the public.

Notable examples of YLD success are: (1) its Disaster Relief Committee, which brings together significant volunteer, pro bono resources to help those in distress every time a disaster hits North Carolina; (2) annual scholarships for the children of slain or permanently disabled law enforcement officers, made possible by grants from the NCBF's Endowment; (3) the YLD Law and the Aging Committee's *Senior Citizens Handbook*, a resource for seniors and their caregivers which gives helpful legal advice; and (4) "Law Week" celebrations, which include moot court competitions for high school students, essay contests for middle and high school students and poster contests for elementary students.

Helping others who may not be able to help themselves is the cornerstone of successful Young Lawyers Division activities over many years. It is significant, but not surprising, that since its creation in 1954, the YLD has had four of its chairs eventually serve as president of the association, and two as president of the North Carolina State Bar.

In 1990, the NCBA Board of Governors authorized the creation of the Senior Lawyers Division for members 55 years of age or older, responding to the need for yet another special area of activity related to age. The primary goal, however, was to keep senior lawyers active in programs and activities of the profession and the association. The first chair was William F. Womble. By the turn of the century, the Senior Lawyers Division membership had grown to nearly 500.

Welcoming new citizens has often been a part of the annual YLD Law Week ceremony.

Other Notable Section and Division News of the 1990s

In 1993 the Labor and Employment Law Section, established in 1982, celebrated the completion of a longterm public service project with the publication of *Employment Law for North Carolina Nonprofits: A Handbook for Managers and Board Members of Nonprofit Organizations*, a cooperative project with the North Carolina Center for Nonprofits.

The Legal Assistants Division was created in 1998. This somewhat controversial affiliate membership category was created after three separate and distinct votes of the board over a period of 15 years. The argument for the need to help make

Since 1990, the Senior Lawyers Division, which has grown to more than 400 members, has provided camaraderie for senior lawyers. Pictured here are those who attended the 1990 organizational meeting. From the bottom, left to right: Chair Wes Moser, Chair-Elect Ralph Strayhorn, Secretary-Treasurer Charles Hostetler, Harold Hall, Lucius Pullen, Clary Holt, John Riggs, Linville Roach, Howard Doyle, Charles White, Elmer Oettinger, Paul Bell and Victor Bryant. Top row: Tom Adams, Bob Bowers, Ed Allman, Bobbie Redding, George Herndon, Harry Groves, Joe Parker, E.K. Powe, W.W. Taylor Jr. and Bill Womble.

In 1976, Legal Services of North Carolina was created by the North Carolina Bar Association in order to meet the civil legal needs of people living in poverty. Established as a not-for-profit organization and governed by a bipartisan board of directors, the incorporation of LSNC was the end result of a study by the NCBA conducted from 1974 to 1976.

From 1976 to 1981, LSNC expanded so that all 100 counties in North Carolina could be served by legal services field programs. Just after the expansion effort was complete, the organization was faced with a 25-percent budget cut. The bar helped the organization through its budget crisis through the donation of funds and through private attorney involvement in the delivery of legal assistance to the poor. During this period, the NCBA established a formal pro bono project.

LSNC survived the loss of funds and, in 1986, engaged in a self-study which resulted in the adoption of goals and objectives for providing quality legal services for clients.

During the next 10-year period, LSNC created new partnerships with entities also concerned with the principle of equal access to justice. The organization grew and stabilized with the support and funding of the State Bar's IOLTA (Interest on Lawyers' Trust Accounts) funds and the N.C. General Assembly's decision to allocate revenue to LSNC to help expand access to justice to poor North Carolinians.

In 1996, LSNC funds were again reduced, this time by 35 percent, and again, with the help of the North Carolina Bar Association, the IOLTA program and with some restructuring, Legal Services of North Carolina has survived.

"Creating LSNC was the major accomplishment of the N.C. Bar Association during that period of time," said Walter Brinkley, who served as president of the NCBA in 1974-75. "It was the most significant undertaking I have been involved with as far as the organized bar is concerned."

It was a lengthy process that led to the creation of Legal Services of North Carolina. Rocky Mount attorney Bill Thorp started a legal aid service on his own initiative for Nash and Edgecombe counties in 1970. There were also federally funded legal services offices in Charlotte, Durham and Winston-Salem. Thorns Craven of Winston-Salem and Thorp joined forces to try to get a statewide legal services program. "The logical way to do that was to work through the NCBA," said Thorp, who served on the NCBA Board of Governors at the time.

NCBA President Joe Moore appointed Thorp to chair the Legal Services Committee, which was able to secure a grant to study North Carolina's need for legal services. A subsequent commission, which included Justice Joe Branch, Judge Hamilton Hobgood, future NCBA president Jim Talley and federal magistrate Herman Smith among others, was appointed.

Some of the members of the commission were not big supporters of the idea of legal services, Thorp said. "They were skeptical," he said. "Some reflected the attitude of a lot of members of the bar that legal services was a financial threat to the practice of law."

Eventually, the commission members were convinced that legal services was the right thing to do. "It was all a question of understanding," Thorp said. A plan setting up North Carolina Legal Services, Inc. was approved at the June, 1976, NCBA Board of Governors meeting. Brinkley, who a year earlier had finished his term as president of the North Carolina Bar Association, was selected to be president of North Carolina Legal Services, Inc., which became Legal Services of North Carolina, Inc.

"All the presidents and other leaders of the NCBA have given fantastic support to legal services ever since," Thorp said.

The U.S. and N.C. Constitutions provide for equal protection of the laws for all people. In order to bring life to that fundamental principle, poor people must have access to legal representation. Assuring equal access to justice for all citizens is a fundamental responsibility of government and is essential to maintain respect for law and public institutions.

As one state senator said, "Without Legal Services, where would 1.3 million North Carolinians—15 percent of our populace—go for legal help?"

career professionals who work under the direct supervision of lawyers more professional finally carried the day. By the close of the century, the Legal Assistants Division provided member services to nearly 600 paralegals, each helping lawyers deliver a higher quality product in less time at a lower cost.

In 1998, the association, never resting on its laurels, appointed new committees such as Sports and Entertainment Law, Government Attorneys, Hispanic Attorneys, and Lawyers in the Schools to mention only a few. The diverse needs and concerns of more than 11,500 members continue to challenge an ever-growing organization that every day must reconfirm its relevance to North Carolina lawyers and law firms.

Representing the Underrepresented

The work of the Bar Association in two significant areas speaks to the association's commitment to groups that have historically been underrepresented in the legal profession. The Minorities in the Profession Committee has undertaken many projects to help ensure an increased number and visibility of minorities in the profession. Projects such as Regional Law Career Conferences for high school students, Bar Exam Writing Clinics, and Minority Clerkship Programs for law students have helped meet some of the need. In 1996, the Race Relations Commission, jointly sponsored with the North Carolina Association of Black

Legal hotlines on TV connect volunteer lawyers with the public. Volunteers Chris Burti, Gary Davis, Thomas Archie and William Watson respond to calls at Washington station WITN's Greenville satellite studio in Spring 1998.

Lawyers, produced a provocative report and seminar designed to help lawyers, law firms and the profession deal with current inequities and future opportunities for minorities. The association's Minority Demonstration Project Task Force, also jointly sponsored with the North Carolina Association of Black Lawyers, helped identify business opportunities for minority firms and minority attorneys in majority firms.

The Committee on Women in the Profession also sought to ensure equality for what has been another underrepresented segment of the bar. During the association's 100th anniversary year in 1999, approximately 25 percent of the profession was female, while 48 percent of those in law school were female. Leadership opportunities in law firms and in the profession is of continuing concern. Glass ceilings have started to crack, but there remains much to be done. Surveys, suggested policies for law firms, published articles and seminar speakers focusing on gender equity are projects which have been offered by the association through the work of this committee.

Ensuring Members' Quality of Life

Another example of the NCBA's unanticipated call to service came in 1990 when the North Carolina Bar Association's Health Benefit Trust was formed to help North Carolina lawyers get control of rapidly escalating health care costs and to maximize benefits for themselves, their families and employees. This self-funded trust was the first such trust formed by a statewide bar association and successfully bridged a three-year period of time when health care coverage was in transition, amidst rapid change in the American health insurance system. HBT Board of Trustees Chair H. Gray Hutchison Jr. provided the skilled leadership necessary for the trust to succeed and conclude its service in 1993.

In response to concerns about the level of dissatisfaction with law practice among some attorneys, 1989 NCBA President Larry McDevitt formed a task

NCBA President Larry B. Sitton (1998-1999) appointed the new Hispanic Lawyers Committee in 1998 to help meet the needs of both lawyers of Hispanic descent and lawyers who serve the state's growing Hispanic population. Pictured left to right are Judge Ann Marie Calabria, Robert F. Willis and Chair Georgia J. Lewis.

LEADERSHIP AT THE TOP

The success of the North Carolina Bar Association has been due in large part to outstanding volunteer leadership, particularly from its presidents. History records that it is an office that has sought the person, and *not* the person seeking the office.

History also records, with only one exception in recent times, that the election has been uncontested. Not to say that there were not enough qualified individuals willing to serve, but rather that the association chose not to put itself — and its members — through divisive campaigns where one will "win" and one must "lose." Instead, great efforts have been made by one nominating committee after another to ensure "representative leadership." Leadership has come, as it should, from those who have been most active in the affairs of the N.C. Bar Association, those most deeply committed to the mission of the organization, and from among those most highly respected within the profession.

In the early days, special efforts were made to elect individuals from different counties to clearly show, to a diverse and growing membership, that support and leadership for the association came from every corner of the state. This practice eventually evolved, in modern times, to an unwritten system of alternating between geographical regions of the state, first east and west, then east, central and west, and ultimately to a system of "the best person for the job," without regard to location. Every effort is made to be as inclusive as possible, respecting — among others things — place of residence, race, gender, practice area and firm size.

Today, in accordance with the association's bylaws, the nomination of the president-elect is made by a nominating committee composed of all living past presidents and chaired by the immediate past president.

The committee begins its work each year with the careful review of a lengthy list of possible nominees. The group of those being considered consists of outstanding past or present members of the NCBA Board of Governors who have distinguished themselves in service to the association and who have clearly demonstrated the potential to effectively lead a large professional association of diverse interests. All those considered must embody the highest standards of the profession.

Later in the year, the Past Presidents' Council, functioning as a screening committee of past presidents, narrows the list to four to six potential candidates. Finally, the full committee, composed of all past presidents, selects a nominee and an alternate. It is reported that no one has ever declined the nomination.

Again, in accordance with the bylaws, the prospective nominee's name is announced at the opening session of the NCBA Annual Meeting. The election is held at a subsequent business session. Other nominations, if any, are accepted from the floor.

While some bar associations in other states have their presidential candidates campaign for election, the North Carolina Bar Association's system of selection and election has served the membership well. One recent president commented, "With such a strong network of support from past presidents, one could never fail as a president." Strong and effective leaders have been a cornerstone of the NCBA and promise to continue to be in the 21st century.

force and commissioned an extensive "quality of life" study. The resulting Quality of Life Task Force final report has become a national model and an oft-requested resource. The task force's 1991 *Report of the Quality of Life Task Force and Recommendations* not only raised the level of awareness for this issue within the bar, but also identified specific areas to be addressed. One such area resulted in a program, funded initially by the NCBF Endowment, for bar members and their families called *BarCARES*, Confidential Attorney Resource and Enrichment Services. The concept is simple — help those who find they can no longer help themselves with personal, family or professional problems and help alleviate a problem before it causes professional consequences. Am I my brother's keeper? The answer from the association was a resounding "yes." When one brother or sister at the bar falls, all lawyers fall. Early leaders for lawyer effectiveness and quality of life issues were task force chairman Larry Sitton, Charlie Hinton, Steve Coggins and Steve Crihfield.

A Tradition of Service for a Century and Beyond

No history of the North Carolina Bar Association would be complete without mention of the highly successful annual meetings (conventions) held each June. These meetings have rotated by tradition between the mountains and the coast. In modern times, the site of the mountain convention has always been Asheville, and since 1928 the headquarters hotel has always been, with one exception, the Grove Park Inn Resort. Since 1975 the beach convention has been held in North Myrtle Beach, S.C. at either the Myrtle Beach Hilton or Kingston Plantation. Annual meetings provide all members a chance to socialize, network, relax, conduct the business of the bar, and receive the latest in continuing legal education while enjoying a fam-

Attorney William M. Claytor of Charlotte represented all North Carolina lawyers during the 1996 Atlanta Olympic torch run.

Members of the N.C. Supreme Court joined Greensboro lawyers to build a Habitat for Humanity house in Greensboro on September 21, 1991. The future homeowner and her child share their excitement with the justices.

ily vacation. More than 600 lawyers attend an annual meeting on average, but attendance exceeded 1,000 at North Myrtle Beach in 1986.

These are but a few of the activities of the N.C. Bar Association and its Bar Foundation which bring us to the year 1999. One hundred years of service to a diverse and demanding profession required creativity and enthusiasm just to meet the challenge. There are more, many more, examples of service, hills that were climbed and volunteers that so generously gave of themselves to make life better for others. The North Carolina Bar Association is not a building, a project, a service or a vision — it is lawyers. It is lawyers who voluntarily belong, and who voluntarily serve so that others may follow and support, in their own way, the noble traditions and high calling of the legal profession and the North Carolina Bar Association.

∞

Lucky prize winners of a hot-air balloon ride at the 1989 convention in Asheville await the take-off signal with, from left, Nancy Walker, Past President James E."Bill" Walker, Root Edmonson and William L. "Bill" Thorp urging them onward and upward.

Celebrating a Century of Service

The Centennial Celebration actually kicked off with a 99th birthday party. Centennial Chairs Judge Wade Barber and Nancy Black Norelli, center and right, hold the association's cake as NCBA President Betty Quick looks on.

In June 1997, a committee was formed to guide the North Carolina Bar Association into its second century of service to the public and the profession. This Centennial Committee, chaired by Superior Court Judge Wade Barber and Charlotte attorney Nancy Black Norelli, was charged with determining the most appropriate ways to celebrate this landmark event.

The goals of the association's Centennial Celebration, as developed by the committee, were to (1) inspire lawyers to the highest ideals of professionalism and service, (2) create a sense of urgency about lawyers' fundamental role in sustaining the rule of law in our free society, (3) challenge all citizens to strengthen our system of justice for the 21st century, and (4) celebrate the accomplishments of lawyers and the accomplishments and vitality of the Bar Association.

Subcommittees were formed. A time line was established. Fundraising efforts began. Volunteer attorneys from across the state devoted countless hours of time and attention to this rather daunting task. All were determined to make 1999 a year that members would remember well into the 21st century.

In the months that followed, plans for the celebration began to take shape. It was determined that three major events — a kickoff gala, a historic marker dedication/recommitment ceremony and a Centennial Symposium — would serve as the centerpieces of the year's festivities. Several other events and activities, sponsored and coordinated by subgroups of the association, would be interspersed throughout the year. In addition, annual NCBA events, such as Law Week and the convention, would draw heavily upon the Centennial theme, "Seeking Liberty and Justice."

It was also decided that, for the first time, a comprehensive history of the Bar Association would be researched and written, a thorough examination of the association's first 100 years, in both words and pictures. An author was selected and work began. Members were

Nancy and Richard E. Thigpen Jr. were stylish in their turn-of-the-century costumes at the January 1999 Centennial Kickoff event.

NCBA Executive Director Allan Head, N.C. Supreme Court Chief Justice Burley Mitchell and Centennial Kickoff Chair Parks Helms pause from their conversation under the newly unveiled historic marker February 10, 1999 at the corner of Salisbury and Edenton streets in Raleigh.

159

At the January 1999 leadership assembly, Dr. John Kuykendall, president emeritus of Davidson College was inspirational as he spoke in the Bar Center, which had been transformed into a "walk in the park" scene from 1899.

interviewed. Archives were searched. Minutes, annual reports and association publications were painstakingly reviewed. Never before had so much information about the association's past been gathered together.

Faster than most expected, 1999 soon arrived and the real fun was set to begin. The first big event on the calendar gave members the opportunity to travel back through time to the era of the association's founding.

Kickoff Gala and Leadership Assembly

Park benches lined cobblestone paths, amid trees and fountains and gas-powered street lamps. From the gazebo, the band played on, as guests arrived by trolley in top hats and taffeta. For one glorious evening, the sights and sounds of 1899 came alive again at the Bar Center in Cary.

Meticulously transformed into a turn-of-the-century park, the Bar Association's headquarters was almost unrecognizable on this mid-January evening. Guests arrived in costumes reminiscent of everything from Confederate soldiers and Ellis Island immigrants to prairie pioneers, Gibson girls and Wild West "madams." Top-hatted gentlemen and befeathered, beribboned ladies called the *Gilded Age* to mind.

Afterward, at a nearby hotel, similarly bedecked in turn-of-the-century trappings, guests enjoyed a four-course dinner and Vaudeville-style entertainment, complete with magicians, jugglers, dancers and a barbershop quartet. Dancing and dessert followed toasts to the profession. Revelers concluded their night with cigars and cognac, or dances to the big band sounds of the North Carolina Jazz Repertory Orchestra.

A leadership assembly the following morning began with a keynote address by Dr. John Kuykendall, president emeritus of Davidson College. His inspiring speech, titled "Amateur Humanity In A Professional World" set the tone for the day's events.

A panel discussion moderated by Bill Friday (and later aired on the UNC-TV network show *North Carolina People*) examined civility in the profession. Panelists included attorneys James Ferguson of Charlotte, Betty Quick of Winston-Salem and Wade Smith of Raleigh.

Attorneys and audience members were encouraged to look inward and address the issues facing lawyers and the legal profession, and to identify potential problems that will be carried forward into the future. The issues of civility, leadership and passion for the profession were presented and discussed.

Nearly 400 lawyers recommitted themselves to service to the public as Chief Justice Burley Mitchell led them in a reaffirmation of the attorney's oath during the February 10, 1999 Historic Marker Dedication Ceremony.

Following the panel discussion, David Gergen, editor, professor and political pundit, traced the last 100 years in North Carolina using the Centennial theme of "Seeking Liberty And Justice."

The kickoff event, chaired by Charlotte attorney Parks Helms, was sponsored by First Union Corp. with a gift of $75,000.

Historic Marker Dedication

Hundreds of lawyers from across the state joined the state's Supreme Court justices at an outdoor ceremony in downtown Raleigh on Wednesday, February 10. Led by N.C. Supreme Court Chief Justice Burley B. Mitchell Jr. attendees reaffirmed their legal vows to uphold the Constitution, strive for justice, practice the highest levels of professionalism and further commit themselves to public and community service.

On the beautiful and unseasonably warm afternoon, lawyers gathered outside the Labor Building at the corner of Edenton and Salisbury Streets, the former home of the N.C. Supreme Court and the site of the N.C. Bar Association's organizational meeting on February 10, 1899.

A North Carolina state historic marker commemorating the Bar Association's 100 years was then unveiled by several past presidents of the association.

Preceding the outdoor ceremony, a special program took place at the Old House Chambers in the State Capitol Building. The program featured the presentation of a gubernatorial proclamation by Lt. Gov. Dennis Wicker, along with patriotic music and theatrical reenactments of historic North Carolina legal cases.

Past Presidents prepare to unveil a permanent historic marker during a ceremony on February 10, 1999, honoring the 100th anniversary of the organizational meeting of the N.C. Bar Association. Pictured left to right are: Richard E. Thigpen Jr., James K. Dorsett Jr., Robert F. Baker, John Q. Beard, Elizabeth L. Quick, William F. Womble, W.W. Taylor Jr., Walter F. Brinkley, Isaac T. Avery Jr. and Ralph N. Strayhorn Jr.

Museum Exhibit

James B. Maxwell of Durham is congratulated by NCBA past presidents after being introduced as the president-elect during the Centennial Annual Meeting in Asheville in June 1999.

Another lasting tribute to the profession and the association, a series of law-related museum panels, was unveiled at a reception at the N.C. Museum of History following the Historic Marker Dedication on February 10.

Providing attorneys and members of the public with an opportunity to learn about the tremendous changes in the profession through the years, the exhibit, titled "Seeking Liberty and Justice: The Legal Profession in North Carolina" was on display at the museum through the end of May.

The museum developed the panel exhibit in conjunction with the N.C. Bar Association's Centennial Exhibit Committee (chaired by Asheville attorney Michelle Rippon) to commemorate the 100th anniversary of the association's founding. The exhibit was sponsored by BB&T.

After its initial run in Raleigh, the exhibit traveled to the NCBA Annual Meeting at Asheville's Grove Park Inn in June. It then traveled around the state to schools, libraries and other organizations.

Seventy-one color and black-and-white illustrations enhanced the exhibit text, conveying the complexity and the many changes of the state's legal system since North Carolina's founding. The exhibit presented topics such as the origins of law and the court system; learning the law; the growth of law practices; pub-

Children of all ages enjoyed a beautiful afternoon of food, balloons, music and magic during a family picnic at The North Carolina Arboretum in Asheville during the 1999 annual meeting.

lic perceptions of lawyers; and lawyers' involvement in community service. The panels traced the growth of North Carolina's court system and described how attorneys have made the law more accessible to North Carolinians.

Centennial Annual Meeting

The Grove Park Inn in Asheville first played host to an NCBA annual meeting in 1928. Since that year, it has hosted the convention 21 times, more than any other facility. It thus seemed fitting that the Centennial year's annual meeting would return to the popular mountainside resort.

Featured speakers included Maureen F. Allyn, chief economist and managing director of Scudder Kemper Investments, Inc.; John Kuykendall, president emeritus of Davidson College; Alexander M. Sanders, president of the College of Charleston; and William K. Slate, president of the American Arbitration Association.

As part of the celebration, a new public education video, complete with a song written for the association titled "The Rule of Law," was premiered. The video is used at schools around the state to educate middle-school students on the roles that lawyers play in America.

A time capsule bearing the association's Centennial logo was packed with NCBA memorabilia and buried at the resort, not to be opened until the year 2099. A photo of convention attendees taken at The North Carolina Arboretum in Asheville was placed in the capsule.

Other Centennial Activities

These rather large-scale events were not the only ones featured during the Centennial year. Many other activities and programs, organized by sections, divisions or committees, were scheduled throughout the year.

A High School Law Career Conference for minority students was conducted by the association's Minorities in the Profession Committee in March. The program featured a mock trial and a look back at the history of African-American lawyers in North Carolina, with a focus on those who opened the doors for black law students.

The annual Law Week program sponsored by the Young Lawyers Division took on the Centennial theme of "Seeking Liberty and Justice" when conducting its moot court, poster art, essay and photo essay contests for school students across the state. Law Week occurs each year during the first week in May, culminating with Law Day festivities on the Friday of that week.

Governor's Proclamation paid tribute to the North Carolina Bar Association and recognized 1999 as its Centennial Celebration Year.

A statewide blood drive was organized and sponsored by the NCBA's Health Law Section in July. Lawyers from across the state were encouraged to roll up their sleeves and donate to the Red Cross at a time of the year when blood supplies are traditionally low.

Chief Justice Burley Mitchell, on behalf of the N.C. Bar Association, receives a proclamation from Gov. Jim Hunt which honors the association and its Centennial Celebration.

Dispute Resolution Month was held in October and featured volunteers conducting alternative dispute resolution workshops across the state. It also featured an education effort about the variety of community and court-annexed resolution programs available in the state.

A Hospice Estate Planning Project featured volunteers from the Estate Planning & Fiduciary Law Section assisting needy hospice patients and their families with estate planning matters such as wills, guardianships and powers of attorney.

Habitat for Humanity received help from volunteer attorneys from the General Practice, Solo & Small Firm Section who compiled a set of legal forms for use by Habitat programs and their local volunteer attorneys across North Carolina.

Centennial Symposium

North Carolina attorneys wrapped up their celebration of the first 100 years of the Bar Association in October at the Centennial Symposium held at Camp Seafarer near Arapahoe. The weekend program gave attendees an opportunity to reflect on the association's first century of service. It featured discussion of a variety of controversial and thought-provoking subjects facing the association and the profession.

Finally, a second time capsule was buried at the Bar Center. It included this book to be read by lawyers in the year 2099.

THE CENTENNIAL OAK
In honor of the 100th Anniversary
of the
North Carolina Bar Association

June 18, 1999

The Grove Park Inn Resort & Spa

At the Grove Park Inn in Asheville, from right, Wade Barber, John Jernigan, Larry Sitton and Nancy Norelli buried a time capsule filled with NCBA memorabilia and messages from current leaders to bar leaders in the year 2099.

SELECTED BIBLIOGRAPHY

By far the most valuable primary sources for any history of the North Carolina Bar Association are the *Reports* of the annual meetings from 1899 to 1948; *BarNotes* and its successor, *North Carolina Lawyer*, and Annual Reports of recent years. The *Reports* typically contain not only the records of debates and business transacted at the annual meetings but have full listings of membership, attendees, committees and members, and memorial biographical sketches, along with the text of the annual message by the president and many other speakers. Recent newsletters have more information about current issues and the role of the Bar Association but less about the annual meetings. Important secondary works are: Fannie Memory Blackwelder (now Memory Mitchell), "Organization and Early Years of the North Carolina Bar Association," *North Carolina Historical Review*, 34 (1957): 36-57; Edwin C. Bryson, "The Organized Bar in North Carolina" *North Carolina Law Review*, 30 (1952): 335-355; and William M. Storey, "Early Years/Recent Years of the North Carolina Bar Association," *BarNotes*, 14 (1962): 40-56.

The story of the legal profession in North Carolina appears in part in many of the standard histories of the state as well as in scattered articles in the *State Magazine* and in *The North Carolina Historical Review*. Events and individuals whose dates are known can be found through appropriate newspaper and clipping files. Biographies of many individuals associated with the Bar Association can be found in William S. Powell, ed., *Dictionary of North Carolina Biography* (Chapel Hill: University of North Carolina Press, 1979-1996) and in the biography index and newspaper clipping files of the North Carolina Collection, Academic Affairs Library, University of North Carolina at Chapel Hill. Each of the state's law schools has a history in some form and their alumni and public relations offices have much information about the activities of their graduates. The files of the Bar Association contain much information about individuals involved in association organizations and activities. Good summary articles by two association members are Fannie Memory Farmer (Memory Mitchell), "Legal Education in North Carolina, 1820-1860," *North Carolina Historical Review*, 28 (1951): 278-281; Ibid., "The Bar Examination and Beginning Years of Legal Practice in North Carolina, 1820-1860," *North Carolina Historical Review*, 29 (1952): 159-170; and Albert Coates, "Beginnings of Legal Education in North Carolina," 24 *North Carolina Law Review* 24 (1946): 307-326 and 47 Ibid., 29 (1968): 59-61.

For background on the history of the state in the 19th and 20th century, readers should consult William S. Powell, *North Carolina Through Four Centuries* (Chapel Hill: University of North Carolina Press, 1993); H. G. Jones, *North Carolina Illustrated*, 1524-1984 (Chapel Hill: University of North Carolina Press, 1983). For a history of the state linked to many of the state's historic sites, the series *The Way We Lived in North Carolina*, edited by Sydney Nathans (Chapel Hill: University of North Carolina Press, 1983) is most useful, particularly these volumes: *Express Lanes & Country Roads: The Way We Lived in North Carolina*, 1920-1970, by Thomas C. Parramore; *Close to the Land: The Way We Lived in North Carolina*, 1820-1870, by Thomas H. Clayton; and *The Quest for Progress: The Way We Lived in North Carolina*, 1870-1920, by Sydney Nathans.

PHOTOGRAPH CREDITS

Dust jacket, North Carolina Bar Association; **x**, North Carolina Division of Archives and History; **1**, North Carolina Division of Archives and History; **2**, North Carolina Collection, University of North Carolina Library at Chapel Hill; **3**, North Carolina Supreme Court Library and the North Carolina Division of Archives and History; **4**, University of North Carolina at Chapel Hill; **5**, North Carolina Collection, University of North Carolina Library at Chapel Hill; **6**, (t, b) North Carolina Division of Archives and History; **7**, (t, b) North Carolina Historic Sites and the North Carolina Division of Archives and History; **8**, (t, b) North Carolina Division of Archives and History; **9**, North Carolina Division of Archives and History; **10** (t, m) North Carolina Collection, University of North Carolina Library at Chapel Hill, (b) North Carolina Supreme Court Library and the North Carolina Museum of History; **11**, (t, m, b) North Carolina Collection, University of North Carolina Library at Chapel Hill; **12**, (t) North Carolina Division of Archives and History, (b) North Carolina Collection, University of North Carolina Library at Chapel Hill; **13**, James C. MacRae and James C. MacRae Jr.; **15**, (t, b) North Carolina Collection, University of North Carolina Library at Chapel Hill; **16**, (t) North Carolina Collection, University of North Carolina Library at Chapel Hill, (b) Greensboro Historical Museum; **17**, (t) North Carolina Collection, University of North Carolina Library at Chapel Hill, (b) Wake Forest University School of Law; **18**, Wake Forest University School of Law; **19**, North Carolina Collection, University of North Carolina Library at Chapel Hill; **20**, B.T. Fowler; **21**, Fred D. Poisson Sr.; **22**, (l) North Carolina Division of Archives and History, (r) North Carolina Historic Sites and the North Carolina Division of Archives and History; **23**, (t, b) North Carolina Division of Archives and History; **24**, (t) North Carolina Museum of History, (b) North Carolina Collection, University of North Carolina Library at Chapel Hill; **25**, (t) North Carolina Collection, University of North Carolina Library at Chapel Hill, (b) Edgecombe County Arts Council and Herbert H. Taylor Jr.; **26**, (tl) North Carolina Collection, University of North Carolina Library at Chapel Hill, (tr) Robinson/Spangler Carolina Room, Public Library of Charlotte and Mecklenburg County, (b) North Carolina Division of Archives and History; **27**, (t, b) North Carolina Division of Archives and History; **28**, North Carolina Division of Archives and History; **29**, North Carolina Division of Archives and History; **30**, R.F. Hoke Pollock; **32**, North Carolina Collection, University of North Carolina Library at Chapel Hill; **33**, Robinson/Spangler Carolina Room, Public Library of Charlotte and Mecklenburg County; **34**, North Carolina Museum of History; **35**, North Carolina Supreme Court Library; **36**, (t) North Carolina Bar Association, (b) North Carolina Division of Archives and History; **37**, North Carolina Collection, University of North Carolina Library at Chapel Hill; **38**, (t) North Carolina Division of Archives and History, (m, b) Durwood Barbour; **39**, (t) North Carolina Bar Association, (b) North Carolina Division of Archives and History; **40-41**, Library of Congress; **42**, (t, b) Durwood Barbour, (m) B.T. Fowler; **44**, North Carolina Bar Association; **45**, (t) North Carolina Museum of History, (b) North Carolina Bar Association; **46**, North Carolina Collection, University of North Carolina Library at Chapel Hill; **47**, (t, b) North Carolina Bar Association; **48**, Greensboro Historical Museum; **49**, (t) North Carolina Bar Association, (b) North Carolina Collection, University of North Carolina Library at Chapel Hill; **50**, North Carolina Bar Association; **51**, Thomas M. Hull; **52**, North Carolina Division of Archives and History; **53**, North Carolina Division of Archives and History; **54**, (tl) North Carolina Museum of History, (tr) The Granger Collection, (b) North Carolina Division of Archives and History; **55**, (t, m, b) Womble, Carlyle, Sandridge & Rice, PLLC; **56**, (t) North Carolina Bar Association, (b) North Carolina Collection, University of North Carolina Library at Chapel Hill; **57**, Badger-Iredell Foundation, Inc.; **58**, North Carolina Collection, University of North Carolina Library at Chapel Hill; **59**, Robinson/Spangler Carolina Room, Public Library of Charlotte and Mecklenburg County; **60**, (tr) North Carolina Museum of History, (m) Duke University Special Collections Library, (b) North Carolina Supreme Court Library and the North Carolina Division of Archives and History; **61**, (t) North Carolina Collection, University of North Carolina Library at Chapel Hill, (b) North Carolina Bar Association; **62**, North Carolina Division of Archives and History; **63**, (t) North Carolina Division of Archives and History, (b) Sam J. Ervin III; **64**, North Carolina Division of Archives and History; **65**, (t) Robinson/Spangler Carolina Room, Public Library of Charlotte and Mecklenburg County, (b) Duke University Archives; **66**, Armistead Jones Maupin; **67**, James E. Cross Jr.; **68**, Norman Rockwell Museum at Stockbridge. Printed by permission of the Norman Rockwell Family Trust. ©1927 Norman Rockwell Family Trust.; **69**, (t) North Carolina Division of Archives, (b) North Carolina Collection, University of North Carolina Library at Chapel Hill; **70**, (t) North Carolina Collection, University of North Carolina Library at Chapel Hill, (b) North Carolina Collection, University of North Carolina Library at Chapel Hill; **71**, North Carolina Division of Archives and History; **72**, (t) North Carolina Bar Association, (b) North Carolina Bar Association; **73**, (t) North Carolina Bar Association, (b) Robinson/Spangler Carolina Room, Public Library of Charlotte and Mecklenburg County; **74**, (t) North Carolina Division of Archives and History, (b)

Duke University School of Law; **75**, Grove Park Inn; **76**, North Carolina Bar Association; **77**, North Carolina Collection, University of North Carolina Library at Chapel Hill; **78**, Robinson/Spangler Carolina Room, Public Library of Charlotte and Mecklenburg County; **79**, North Carolina Division of Archives and History; **80**, North Carolina Supreme Court Library and the North Carolina Division of Archives and History; **81**, Greensboro Historical Museum; **82**, North Carolina Museum of History; **84**, Odum Photo Study, Southern Historical Collection, University of North Carolina Library at Chapel Hill; **85**, Odum Photo Study, Southern Historical Collection, University of North Carolina Library at Chapel Hill; **86**, Richard Elton Thigpen; **87**, North Carolina Bar Association; **88**, (t) North Carolina Bar Association, (b) North Carolina Division of Archives and History; **89**, (t) North Carolina Division of Archives and History, (b) Duke University Archives; **90**, North Carolina Bar Association; **91**, Duke University School of Law; **92**, B.T. Fowler; **93**, (t) Duke University Archives, (b) B.T. Fowler; **94**, (t) Duke University Archives, (b) North Carolina Central University School of Law; **95**, Odum Photo Study, Southern Historical Collection, University of North Carolina Library at Chapel Hill; **96**, (t) North Carolina Division of Archives and History, (b) Odum Photo Study, Southern Historical Collection, University of North Carolina Library at Chapel Hill; **97**, Odum Photo Study, Southern Historical Collection, University of North Carolina Library at Chapel Hill; **98**, James K. Dorsett Jr.; **99**, Franklin D. Roosevelt Library; **100**, (t) Jonas Papers, Southern Historical Collection, University of North Carolina Library at Chapel Hill, (b) North Carolina Bar Association; **101**, (t) North Carolina Division of Archives and History, (b) B.T. Fowler; **102**, (t) North Carolina Division of Archives and History, (b) Walter L. Hannah; **103** (t) Mrs. John A. Kleemeier Jr., (b) North Carolina Division of Archives and History; **104**, North Carolina Central University School of Law; **105**, North Carolina Bar Association; **106**, (t) Duke University Archives, (b) North Carolina Bar Association; **108**, North Carolina Division of Archives and History; **109**, North Carolina Collection, University of North Carolina Library at Chapel Hill; **110**, North Carolina Collection, University of North Carolina Library at Chapel Hill; **111**, North Carolina Bar Association; **112**, (t) B.T. Fowler, (b) North Carolina Bar Association; **113**, (t) North Carolina Collection, University of North Carolina Library at Chapel Hill, (b) North Carolina Bar Association; **114**, (t) North Carolina Division of Archives and History, (b) North Carolina Division of Archives and History; **115**, North Carolina Collection, University of North Carolina Library at Chapel Hill; **116**, Jonas Papers, Southern Historical Collection, University of North Carolina Library at Chapel Hill; **117**, North Carolina Bar Association; **118**, (t) North Carolina Bar Association, (b) Elizabeth O. Rollins; **120**, (t) B.C. Allen Jr., (b) John H. Zollicoffer Jr.; **121**, Mrs. H.E. (Violette K.) Phillips; **122**, (t) North Carolina Division of Archives and History, (b) Duke University Archives; **124**, (t) North Carolina Bar Association, (b) Julie Dumont Rabinowitz/North Carolina Bar Association; **125**, (t, b) North Carolina Bar Association; **126**, North Carolina Bar Association; **128**, Duke University Archives; **129**, (l) North Carolina Bar Association, (r) Herbert H. Taylor Jr.; **130**, Jane Morrison Moore; **131**, (t) North Carolina Supreme Court Library and the North Carolina Museum of History, (b) North Carolina Bar Association; **132**, (t, b) North Carolina Bar Association; **133**, James E. Long; **135**, (t) North Carolina Bar Association, (b) Robinson/Spangler Carolina Room, Public Library of Charlotte and Mecklenburg County; **136**, (t) North Carolina Collection, University of North Carolina Library at Chapel Hill, (b) North Carolina Central University School of Law; **137**, North Carolina Supreme Court Library and the North Carolina Museum of History; **138**, North Carolina Supreme Court Library and the North Carolina Museum of History; **139**, (t) J. Donald Cowan Jr., (b) Richard Vinroot; **140**, (tr, tl) Norman Adrian Wiggins School of Law, Campbell University, (b) UPI-Bettman; **142**, North Carolina Bar Association; **143**, (t, m, b) North Carolina Bar Association; **144**, (t, m, b) North Carolina Bar Association; **145**, Clifton Barnes/North Carolina Bar Association; **147**, (t, m), Clifton Barnes/North Carolina Bar Association, (b) Gordon H. Schenck Jr.; **148**, (t, m, b) Clifton Barnes/North Carolina Bar Association; **149**, American Bar Association; **150**, (t) David MacDonald/North Carolina Bar Association, (b) Clifton Barnes/North Carolina Bar Association; **151**, William F. Womble; **152**, (t, b) Clifton Barnes/North Carolina Bar Association; **153**, (t) Clifton Barnes/North Carolina Bar Association, (b) Russell Wong/North Carolina Bar Association; **155**, (t) Cathy Larsson/North Carolina Bar Association, (b) Clifton Barnes/North Carolina Bar Association; **156**, Coca-Cola Company, ©1996; **157**, (t) Greensboro Bar Association, (b) Clifton Barnes/North Carolina Bar Association; **158**, David MacDonald/North Carolina Bar Association; **159**, (t, b) Clifton Barnes/North Carolina Bar Association; **160**, (t) Clifton Barnes/North Carolina Bar Association, (b) David MacDonald/North Carolina Bar Association; **161**, (t) Clifton Barnes/North Carolina Bar Association, (b) Cathy Larsson/North Carolina Bar Association; **162**, (t) Cathy Larsson/North Carolina Bar Association, (m) K.D. Zotter, (b) David MacDonald/North Carolina Bar Association; **163**, (t, b) Cathy Larsson/North Carolina Bar Association.

APPENDIX

PRESIDENTS OF THE
NORTH CAROLINA BAR ASSOCIATION

Platt D. Walker*
Charlotte
1899

Charles F. Warren*
Washington
1899-1900

Charles M. Stedman*
Greensboro
1900-01

Charles M. Busbee*
Raleigh
1901-02

Charles Price*
Salisbury
1902-03

W. D. Pruden*
Edenton
1903-04

Hamilton C. Jones*
Charlotte
1904

Thomas S. Kenan*
Raleigh
1904-05

Clement Manly*
Winston
1905-06

George Rountree*
Wilmington
1906-07

Charles A. Moore*
Asheville
1907-08

Louis H. Clement*
Salisbury
1908-09

John W. Hinsdale*
Raleigh
1909-10

Charles W. Tillett*
Charlotte
1910-11

Francis D. Winston*
Windsor
1911-12

James S. Manning*
Raleigh
1912-13

Thomas S. Rollins*
Asheville
1913-14

J. Crawford Biggs*
Durham
1914-15

Harry Skinner*
Greenville
1915-16

Aubrey L. Brooks*
Greensboro
1916-17

Angus W. McLean*
Lumberton
1917-18

E. F. Aydlett*
Elizabeth City
1918-19

William P. Bynum*
Greensboro
1919-20

Thomas W. Davis*
Wilmington
1920-21

(* deceased)

John A. MacRae*
Charlotte
1921-22

L. R. Varser*
Lumberton
1922-23

Edward S. Parker*
Greensboro
1923-24

George V. Cowper*
Kinston
1924-25

William M. Hendren*
Winston-Salem
1925-26

John D. Bellamy*
Wilmington
1926-27

Mark W. Brown*
Asheville
1927-28

Alexander B. Andrews*
Raleigh
1928-29

T. L. Caudle*
Wadesboro
1929

Kenneth C. Royall*
Goldsboro
1929-30

Charles G. Rose*
Fayetteville
1930-31

Silas G. Bernard*
Asheville
1931-32

Kemp D. Battle*
Rocky Mount
1932-33

J. Elmer Long*
Durham
1933-34

Charles W. Tillett Jr.*
Charlotte
1934-35

J. Melville Broughton*
Raleigh
1935-36

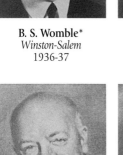
B. S. Womble*
Winston-Salem
1936-37

Francis E. Winslow*
Rocky Mount
1937-38

Kingsland Van Winkle*
Asheville
1938-39

Fred I. Sutton*
Kinston
1939-40

Hamilton C. Jones III*
Charlotte
1940-41

Willis Smith*
Raleigh
1941-42

Linville K. Martin*
Winston-Salem
1942

Fitzhugh E. Wallace*
Kinston
1942-43

W. Frank Taylor*
Goldsboro
1943-44

Irving E. Carlyle*
Winston-Salem
1944-45

Louis J. Poisson Jr.*
Wilmington
1945-46

Charles R. Jonas*
Lincolnton
1946-47

John C. Rodman*
Washington
1947-48

Richard Elton Thigpen
Charlotte
1948-49

(* deceased)

Thomas H. Leath*
Rockingham
1949-50

Francis J. Heazel*
Asheville
1950-51

W.A. Leland McKeithen*
Pinehurst
1951-52

J. Spencer Bell*
Charlotte
1952-53

William L. Thorp*
Rocky Mount
1953-54

Joel B. Adams*
Asheville
1954-55

Albert W. Kennon*
Durham
1955-56

Nelson Woodson*
Salisbury
1956-57

W. W. Taylor Jr.
Warrenton
1957-58

Beverly C. Moore Sr.
Greensboro
1958-59

James K. Dorsett Jr.
Raleigh
1959-60

James B. McMillan*
Charlotte
1960-61

Herman S. Merrell*
Rocky Mount
1961-62

Isaac T. Avery Jr.
Statesville
1962-63

Henry L. Anderson*
Fayetteville
1963-64

George A. Long*
Burlington
1964-65

A. Pilston Godwin Jr.*
Raleigh
1965-66

William F. Womble
Winston-Salem
1966-67

James M. Poyner*
Raleigh
1967-68

William J. Adams Jr.*
Greensboro
1968-69

Lindsay C. Warren Jr.
Goldsboro
1969-70

J. Mack Holland Jr.
Gastonia
1970-71

Ralph N. Strayhorn
Winston-Salem
1971-72

Harold K. Bennett*
Asheville
1972-73

Joseph C. Moore Jr.*
Raleigh
1973-74

Walter F. Brinkley
Lexington
1974-75

Edward N. Rodman
Washington
1975-76

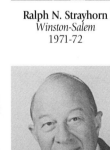

Ralph M. Stockton Jr.
Winston-Salem
1976-77

Herbert H. Taylor Jr.
Tarboro
1977-78

Clarence W. Walker Jr.
Charlotte
1978-79

(* deceased)

John R. Haworth
High Point
1979-80

Dewey W. Wells
Winston-Salem
1980-81

James E. Walker*
Charlotte
1981-82

Robert F. Baker
Durham
1982-83

Charles L. Fulton
Raleigh
1983-84

E. Osborne Ayscue Jr.
Charlotte
1984-85

Robert C. Vaughn Jr.
Winston-Salem
1985-86

John Q. Beard
Raleigh
1986-87

E. James Moore
North Wilkesboro
1987-88

Richard E. Thigpen Jr.
Charlotte
1988-89

Larry S. McDevitt
Asheville
1989-90

George B. Mast
Smithfield
1990-91

Rhoda B. Billings
Winston-Salem
1991-92

J. Donald Cowan Jr.
Greensboro
1992-93

Charles E. Burgin
Marion
1993-94

James M. Talley Jr.
Charlotte
1994-95

John S. Stevens
Asheville
1995-96

L. P. Hornthal Jr.
Elizabeth City
1996-97

Elizabeth L. Quick
Winston-Salem
1997-98

Larry B. Sitton
Greensboro
1998-99

John L. Jernigan
Raleigh
1999-2000

James B. Maxwell
Durham
2000-01

CHIEF JUSTICES OF THE NORTH CAROLINA SUPREME COURT

1818-29 John Louis Taylor	1893-95 James E. Shepherd	1951-54 William A. Devin	1975-79 Susie M. Sharp
1829-33 Leonard Henderson	1895-1901 William T. Faircloth	1954-56 M.V. Barnhill	1979-86 Joseph Branch
1833-52 Thomas Ruffin	1901-03 David M. Furches	1956-62 J. Wallace Winborne	1986 Rhoda B. Billings
1852-58 Frederick Nash	1903-24 Walter Clark	1962-66 Emery B. Denny	1986-94 James G. Exum Jr.
1858-78 Richmond M. Pearson	1924-25 William A. Hoke	1966-69 R. Hunt Parker	1995-99 Burley B. Mitchell Jr.
1878-89 William N.H. Smith	1925-51 Walter P. Stacy	1969-74 William H. Bobbitt	1999 Henry E. Frye
1889-93 Augustus S. Merrimon			

SECRETARY/TREASURERS AND EXECUTIVE DIRECTORS OF THE NORTH CAROLINA BAR ASSOCIATION

J. Crawford Biggs
1899-1906

Thomas W. Davis
1906-20

Alexander B. Andrews
1920-21

Henry M. London
1921-40

Allston J. Stubbs
1940-44

Edward L. Cannon
1944-53

Charles W. Daniel
1953-55

William M. Storey*
1955-81

Allan B. Head*
1981-

(* full time)

GOVERNORS OF THE STATE OF NORTH CAROLINA
(* indicates those who were lawyers)

Years	Name	Home County
1776-80	Richard Caswell*	Dobbs (now Lenoir)
1780-81	Abner Nash	Craven
1781-82	Thomas Burke	Orange
1782-84	Alexander Martin	Guilford
1784-87	Richard Caswell*	Dobbs (now Lenoir)
1787-89	Samuel Johnston	Chowan
1789-92	Alexander Martin	Guilford
1792-95	Richard Dobbs Spaight	Craven
1795-98	Samuel Ashe*	New Hanover
1798-99	William R. Davie*	Halifax
1799-1802	Benjamin Williams	Moore
1802-05	James Turner	Warren
1805-07	Nathaniel Alexander	Mecklenburg
1807-08	Benjamin Williams	Moore
1808-10	David Stone*	Bertie
1810-11	Benjamin Smith	Brunswick
1811-14	William Hawkins	Warren
1814-17	William Miller*	Warren
1817-20	John Branch*	Halifax
1820-21	Jesse Franklin	Surry
1821-24	Gabriel Holmes*	Sampson
1824-27	Hutchins G. Burton*	Halifax
1827-28	James Iredell*	Chowan
1828-30	John Owen*	Bladen
1830-32	Montfort Stokes*	Wilkes
1832-35	David L. Swain*	Buncombe
1835-36	Richard Dobbs Spaight Jr.*	Craven
1836-41	Edward B. Dudley	New Hanover
1841-45	John M. Morehead*	Guilford
1845-49	William A. Graham	Orange
1849-51	Charles Manly*	Wake
1851-54	Davis S. Reid*	Rockingham
1854-55	Warren Winslow	Cumberland
1855-59	Thomas Bragg*	Northampton
1859-61	John W. Ellis	Rowan
1861-62	Henry T. Clark	Edgecombe
1862-65	Zebulon B. Vance*	Buncombe
1865	William W. Holden	Wake
1865-68	Jonathan Worth*	Wake
1868-71	William W. Holden	Wake
1871-74	Tod R. Caldwell*	Burke
1874-77	Curtis H. Brogden	Wayne
1877-79	Zebulon B. Vance*	Mecklenburg
1879-85	Thomas J. Jarvis*	Pitt
1885-89	Alfred M. Scales*	Rockingham
1889-91	Daniel G. Fowle*	Wake
1891-93	Thomas M. Holt	Alamance
1893-97	Elias Carr	Edgecombe
1897-1901	Daniel L. Russell*	Brunswick
1901-05	Charles B. Aycock*	Wayne
1905-09	Robert B. Glenn	Forsyth
1909-13	William W. Kitchen*	Person
1913-17	Locke Craig*	Buncombe
1917-21	Thomas W. Bickett*	Franklin
1921-25	Cameron Morrison*	Mecklenburg
1925-29	Angus W. McLean*	Robeson
1929-33	O. Max Gardner*	Cleveland
1933-37	J.C.B. Ehringhaus*	Pasquotank
1937-41	Clyde R. Hoey*	Cleveland
1941-45	J. Melville Broughton*	Wake
1945-49	R. Gregg Cherry*	Gaston
1949-53	W. Kerr Scott	Alamance
1953-54	William B. Umstead*	Durham
1954-61	Luther H. Hodges	Rockingham
1961-65	Terry Sanford*	Cumberland
1965-69	Dan K. Moore*	Jackson
1969-73	Robert W. Scott	Alamance
1973-77	James E. Holshouser Jr.*	Watauga
1977-85	James B. Hunt Jr.*	Wilson
1985-93	James G. Martin	Iredell
1993-	James B. Hunt Jr.*	Wilson

SECTION CHAIRS SINCE ESTABLISHMENT OF SECTIONS

ADMINISTRATIVE LAW
(1/89)   Ralph McDonald
1989-90   Ralph McDonald
1990-91   Ann Reed
1991-92   Michael Crowell
1992-93   Daniel F. McLawhorn
1993-94   Curtis B. Venable
1994-95   M. Jackson Nichols
1995-96   Sabra Jean Faires
1996-97   William L. Hopper
1997-98   Thomas R. West
1998-99   Charles D. Case
1999-2000   Jane T. Friedensen

ANTITRUST & TRADE REGULATION LAW
(10/90)   John F. Graybeal
1991-92   Rodrick J. Enns
1992-93   Douglas W. Kenyon
1993-94   John M. Murchison Jr.
1994-95   Everett J. Bowman
1995-96   M. Elizabeth Gee
1996-97   M. LeAnn Nease
1997-98   Norman B. Smith
1998-99   Noel L. Allen
1999-2000   Robin K. Vinson

BANKRUPTCY
(10/79)   Trawick H. Stubbs Jr.
1980-81   Richard M. Hutson Jr.
1981-82   William B. Hawfield Jr.
1982-83   J. Larkin Pahl
1983-84   Donald R. Billings
1984-85   David R. Badger
1985-86   Algernon L. Butler Jr.
1986-87   R. Bradford Leggett
1987-88   Robert H. Gourley
1988-89   Michael P. Flanagan
1989-90   James C. Frenzel
1990-91   Albert F. Durham
1991-92   Sally A. Conti
1992-93   John A. Northen
1993-94   J. William Porter
1994-95   William S. Aldridge
1995-96   Thomas W. Waldrep
1996-97   Rebecca S. Henderson
1997-98   David M. Warren
1998-99   Walter W. Pitt Jr.
1999-2000   David G. Gray

BUSINESS LAW
(10/79)   Doris R. Bray
1980-81   Doris R. Bray
1981-82   Alfred L. Purrington III
1982-83   Alfred L. Purrington III
1983-84   J. Donnell Lassiter
1984-85   J. Donnell Lassiter
1985-86   John L. Jernigan
1986-87   John L. Jernigan
1987-88   Edward C. Winslow III
1988-89   Edward C. Winslow III
1989-90   Zeb E. Barnhardt Jr.
1990-91   Zeb E. Barnhardt Jr.
1991-92   J. Norfleet Pruden III
1992-93   J. Norfleet Pruden III
1993-94   Gerald F. Roach
1994-95   Gerald F. Roach
1995-96   William M. Flynn
1996-97   William M. Flynn
1997-98   William G. Pappas
1998-99   William G. Pappas
1999-2000   Stephen D. Poe

CONSTITUTIONAL RIGHTS & RESPONSIBILITIES
(10/95)   J. McNeill Smith Jr.
1996-97   J. McNeill Smith Jr.
1997-98   Frank P. Ward Jr.
1998-99   Deborah K.Ross
1999-2000   Hugh Stevens

CONSTRUCTION LAW
(10/87)   Mark C. Kirby
1988-89   Mark C. Kirby
1989-90   Charles R. Holton
1990-91   W. Winburne King III
1991-92   James S. Schenck IV
1992-93   Kenneth R. Wooten
1993-94   Evelyn M. Coman
1994-95   Karen E. Carey
1995-96   Michael R. Pendergraft
1996-97   Richard W. Wilson
1997-98   John I. Mabe Jr.
1998-99   Dudley Humphrey
1999-2000   Carson Carmichael III

CORPORATE COUNSEL
(10/89)   James W. Kiser
1990-91   James W. Kiser
1991-92   John B. Yorke
1992-93   John R. Lassiter
1993-94   Dwight W. Allen
1994-95   William E. Poe Jr.
1995-96   Fred Alphin Jr.
1996-97   Beverly C. Moore
1997-98   T. Carlton Younger Jr.
1998-99   Alice W. Grogan
1999-2000   Ted P. Pearce

CRIMINAL JUSTICE
(1/81)   Rhoda B. Billings
1981-82   Locke T. Clifford
1982-83   Locke T. Clifford
1983-84   C. D. Heidgerd
1984-85   Stephen T. Smith
1985-86   Fred G. Crumpler Jr.
1986-87   Charles A. Lloyd
1987-88   Charles A. Lloyd
1988-89   L. Michael Dodd
1989-90   L. Michael Dodd
1990-91   J. Kirk Osborn
1991-92   J. Kirk Osborn
1992-93   Robert B. Rader
1993-94   J. Matthew Martin
1994-95   J. Matthew Martin
1995-96   Lyle J. Yurko
1996-97   D. Thomas Lambeth Jr.
1997-98   Ernest L. Conner Jr.
1998-99   Mark T. Calloway
1999-2000   Joseph B. Cheshire V

DISPUTE RESOLUTION
(1/93)   J Anderson Little
1993-94   J. Anderson Little
1994-95   Reagan H. Weaver
1995-96   Rosemary G. Kenyon
1996-97   J. Dickson Phillips III
1997-98   Dorothy C. Bernholz
1998-99   James E. Gates
1999-2000   John C. Schafer

EDUCATION LAW
(9/87)   John W. Hardy
1988-89   Elizabeth C. Bunting
1989-90   Elizabeth C. Bunting
1990-91   Phillip R. Dixon Sr.
1991-92   Homa J. Freeman Jr.
1992-93   Julia M. Shovelin
1993-94   Dorothy C. Bernholz
1994-95   Douglas S. Punger
1995-96   L. Wardlaw Lamar
1996-97   Fredrick G. Johnson
1997-98   Thomas M. Stern
1998-99   Neil B. Whitford
1999-2000   Cynthia S. Lopez

ELDER LAW
(6/96)   A. Frank Johns
1997-98   A. Frank Johns
1998-99   Laurence S. Graham
1999-2000   Carol A. Schwab

ENVIRONMENTAL & NATURAL RESOURCES LAW
(6/87)   William G. Ross Jr.
1988-89   John S. Curry
1989-90   Daniel F. McLawhorn
1990-91   Harold N. Bynum
1991-92   Deborah Lark Hayes
1992-93   Yvonne C. Bailey
1993-94   William A. Raney Jr.
1994-95   Richard C. Gaskins
1995-96   Prentiss Anne Allen
1996-97   Derb S. Carter Jr.
1997-98   Stephen W. Earp
1998-99   Robin W. Smith
1999-2000   Frank H. Sheffield Jr.

ESTATE PLANNING & FIDUCIARY LAW
(10/79)   Robert C. Vaughn Jr.
1980-81   Robert B. Lloyd Jr.
1981-82   Dean A. Rich
1982-83   William P. Skinner Jr.
1983-84   Neill G. McBryde
1984-85   Jeff D. Batts
1985-86   David S. Evans
1986-87   Thomas W. Sinks
1987-88   Molly B. Griffin
1988-89   Michael H. Godwin
1989-90   W. Woods Doster
1990-91   George A. Ragland
1991-92   Richard A. Bigger
1992-93   Cornelius W. Coghill
1993-94   Jo Ann Harllee
1994-95   J. Stanley Atwell
1995-96   Christy Eve Reid
1996-97   Michael A. Colombo
1997-98   Rudy L. Ogburn
1998-99   Thomas R. Crawford
1999-2000   Julie Z. Griggs

FAMILY LAW
(4/80)   James B. Maxwell
1980-81   James B. Maxwell
1981-82   Elizabeth O. Rollins
1982-83   Thomas R. Cannon
1983-84   Robert E. Riddle
1984-85   John H. Parker
1985-86   Carlyn G. Poole
1986-87   Howard L. Gum
1987-88   Howard L. Gum
1988-89   Lunsford Long
1989-90   James Edgar Moore
1990-91   Robert W. Bryant Jr.
1991-92   Lynn P. Burleson
1992-93   Edward P. Hausle
1993-94   Barbara R. Morgenstern
1994-95   Joslin Davis
1995-96   Marcia H. Armstrong
1996-97   Wiley P. Wooten
1997-98   Pamela H. Simon
1998-99   Robin J. Stinson
1999-2000   J. Wade Harrison

GENERAL PRACTICE, SOLO & SMALL FIRM
(9/84)   John W. Lunsford
1984-85   John W. Lunsford
1985-86   John L. Sarratt
1986-87   John L. Sarratt
1987-88   Louis A. Bledsoe Jr.
1988-89   Louis A. Bledsoe Jr.
1989-90   Thomas A. Lockhart Jr.
1990-91   Thomas A. Lockhart Jr.
1991-92   John E. Nobles Jr.
1992-93   Michelle Rippon
1993-94   Michael M. Jones
1994-95   Gerald R. McKinney
1995-96   Charles S. Rountree III
1996-97   Henry P. Van Hoy II
1997-98   Stacy C. Cordes
1998-99   Malvern F. King Jr.
1999-2000   Carolyn B. Winfrey

HEALTH LAW
(4/84)   Noah H. Huffstetler III
1984-85   Noah H. Huffstetler III
1985-86   James T. Cheatham
1986-87   Arlene J. Diosegy
1987-88   Arlene J. Diosegy
1988-89   Thomas L. Young
1989-90   Craig A. Reutlinger
1990-91   Ann Y. Young
1991-92   William R. Shenton
1992-93   Randolph A. Redpath
1993-94   John L. Crill
1994-95   Jan E. Yarborough
1995-96   J. Charles Waldrup
1996-97   Thaddeus B. Hodgdon
1997-98   Christy M. Gudaitis
1998-99   Samuel O. Southern
1999-2000   Barbara B. Garlock

INTELLECTUAL PROPERTY LAW
(10/89)   John B. Maier
1990-91   John B. Maier
1991-92   Dalbert U. Shefte
1992-93   Philip Summa
1993-94   Charles R. Rhodes
1994-95   David A. Harlow
1995-96   Howard A. MacCord Jr.
1996-97   A. Peter Tennent
1997-98   Lynn E. Barber
1998-99   Gabriel A. Avram
1999-2000   William S. Byassee

INTERNATIONAL LAW & PRACTICE
(1/92)   Noel L. Allen
1992-93   Noel L. Allen
1993-94   Noel L. Allen
1994-95   Gary W. Jackson
1995-96   George K. Walker
1996-97   George K. Walker
1997-98   Ann Marie Nader
1998-99   William D. Harazin
1999-2000   Richard J. Boles

JUVENILE JUSTICE & CHLDREN'S RIGHTS
(10/97)   Katherine S. Holliday
1998-99   Katherine S. Holliday
1999-2000   Phillip H. Redmond Jr

LABOR & EMPLOYMENT LAW
(6/82)   John J. Doyle Jr.
1982-83   John J. Doyle Jr.
1983-84   Jonathan R. Harkavy
1984-85   Jonathan R. Harkavy
1985-86   David A. Irvin
1986-87   C. Frank Goldsmith Jr.
1987-88   M. Daniel McGinn
1988-89   Joyce M. Brooks
1989-90   W. Randolph Loftis Jr.
1990-91   Victor J. Boone
1991-92   Albert R. Bell Jr.
1992-93   Geraldine Sumter
1993-94   A. Bruce Clarke
1994-95   Michael G. Okun
1995-96   Charles D. Barrett
1996-97   Robert M. Elliot
1997-98   John R. Archambault
1998-99   Heather Newton
1999-2000   William H. Sturges

LAW PRACTICE MANAGEMENT
(10/83)   Charles T. Lane
1983-84   Charles T. Lane
1984-85   Laurence S. Graham
1985-86   Laurence S. Graham
1986-87   Charles B. Neely Jr.
1987-88   Charles B. Neely Jr.
1988-89   Fred J. Smith Jr.
1989-90   W. Sidney Aldridge
1990-91   Henry C. Campen Jr.
1991-92   Robert B. Hobbs Jr.
1992-93   Kenneth Kyre Jr.

1993-94   Marcus B. Liles III
1994-95   James H. Hughes
1995-96   Paul C. Ridgeway
1996-97   Carol K. Silverstein
1997-98   Tamara P. Barringer
1998-99   J.Gregory Wallace
1999-2000   Guido De Maere

LITIGATION
(1/81)   William F. Maready
1981-82   William F. Maready
1982-83   Charles F. Blanchard
1983-84   Ronald C. Dilthey
1984-85   George B. Mast
1985-86   J. Donald Cowan Jr.
1986-87   Paul J. Michaels
1987-88   Jackson N. Steele
1988-89   Grover C. McCain Jr.
1989-90   Marshall A. Gallop Jr.
1990-91   H. Clay Hemric Jr.
1991-92   Robert W. Sumner
1992-93   Elizabeth F. Kuniholm
1993-94   Alan W. Duncan
1994-95   M. Melinda Lawrence
1995-96   Susan K. Burkhart
1996-97   Janet Ward Black
1997-98   Peter G. Pappas
1998-99   Hoyt G. Tessener
1999-2000   J. Nicholas Ellis

REAL PROPERTY
(10/79)   David G. Martin
1980-81   Charles E. Melvin Jr.
1981-82   James L. Davis
1982-83   M. Jay DeVaney
1983-84   Alfred G. Adams
1984-85   R. Woody Harrison Jr.
1985-86   E. Garrett Walker
1986-87   J. Clark Brewer
1987-88   Leon M. Killian III
1988-89   William S. Cherry Jr.
1989-90   Tyler B. Warren
1990-91   Daniel D. Khoury
1991-92   Robert G. Brinkley
1992-93   David R. Dorton
1993-94   Brian P. Evans
1994-95   Howard L. Borum
1995-96   Franklin E. Martin
1996-97   E. Allen Prichard
1997-98   Clint D. Routson
1998-99   Steven I. Reinhard
1999-2000   Margaret S. Burnham

TAX
(10/79)   Richard E. Thigpen Jr.
1980-81   David W. Hardee
1981-82   David W. Hardee
1982-83   W. Gerald Thornton
1983-84   Paul H. Livington Jr.
1984-85   Ocie F. Murray Jr.
1985-86   J. Randall Groves
1986-87   C. Wells Hall III
1987-88   C. Wells Hall III
1988-89   Donald M. Etheridge Jr.
1989-90   Steve C. Horowitz
1990-91   Michael D. Gunter
1991-92   David D. Dahl
1992-93   Walter H. Nunnallee
1993-94   Joseph D. Joyner Jr.
1994-95   W. Y. Alex Webb
1995-96   John A. Cocklereece Jr.
1996-97   W. B. Rodman Davis
1997-98   D. Royce Powell
1998-99   Linda F. Nelson
1999-2000   Stephen T. Byrd

WORKERS' COMPENSATION
(8/95)   Sandra M. King
1996-97   Robert S. Hodgman
1997-98   George W. Dennis III
1998-99   Joseph B. Roberts
1999-2000   Richard M. Lewis

SENIOR LAWYERS DIVISION CHAIRS

6/90-91	D. Wescott Moser		1994-95	William F. Womble		1998-99	Robert D. Darden Jr.
1991-92	D. Wescott Moser		1995-96	Dean A. Rich		1999-2000	Charles E. Nichols
1992-93	Paul B. Bell		1996-97	Robert A. Collier Jr.			
1993-94	Oscar Edwin Starnes		1997-98	Richmond G. Bernhardt Jr.			

NORTH CAROLINA BAR ASSOCIATION

YOUNG LAWYERS DIVISION CHAIRS

1953-55	Charles F. Blanchard, Raleigh		1978-79	Malvern F. King Jr., Durham
1955-56	Don T. Evans, Rocky Mount		1979-80	J. Donald Cowan, Greensboro
1956-57	Ralph N. Strayhorn, Durham		1980-81	Robert A. Wicker, Greensboro
1957-58	William E. Poe, Charlotte		1981-82	A. P. Carlton Jr., Raleigh
1958-59	Lawrence McN. Johnson, Aberdeen		1982-83	John L. Sarratt, Greensboro
1959-60	William S. Stewart, Chapel Hill		1983-84	Mary I. Murrell, Monroe
1960-61	J. Carlton Fleming, Charlotte		1984-85	C. Wells Hall III, Charlotte
1961-62	Hubert B. Humphrey, Greensboro		1985-86	Reid L. Phillips, Greensboro
1962-63	John R. Ingram, Asheboro		1986-87	G. Gray Wilson, Winston-Salem
1963-64	J. Albert House Jr., Roanoke Rapids*		1987-88	Carl N. Patterson, Raleigh
1964-65	F. Gordon Battle, Chapel Hill		1988-89	Gary K. Joyner, Raleigh
1965-66	Roy W. Davis Jr., Asheville		1989-90	Jeffrey C. Howard, Winston-Salem
1966-67	John V. Hunter III, Raleigh		1990-91	R. Donavon Munford Jr., Raleigh
1967-68	R. Beverly R. Webb, Charlotte		1991-92	Peter G. Pappas, Greensboro
1968-69	Edward R. Hardin, High Point		1992-93	Ellen P. Hamrick, Greensboro
1969-70	Alfred S. Bryant, Durham		1993-94	Adrian N. Wilson, Raleigh
1970-71	James M. Kimzey, Raleigh		1994-95	Stuart B. Dorsett, New Bern
1971-72	Robert F. Baker, Durham		1995-96	Margaret Robison Kantlehner, Greensboro
1972-73	James M. Talley Jr., Charlotte		1996-97	Byron B. Kirkland, Raleigh
1973-74	J. Mac Boxley, Raleigh		1997-98	Susan S. McFarlane, Louisburg
1974-75	Joseph W. Moss, Greensboro		1998-99	Martin H. Brinkley, Raleigh
1975-76	Laurence S. Graham, Greenville		1999-2000	Caryn C. McNeill, Raleigh
1976-77	C. Thomas Ross, Winston-Salem		(* deceased)	
1977-78	Richard F. Harris III, Charlotte			

NORTH CAROLINA
BAR ASSOCIATION

LEGAL ASSISTANTS DIVISION CHAIRS

1998-99	Sharon L. Wall	Raleigh
1999-2000	Richard H. Reich	Winston-Salem

NORTH CAROLINA BAR ASSOCIATION STAFF
June 1999

EXECUTIVE OFFICE
Allan B. Head, *Executive Director*
Elaine R. Nanney, *Assistant Executive Director*
Julie Dumont Rabinowitz, *Director of Membership Services & Benefits*
Kaye B. Barbour, *NCBA Administrative Assistant*
Sherry V. Leonard, *Assistant to the Assistant Executive Director*
Kimberly H. Vaughan, *Assistant to the Executive Director*
Betty D. Wood, *Receptionist*

ADMINISTRATION
Guy R. Sodano, *Director of Administration*
Virginia E. Craig, *Accounting Manager*
Robin J. Polilli, *Assistant Accounting Manager*
Traci L. Cooley, *Accounting Assistant*
Al B. Kurzawa, *Computer Systems Manager*
Sally H. Maddox, *Programmer/Analyst*
Scott J. Reichard, *Web Page Assistant*
Dorise Utley, *Assistant to the Director of Administration*
Ginger M. McSwain, *Data Entry Specialist*
Lisa M. Ratliff, *Computer Systems Operator*
Beth H. Simmons, *Human Resources Manager*
Bobby Gill, *Printing Coordinator**

COMMUNICATIONS
W. Clifton Barnes III, *Director of Communications*
E. Lee Kennedy, *Assistant Director, Internal*
A. Cathleen Larsson, *Assistant Director, External*
Linda W. Bridges, *Assistant to the Director of Communications*
Joann Petilli, *Assistant to the Assistant Director of Communications Internal*

CONTINUING LEGAL EDUCATION
Raymond C. Ruppert, *Director of Continuing Legal Education*
Sally E. Davis, *Assistant Director*
Melissa Noderer, *Assistant Director*

Merley L. Brown, *Video Coordinator*
Donita J. Dixon, *Registrar*
Ellen S. Doyle, *Assistant to the Assistant Directors*
Geraldine M. Gram, *Assistant to the Assistant Directors*
Ruby D. Hawkins, *Assistant to the Assistant Directors*
Sandra C. Holloway, *Assistant to the Director of Continuing Legal Education*
Brenda L. Sohacki, *Marketing Coordinator*

DEVELOPMENT
Thomas M. Hull, *Director of Development*
Emily B. Babcock, *Assistant to the Director of Development*
Candice D. Whitfield, *Campaign Associate*

GOVERNMENTAL AFFAIRS
William G. Scoggin, *Director of Governmental Affairs*
Laura E. Hartsell, *Assistant Director*
L. R. "Becky" Blankenship, *Assistant to the Director of Governmental Affairs*

PUBLIC SERVICE ACTIVITIES
Michelle S. Cofield, *Director of Public Service Activities*
Doris J. Anderson, *Assistant Director*
Persis N. Betts, *Lawyer Referral Service*
Dare L. Hamilton, *Assistant to the Director of Public Service Activities*
Nancy F. Hodges, *Lawyer Referral Service*
M. Katheryn Ruppert, *Lawyer Referral Service*
Sandra L. Saxton, *Lawyer Referral Service*

SECTIONS/DIVISIONS
Jane B. Weathers, *Director of Section & Division Activities*
Lynda B. Stogner, *Assistant Director*
Jacquelyn Terrell-Fountain, *Assistant Director*
J. Michelle Bedford, *Assistant to the Assistant Directors*
Marsha A. Lewandowski, *Assistant to the Director*

* Longest-serving (32 years) staff member in the history of the North Carolina Bar Association (as of June 1, 1999).

NORTH CAROLINA BAR ASSOCIATION
JUDGE JOHN J. PARKER MEMORIAL AWARD RECIPIENTS

The highest award given by the North Carolina Bar Association. (Not awarded every year)

1959 J. Spencer Bell*, Charlotte	1972 Carroll Wayland Weathers*, Winston-Salem	1991 Franklin T. Dupree Jr.*, Raleigh
1961 Hoyt Patrick Taylor Jr., Wadesboro	1975 James Dickson Phillips Jr., Chapel Hill	1992 Carmon J. Stuart, Greensboro
1962 Robert Franklin Moseley*, Greensboro	1977 Hamilton Harris Hobgood*, Louisburg	1993 Russell M. Robinson II, Charlotte
1963 J. Will Pless Jr.*, Marion	1978 Susie Marshall Sharp*, Raleigh	1994 Julius L. Chambers, Durham
1964 Albert Coates*, Chapel Hill	1981 Sam J. Ervin Jr.*, Morganton	1996 William L. Thorp, Chapel Hill
1966 David Maxwell Britt, Fairmont &	1984 William F. Womble, Winston-Salem	1997 James G. Exum Jr., Greensboro
Lindsay C. Warren Jr., Goldsboro	1986 Harry E. Groves, Durham	1999 Norman A. Wiggins, Buies Creek
1969 Raymond Bowden Mallard*, Tabor City	1987 Joseph Branch*, Raleigh	
1971 William Marion Storey*, Raleigh	1989 James B. McMillan*, Charlotte	(* deceased)

GENERAL PRACTICE HALL OF FAME

The General Practice Hall of Fame recognizes lawyers throughout the state based on their exceptional achievements in the law and the areas in which they practice. Although the only requirements are that the candidates have practiced law for 25 years and are still living, the award recognizes lawyers who are role models in our profession.

JUNE 1989
Harold K. Bennett
Asheville
Joseph W. Grier Jr.
Charlotte
Kenneth R. Hoyle
Sanford
Harvey A. Jonas Jr.
Lincolnton
Claud R. Wheatly Jr.
Beaufort
Lindsay C. Warren Jr.
Goldsboro

JUNE 1990
I. Murchison Biggs
Lumberton
Weston P. Hatfield
Winston-Salem
Martin Kellogg Jr.
Manteo
Herbert H. Taylor Jr.
Tarboro

Richard A. Williams Sr.
Newton

JUNE 1991
R. Lewis Alexander
Elkin
Heman R. Clark
Raleigh
E.P. "Sandy" Dameron
Marion
Fred B. Helms
Charlotte
Frank H. Watson
Spruce Pine

JUNE 1992
Wade Edward Brown
Boone
William A. Dees Jr.
Goldsboro
William E. Poe
Charlotte
Robert Leroy McMillan
Raleigh

Louis W. Gaylord Jr.
Greenville
Oscar Edwin Starnes Jr.
Asheville

JUNE 1993
Edwin Osborne Ayscue Jr.
Charlotte
William Lamont Brown
Pinehurst
Robert B. Byrd
Morganton
John Haworth
High Point
James W. Mason
Laurinburg
Ralph M. Stockton Jr.
Winston-Salem

JUNE 1994
Grady B. Stott
Gastonia
William A. Johnson
Lillington

Landon B. Roberts
Asheville
B. Irvin Boyle
Charlotte

JUNE 1995
Louis A. Bledsoe Jr.
Charlotte
Walter F. Brinkley
Lexington
James B. Garland
Gastonia
John R. Jordan Jr.
Raleigh
Edward L. Williamson
Whiteville

JUNE 1996
Stacy C. Eggers Jr.
Boone
Annie Brown Kennedy
Winston-Salem

E.K. Powe
Durham

JUNE 1997
Robert H. Burns Jr.
Whiteville
Max O. Cogburn
Asheville
W. Lunsford Crew
Roanoke Rapids
Wright T. Dixon
Raleigh
Thomas Shull Johnston
Jefferson
J. Brian Scott
Rocky Mount
Gerald F. White Sr.
Elizabeth City

JUNE 1998
Garret Dixon Bailey
Burnsville

Julius Chambers
Charlotte, Durham
Herbert S. Falk Jr.
Greensboro
Worth H. Hester
Elizabethtown
Dewey W. Wells
Blowing Rock

JUNE 1999
John J. Burney Jr.
Wilmington
Herbert L. Hyde
Asheville
Richard S. Jones Jr.
Franklin
William A. Marsh Jr.
Durham
Charles W. Ogletree
Columbia
David L. Ward
New Bern

NORTH CAROLINA BAR ASSOCIATION FOUNDATION
JUSTICE FUND HONOREES

Justice Funds honor those lawyers, past and present, whose careers have demonstrated dedication to the pursuit of justice and outstanding service to the profession and the public.

Arch T. Allen Jr.	Raleigh	1910-	Annie B. Kennedy	Winston-Salem	1924-	George M. Smedes	Goldsboro	1850-1885
Charles B. Aycock	Raleigh	1859-1912	Frank H. Kennedy	Charlotte	1893-1975	Julius C. Smith	Greensboro	1889-1968
E. Osborne Ayscue Sr.	Monroe	1903-70	Hugh L. Lobdell	Charlotte	1908-82	Willis Smith	Raleigh	1887-1953
William H. Bobbitt	Raleigh	1900-92	Clement Manly	Winston-Salem	1853-1928	Willis Smith Jr.	Raleigh	1921-71
Joseph Branch	Raleigh	1915-91	Linville K. Martin	Winston-Salem	1896-1954	William M. Storey	Raleigh	1924-81
Aubrey Lee Brooks	Greensboro	1871-1958	T. Michael McLarry	Raleigh	1950-87	Carol D. Taliaferro	Charlotte	1888-1960
Irving E. Carlyle	Winston-Salem	1896-1971	Beverly C. Moore Sr.	Greensboro	1909-	Richard E. Thigpen	Charlotte	1900-
Julius L. Chambers	Durham	1936-	James O. Moore	Charlotte	1909-88	Newman A. Townsend Jr.	Raleigh	1913-87
Franklin T. Dupree Jr.	Raleigh	1913-95	Joseph C. Moore Jr.	Raleigh	1919-88	William K. Van Allen	Charlotte	1914-
Wade M. Gallant Jr.	Winston-Salem	1930-88	William F. Mulliss	Charlotte	1911-88	Carroll W. Weathers	Winston-Salem	1901-83
Peter Woods Garland	Gastonia	1881-1957	Joseph T. Nall	Washington, DC	1942-89	Elizabeth Dunn White	Greensboro	1954-95
Allan B. Head	Raleigh	1944-	Alfred L. Purrington Jr.	Raleigh	1902-95	B. S. Womble	Winston-Salem	1882-1976
William M. Hendren	Winston-Salem	1871-1939	Leon L. Rice Jr.	Winston-Salem	1912-87	William F. Womble	Winston-Salem	1916-
Robert D. Holleman	Durham	1914-	John M. Robinson	Charlotte	1887-1963			
H. Gardner Hudson	Winston-Salem	1896-1979	William P. Sandridge	Winston-Salem	1904-82			

NORTH CAROLINA BAR ASSOCIATION, YOUNG LAWYERS DIVISION
LIBERTY BELL AWARD RECIPIENTS

1983 Sen. Sam J. Ervin Jr.	1988 Secretary of State Thad Eure	1993 Katherine R. Everett	1998 Sen. Terry Sanford
1984 Chief Justice Susie M. Sharp	1989 Judge Franklin T. Dupree Jr.	1994 Judge Hiram H. Ward	1999 Judge Sam J. Ervin III
1985 William B. Aycock	1990 J. McNeill Smith	1995 Wade E. Brown	
1986 Dr. Robert E. Lee	1991 Justice J. Frank Huskins	1996 Judge J. Dickson Phillips Jr.	
1987 Chief Justice Joseph Branch	1992 L. Richardson Preyer	1997 Herbert H. Taylor Jr.	

PUBLIC SERVICE AWARDS

THE PRO BONO ATTORNEY OF THE YEAR AWARD

1984
Robinson, Bradshaw & Hinson, P.A.

1985
Joe L. Webster

1986
Philip A. Diehl and
Millicent Gibson Diehl

1987
Geoffrey H. Simmons

1988
Marjorie A. Putnam

1989
Law Firm of Poyner & Spruill

1990
Manlin M. Chee

1991
Robert M. "Hoppy" Elliot

1992
Linda Mace McGee

1993
Graham & James, Raleigh office,
and A. Frank Johns

1994
Hollis B. May Jr.

1995
Craig B. Brown

1996
H. Randolph "Dolph" Sumner

1997
James Battle Morgan

1998
The Honorable William B. Reingold

1999
John J. Butler and Peter J.M. Romary

OUTSTANDING LEGAL SERVICES ATTORNEY AWARD

1991
Ellen W. Gerber
Legal Services of Northwest
North Carolina, Winston Salem

1992
Leonard G. Green
East Central Community Legal
Services Branch Office, Smithfield

1993
Charlotte Gail Blake
Legal Services of the Blue Ridge
Boone

1994
Carlene M. McNulty
North State Legal Services
Hillsborough

1995
Barbara J. Degen
Catawba Valley Legal Services
Morganton

1996
Jack S. Hansel
Pamlico Sound Legal Services
Greenville

1997
Stanley B. Sprague
Central Carolina Legal Services
Greensboro

1998
Vilma Suarez
East Central Community Legal
Services, Smithfield

1999
Samuel F. Furgiuele Jr.
Legal Services of the Blue Ridge
Boone

THE CHIEF JUSTICE AWARD

1989
The Thirtieth Judicial District.

1991
The Gaston County Volunteer
Lawyers Program

1992
The Wake County Volunteer
Lawyers Program

1993
The Mecklenburg County Bar
Volunteer Lawyers Program

1994
The Seventh Judicial District Bar

1995
The Twenty-Eighth Judicial District Bar

1996
The McDowell County Bar
Volunteer Lawyers Program

1997
The Gaston County Bar Association

1998
The Forsyth County Bar Association

1999
The Buncombe, Henderson, Madison,
Polk, Rutherford and Transylvania
County Bar Associations

OUTSTANDING PRO BONO SERVICES AWARDS FOR LAW FIRMS

1997
Smith Helms Mulliss & Moore, L.L.P.

1998
Parker, Poe, Adams, Bernstein, L.L.P.

1999
Hunton & Williams

NORTH CAROLINA BAR ASSOCIATION
ANNUAL MEETING LOCATIONS 1899-1999

Year	Dates	Location	City
1899	July 5- 7	Atlantic Hotel	Morehead City
1900	June 27- 29	Battery Park Hotel	Asheville
1901	June 26-28	Seashore Hotel	Wrightsville Beach
1902	July 9-11	Battery Park Hotel	Asheville
1903	July 1- 3	Atlantic Hotel	Morehead City
1904	June 20- 22	Colonial Club	Charlotte
1905	July 5- 7	Toxaway Inn	Lake Toxaway
1906	June 27-29	Seashore Hotel	Wrightsville Beach
1907	July 10-12	Court House	Hendersonville
1908	June 30, July 1, 2	Atlantic Hotel	Morehead City
1909	June 30	Battery Park Hotel	Asheville
1910	June 28	Seashore Hotel	Wrightsville Beach
1911	June 28	Toxaway Inn	Lake Toxaway
1912	July 3-5	Atlantic Hotel	Morehead City
1913	July 2- 4	Battery Park Hotel	Asheville
1914	June 29, 30, July 1	Seashore Hotel	Wrightsville Beach
1915	August 2- 4	Battery Park Hotel	Asheville
1916	June 27-29	Seashore Hotel	Wrightsville Beach
1917	July 3- 5	Battery Park Hotel	Asheville
1918	June 25- 27	Harbor Island Auditorium	Wrightsville Beach
1919	August 5- 7	O. Henry Hotel	Greensboro
1920	June 29, 30, July 1	United States Courtroom	Asheville
1921	July 5- 7	Selwyn Hotel	Charlotte
1922	June 27- 29	Oceanic Hotel	Wrightsville Beach
1923	July 5- 7	Mayview Manor	Blowing Rock
1924	May 1- 3	The Carolina	Pinehurst
1925	July 1- 3	Battery Park Hotel	Asheville
1926	June 30, July 1, 2	Oceanic Hotel	Wrightsville Beach
1927	May 5- 7	The Carolina	Pinehurst
1928	June 28- 30	Grove Park Inn	Asheville
1929	June 27- 29	Oceanic Hotel	Wrightsville Beach
1930	May 1- 3	The Carolina	Pinehurst
1931	July 23- 25	UNC-Chapel Hill	Chapel Hill
1932	July 14- 16	Grove Park Inn	Asheville
1933	July 6- 8	Oceanic Hotel	Wrightsville Beach
1934	June 28- 30	Duke University	Durham
1935	August 17-21	S.S. Reliance	Norfolk to Nova Scotia
1936	July 9- 11	Grove Park Inn	Asheville
1937	June 19-24	S.S. Reliance	Norfolk to Bermuda
1938	May 5- 7	The Carolina	Pinehurst
1939	June 22-24	Ocean Terrace Hotel	Wrightsville Beach
1940	June 28- 30	Mayview Manor	Blowing Rock
1941	May 16- 18	Sedgefield Inn	Greensboro
1942	May 15- 17	The Carolina	Pinehurst
1943	July 16-17	Robert E. Lee Hotel	Winston-Salem
1944	June 16- 17	Sir Walter Hotel	Raleigh
1945	Sept. 7	Sir Walter Hotel	Raleigh
1946	Aug. 29-31	Robert E. Lee Hotel	Winston-Salem
1947	June 26-28	Green Park Hotel	Blowing Rock
1948	June 10-15	S.S. Evangeline	Norfolk to Bermuda
1949	June 9-11	Grove Park Inn	Asheville
1950	June 17-20	Ocean Terrace Hotel	Wrightsville Beach
1951	June 11-14	Mayview Manor	Blowing Rock
1952	June 19-22	The Carolina	Pinehurst
1953	June 12-15	Green Park Hotel	Blowing Rock
1954	June 23-26	Ocean Terrace Hotel	Wrightsville Beach
1955	June 15-18	George Vanderbilt Hotel	Asheville
1956	June 13-16	Ocean Forest Hotel	Myrtle Beach
1957	June 12-15	Mayview Manor	Blowing Rock
1958	June 11-14	Ocean Forest Hotel	Myrtle Beach
1959	June 17-20	Mayview Manor	Blowing Rock
1960	June 15-18	Ocean Forest Hotel	Myrtle Beach
1961	June 28-July 1	Grove Park Inn	Asheville
1962	June 20-23	Ocean Forest Hotel	Myrtle Beach
1963	June 19-22	Grove Park Inn	Asheville
1964	June 17-20	Ocean Forest Hotel	Myrtle Beach
1965	June 30-July 3	Grove Park Inn	Asheville
1966	June 29-July 2	Ocean Forest Hotel	Myrtle Beach
1967	June 21-24	Grove Park Inn	Asheville
1968	June 20-23	Ocean Forest Hotel	Myrtle Beach
1969	June 25-28	Grove Park Inn	Asheville
1970	June 16-20	Ocean Forest Hotel	Myrtle Beach
1971	June 30-July 3	Grove Park Inn	Asheville
1972	June 21-24	Ocean Forest Hotel	Myrtle Beach
1973	July 3-7	Grove Park Inn	Asheville
1974	July 3-6	Landmark Inn	Myrtle Beach
1975	July 2-5	Great Smokies Hilton	Asheville
1976	June 23-26	Myrtle Beach Hilton	N. Myrtle Beach
1977	June 15-18	Grove Park Inn	Asheville
1978	June 14-17	Myrtle Beach Hilton	N. Myrtle Beach
1979	June 20-23	Grove Park Inn	Asheville
1980	June 25-29	Myrtle Beach Hilton	N. Myrtle Beach
1981	June 25-28	Grove Park Inn	Asheville
1982	June 17-20	Myrtle Beach Hilton	N. Myrtle Beach
1983	June 30-July 3	Grove Park Inn	Asheville
1984	June 21-24	Myrtle Beach Hilton	N. Myrtle Beach
1985	June 20-23	Grove Park Inn	Asheville
1986	June 19-22	Myrtle Beach Hilton	N. Myrtle Beach
1987	June 18-21	Grove Park Inn	Asheville
1988	June 23-26	Myrtle Beach Hilton	N. Myrtle Beach
1989	June 29- July 2	Grove Park Inn	Asheville
1990	June 21-24	Myrtle Beach Hilton	N. Myrtle Beach
1991	June 20-23	Grove Park Inn	Asheville
1992	June 18-21	Myrtle Beach Hilton	N. Myrtle Beach
1993	June 17-20	Grove Park Inn	Asheville
1994	June 22-26	Myrtle Beach Hilton	N. Myrtle Beach
1995	June 14-17	Grove Park Inn	Asheville
1996	June 19-23	Radisson Hotel	N. Myrtle Beach
1997	June 19-22	Grove Park Inn	Asheville
1998	June 18-21	Embassy Suites	N. Myrtle Beach
1999	June 16-20	Grove Park Inn	Asheville

Historical note: Exact dates and locations for the 1950-53 annual meetings are unverified.

REPORT OF COMMITTEE ON LEGAL ETHICS

To the North Carolina Bar Association:

The Committee on Legal Ethics respectfully report that they find their labors much lightened by the Codes upon this subject which have been adopted by the Bar Associations of sister States. They present a Code of Legal Ethics for the consideration of this Association, which is substantially the same as that which has been adopted by the Bar Associations of Alabama, Georgia, Virginia and perhaps other States.

Respectfully submitted,

JAMES C. MACRAE, Chairman
Armistad Burwell, Committee
R. H. Battle, Committee
T. B. Womack, Committee
T. M. Argo, Committee

CODE OF ETHICS

Adopted by the North Carolina Bar Association,
June 28th, 1900.

The purity and efficiency of judicial administration, which under our system is largely government itself, depends as much upon the character, conduct, and demeanor of attorneys in their great trust as upon the fidelity and learning of courts or the honesty and intelligence of juries.

"There is, perhaps, no profession, after that of the sacred ministry, in which high-toned morality is more imperatively necessary than that of the law. There is certainly, without any exception, no profession in which so many temptations beset the path to swerve from the lines of strict integrity; in which so many delicate and difficult questions of duty are constantly arising. There are pitfalls and mantraps at every step, and the mere youth, at the very outset of his career, needs often the prudence of self-denial, as well as the moral courage, which belong commonly to riper years. High moral principle is his only safe guide; the only torch to light his way amidst darkness and obstruction." —*Sharswood.*

No rule will determine an attorney's duty in the varying phases of every case. What is right and proper must, in the absence of statutory rules and an authoritative code, be ascertained in view of the peculiar facts, in the light of conscience, and the conduct of honorable and distinguished attorneys in similar cases, and by analogy to the duties enjoined by statute, and the rules of good neighborhood.

The following general rules are adopted by the North Carolina Bar Association for the guidance of its members:

Duties of Attorneys to Courts and Judicial Officers.

1. The respect enjoined by law for courts and judicial officers is exacted for the sake of the office, and not for the individual who administers it. Bad opinion of the incumbent, however well founded, cannot excuse the withholding of the respect due to the office while administering its functions.

2. The proprieties of the judicial station, in a great measure, disable the judge from defending himself against strictures upon his official conduct. For this reason, and because such criticisms tend to impair public confidence in the administration of justice, attorneys should, as a rule, refrain from published criticism of judicial conduct, especially in reference to causes in which they have been of counsel, otherwise than in courts of review, or when the conduct of the judge is necessarily involved in determining his removal from or continuance in office.

3. Marked attention and unusual hospitality to a judge, when the relations of the parties are such that they would not otherwise be extended, subject both judge and attorney to misconstruction, and should be sedulously avoided. A self-respecting independence in the discharge of the attorney's duties, which, at the same time, does not withhold the courtesy and respect due the judge's station, is the only just foundation for cordial, personal, and official relations between Bench and Bar. All attempts by means beyond these to gain special personal consideration and favor of a judge are disreputable.

4. Courts and judicial officers, in the rightful exercise of their functions, should always receive the support and countenance of attorneys against unjust criticism and popular clamor; and it is an attorney's duty to give them his moral support in all proper ways, and particularly by setting a good example in his own person of obedience to law.

5. The utmost candor and fairness should characterize the dealings of attorneys with the courts and with each other. Knowingly citing as authority an overruled case, or reading a repealed statute as in existence; knowingly misquoting the language of a decision or text-book; knowingly misstating the contents of a paper, the testimony of a witness, or the language or arguments of the opposite counsel; offering evidence which it is known the court must reject as illegal, to get it before a jury under guise of arguing its admissibility, and all kindred practices, are deceits and evasions unworthy of attorneys. Purposely concealing or withholding in the opening argument positions intended finally to be relied on, in order that opposite counsel may not discuss them, is unprofessional. In the argument of demurrers, admission of evidence, and other questions of law, counsel should carefully refrain from "side-bar" remarks and sparring discourse to influence the jury or bystanders. Personal colloquies between counsel tend to delay, and promote unseemly wrangling, and ought to be discouraged.

6. Attorneys owe it to the courts, and the public whose business the courts transact, as well as to their own clients, to be punctual in attendance on their causes; and whenever an attorney is late, he should apologize, or explain his absence.

7. One side must always lose the cause; and it is not wise or respectful to the court for attorneys to display temper because of an adverse ruling.

Duty of Attorneys to Each Other, to Clients, and the Public.

8. An attorney should strive, at all times, to uphold the honor, maintain the dignity, and promote the usefulness of the profession; for it is interwoven with the administration of justice, that whatever redounds to the good of one, advances the other; and the attorney thus discharges, not merely an obligation to his brothers, but a high duty to the State and his fellowman.

9. An attorney should not speak slightingly or disparagingly of his profession, or pander in any way to the unjust popular prejudices against it; and he should scrupulously refrain at all times, and in all relations of life, from availing himself of any prejudice or popular misconception against lawyers, in order to carry a point against a brother attorney.

10. Nothing has been more potent in creating and pandering to popular prejudice against lawyers as a class, and in withholding from the profession the full measure of public esteem and confidence which belong to the proper discharge of its duties" than the false claim, often set up by the unscrupulous in defence of questionable tranactions, that it is an attorney's duty to do everything to succeed in his client's cause. An attorney "owes entire devotion to the interests of his client, warm zeal in the maintenance and defence of his cause, and the exertion of the utmost skill and ability," to the end that nothing may be taken or withheld from him save by the rules of law, legally applied. No sacrifice or peril, even to loss of life, itself, can absolve from the fearless discharge of his duty. Nevertheless, it is steadfastly to be borne in mind that the great trust is to be performed within, and not without, the bounds of the law which creates it. The attorney's office does not destroy man's accountability to his Creator, or loosen the duty of obedience to law, and the obligation to his neighbor; and it does not permit, much less demand, violation of law, or any manner of fraud or chicanery, for the client's sake.

11. Attorneys should fearlessly expose before the proper tribunals corrupt or dishonest conduct in the profession; and there should never be any hesitancy in accepting employment against an attorney who has wronged his client.

12. An attorney appearing or continuing as private counsel in the prosecution for a crime of which he believes the accused innocent, forswears himself. The State's attorney is criminal, if he presses for a conviction, when upon the evidence he believes the prisoner innocent. If the evidence is not plain enough to justify a Nolle Prosequi a public prosecutor should submit the case, with such comments as are pertinent, accompanied by a candid statement of his own doubts.

13. An attorney cannot reject the defense of a person accused of a criminal offense because he knows or believes him guilty. It is his duty, by all fair and lawful means, to present such defenses as the law of the land permits, to the end that no one may be deprived of life or liberty but by due process of law.

14. An attorney must decline in a civil cause to conduct a prosecution, when satisfied that the purpose is merely to harass or injure the opposite party, or to work oppression and wrong.

15. It is a bad practice for an attorney to communicate or argue privately with the judge as to the merits of his cause.

16. Newspaper advertisements, circulars, and business cards, tendering professional services to the general public, are proper; but special solicitation of particular individuals to become clients ought to be avoided. Indirect advertisements for business, by furnishing or inspiring editorials or press notices regarding causes in which the attorney takes part, the manner in which they were conducted, the importance of his positions, the magnitude of the interests involved, and all other like self-laudation, is of evil tendency and wholly unprofessional.

17. Newspaper publications by an attorney as to the merits of pending or anticipated litigation, calling for discussion and reply from the opposite party, tend to prevent a fair trial in the courts, and otherwise prejudice the due administration of justice. It requires a strong case to justify such publications; and, when proper, it is unprofessional to make them anonymously.

18. When an attorney is witness for his client, except as to formal matters, such as the attestation or custody of an instrument and the like, he should leave the trial of the cause to other counsel. Except when essential to the ends of justice, an attorney should scrupulously avoid testifying in court in behalf of his client as to any matter.

19. Assertions, sometimes made by counsel in argument, of a personal belief of the client's innocence, or the justice of his cause, are to be discouraged.

20. It is indecent to hunt up defects in titles, and the like, and inform thereof, in order to be employed to bring suit; or to seek out a person supposed to have a cause of action, and endeavor to get a fee to litigate about it. Except where ties of blood, relationship, or trust make it an attorney's duty, it is unprofessional to volunteer advice to bring a law suit. Stirring up strife and litigation is forbidden by law, and disreputable in morals.

21. Communications and confidence between client and attorney are the property and secrets of the client, and cannot be divulged except at his instance; even the death of the client does not absolve the attorney from obligation of secrecy.

22. The duty not to divulge the secrets of clients extends further than mere silence by the attorney, and forbids accepting retainers or employment afterwards from others, involving the client's interest in the matters about which the confidence was reposed. When the secrets or confidence of a former client may be availed of or be material in a subsequent suit, as the basis of any judgment which may injuriously affect his rights, the attorney cannot appear in such cause without the consent of his former client.

23. An attorney can never attack an instrument or paper drawn by him for any infirmity apparent on its face; nor for any other cause where confidence has been reposed as to the facts concerning it. Where the attorney acted as a mere scrivener, and was not consulted as to the facts, and, unknown to him, the transaction amounted to a violation of the laws, he may assail it on that ground in suits between third persons, or between parties to the instrument and strangers.

24. An attorney openly, and in his true character, may render purely professional services before committees regarding proposed legislation, and in advocacy of claims before departments of the government, upon the same principles of ethics which justify his appearance before the courts; but it is immoral and illegal for an attorney so engaged to conceal his attorneyship, or to employ secret personal solicitations, or to use means other than those addressed to the reason or understanding, to influence action.

25. An attorney can never represent conflicting interests in the same suit or transaction, except by express consent of all so concerned, with full knowledge of the facts. Even then such a position is embarrassing and ought to be avoided. An attorney represents conflicting interests, within the meaning of this rule, when it is his duty, in behalf of one of his clients, to contend for that which duty to other clients in the transaction requires him to oppose.

26. "It is not a desirable professional reputation to live and die with that — of a rough tongue, which makes a man to be sought out and retained to gratify the malevolent feeling of a suitor, in hearing the other side well lashed and vilified."

27. An attorney is under no obligation to minister to the malevolence or prejudice of a client in the trial or conduct of a cause. The client cannot be made the keeper of an attorney's conscience in professional matters. He cannot demand as of right that his attorney shall abuse the opposite party, or indulge in offensive personalities. The attorney, under the solemnity of his oath, must determine for himself whether such a course is essential to the ends of justice, and therefore justifiable.

28. Clients, and not their attorneys, are the litigants; and, whatever may be the ill-feeling existing between clients, it is unprofessional for attorneys to partake of it in their conduct and demeanor to each other, or to suitors in the case.

29. In the conduct of litigation, and the trial of causes, the attorneys shall try the merits of the cause, and not try each other. It is not proper to allude to, or comment upon the personal history, or mental or physical peculiarities, or idiosyncrasies, of opposite counsel. Personalities should always be avoided, and the utmost courtesy always extended to an honorable opponent.

30. As to incidental matters pending the trial, not affecting the merits of the cause, or working substantial prejudice to the rights of the client, such as forcing the opposite attorney to trial when he is under affliction or bereavement; forcing the trial on a particular day, to the serious injury of the opposite attorney, when no harm will result from a trial at a different time; the time allowed for signing a bill of exceptions, crossing interrogatories, and the like, the attorney must be allowed to judge. No client has a right to demand that his attorney shall be illiberal in such matters, or that he should do anything therein repugnant to his own sense of honor and propriety; and if such a course is insisted on, the attorney should retire from the cause.

31. The miscarriage to which justice is subject, and the uncertainty of predicting results, admonish attorneys to beware of bold and confident assurances to clients, especially where the employment depends upon the assurance, and the case is not plain.

32. Prompt preparation for trial, punctuality in answering letters and keeping engagements, are due from an attorney to his client, and do much to strengthen their confidence and friendship.

33. An attorney is in honor bound to disclose to the client, at the time of retainer, all the circumstances of his relation to the parties, or interest or connection with the controversy, which might justly influence the client in the selection of his attorney. He must decline to appear in any cause where his obligations or relations to the opposite parties will hinder or seriously embarrass the full and fearless discharge of all his duties.

34. An attorney should endeavor to obtain full knowledge of his client's cause before advising him, and is bound to give him a candid opinion of the merits and probable result of his cause. When the controversy will admit of it, he ought to seek to adjust it without litigation, if practicable.

35. Money, or other trust property, coming into the possession of the attorney should be promptly reported, and never commingled with his private property or used by him, except with the client's knowledge and consent.

36. Attorneys should, as far as possible, avoid becoming either borrowers or creditors of their clients; and they ought scrupulously to refrain from bargaining about the subject matter of the litigation, so long as the relation of attorney and client continues.

37. Natural solicitude of clients often prompts them to offer assistance of additional counsel. This should not be met, as it sometimes is, as evidence of want of confidence; but, after advising frankly with the client, it should be left to his determination.

38. Important agreements affecting the rights of clients should, as far as possible, be reduced to writing; but it is dishonorable to avoid performance of an agreement fairly made, because not reduced to writing, as required by rules of court.

39. Attorneys should not ignore known customs of practice of the Bar of a particular court, even when the law permits, without giving opposing counsel timely notice.

40. An attorney should not attempt to compromise with the opposite party without notifying his attorney, if practicable.

41. When attorneys jointly associated in a cause cannot agree as to any matter vital to the interest of their client, the course to be pursued should be left to his determination. The client's decision should be cheerfully acquiesced in, unless the nature of the difference makes it impracticable for the attorney to co-operate heartily and effectively, in which event it is his duty to ask to be discharged.

42. An attorney ought not to engage in discussion or argument about the merits of the case with the opposite party without notice to his attorney.

43. Satisfactory relations between attorney and client are best preserved by a frank and explicit understanding at the outset, as to the amount of the attorney's compensation; and, where it is possible, this should always be agreed on in advance.

44. In general, it is better to yield something to a client's dissatisfaction at the amount of the fee, though the sum be reasonable, than to engage in a law suit to justify it, which ought always to be avoided, except as a last resort to prevent imposition and fraud.

45. In fixing fees, the following elements should be considered: (1) The time and labor required, the novelty and difficulty of the questions involved, and the skill requisite properly to conduct the cause. (2) Whether the particular case will debar the attorney's appearance for others in cases likely to arise out of the transaction and in which there is a reasonable expectation that the attorney would otherwise be employed; and herein of the loss of other business while employed in the particular case, and the antagonism with other clients growing out of the employment. (3) The customary charges of the Bar for similar services. (4) The real amount involved, and the benefit resulting from the service. (5) Whether the compensation was contingent or assured. (6) Is the client a regular one, retaining the attorney in all his business? No one of these considerations is in itself controlling. They are mere guides in ascertaining what the service was really worth; and, in fixing the amount, it should never be forgotten that the profession is a branch of the administration of justice, and not a mere money-getting trade.

46. Contingent fees may be contracted for; but they lead to many abuses, and certain compensation is to be preferred.

47. Casual and slight services should be rendered without charge by one attorney to another in his personal cause; but when the service goes beyond this, an attorney may be charged as other clients. Ordinary advice and services to the family of a deceased attorney should be rendered without charge in most instances, and where the circumstances make it proper to charge, the fees should generally be less than in case of other clients.

48. Witnesses and suitors should be treated with fairness and kindness. When essential to the ends of justice to arraign their conduct or testimony, it should be done without vilification or unnecessary harshness. Fierceness of manner and uncivil behavior can add nothing to the truthful dissection of a false witness' testimony, and often rob deserved strictures of proper weight.

49. It is the duty of the court and its officers to provide for the comfort of jurors. Displaying special concern for their comfort, and volunteering to ask favors for them while they are present — such as frequent motions to adjourn trials, or take a recess, solely on the ground of the jury's fatigue or hunger, the uncomfortableness of their seats or the court-room, and the like — should be avoided. Such intervention of attorneys, when proper, ought to be had privately with the court, whereby there will be no appearance of fawning upon the jury, nor ground for ill-feeling of the jury toward court or opposite counsel, if such requests are denied. For like reasons, one attorney should never ask another, in the presence of the jury, to consent to its discharge or dispersion; and when such a request is made by the court, the attorneys without indicating their preference, should ask to be heard after the jury withdraws. And all propositions from counsel to dispense with argument should be made and discussed out of the hearing of the jury.

50. An attorney ought never to converse privately with jurors about the case; and must avoid all unnecessary communication, even as to matters foreign to the cause, both before and during the trial. Any other course, no matter how blameless the attorney's motives, gives color for imputing evil designs, and often leads to scandal in the administration of justice.

51. An attorney assigned as counsel for an indigent prisoner ought not to ask to be excused for any light cause, and should always be a friend to the defenseless and oppressed.

INDEX

176

This book was designed and
printed courtesy of

LEXIS Publishing™

LEXIS-NEXIS • MARTINDALE-HUBBELL
MATTHEW BENDER • MICHIE • SHEPARD'S

Charlottesville, Virginia

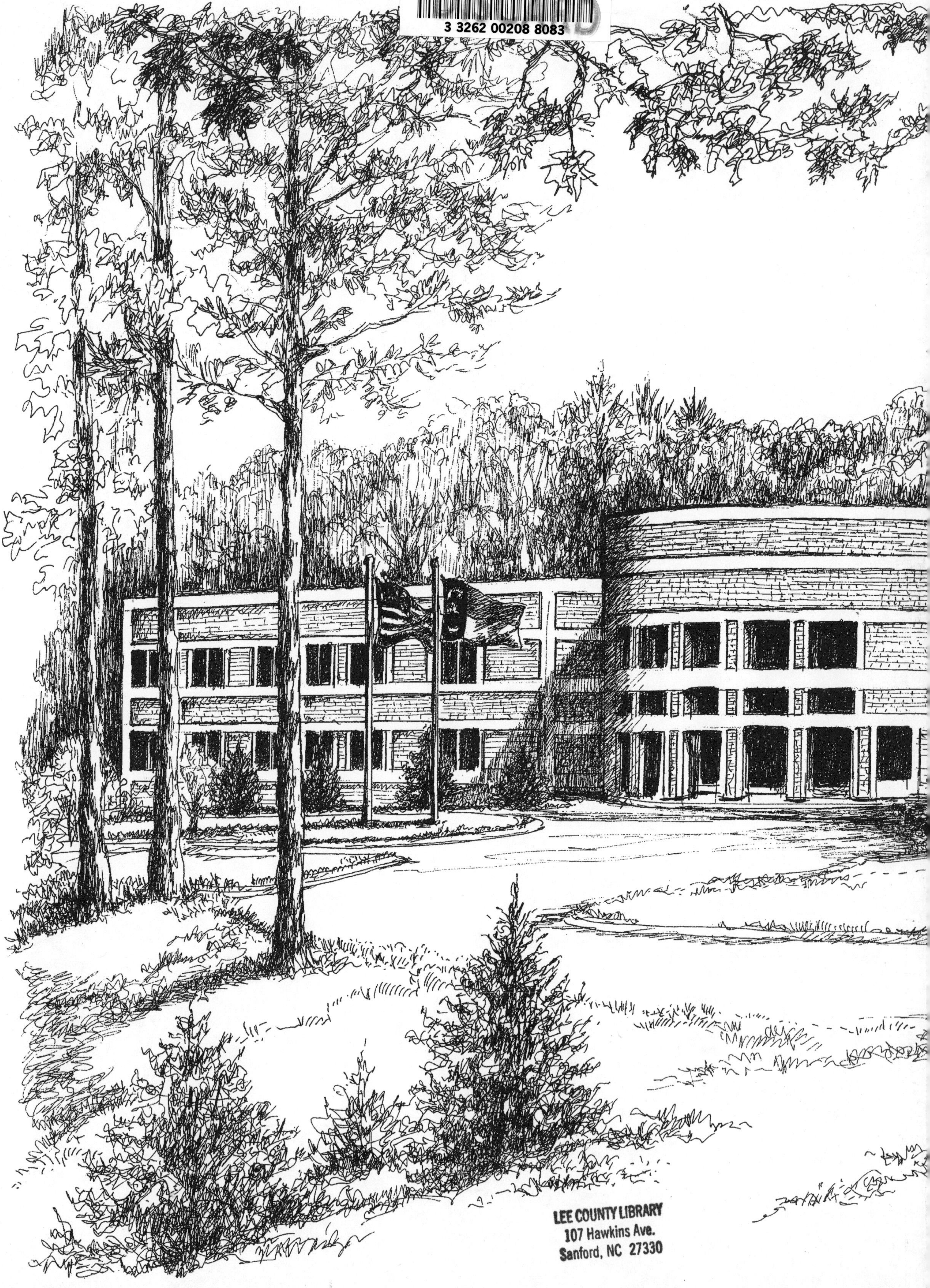